MARY BERRY'S BAKING BIBLE

MARY BERRY'S BAKING BIBLE

FULLY UPDATED WITH OVER
250 NEW AND CLASSIC RECIPES

MARY BERRY

CLARKSON POTTER/PUBLISHERS
New York

Published in the United States by Clarkson Potter/Publishers, an imprint of Random House, a division of Penguin Random House LLC, New York.

ClarksonPotter.com

RandomHouseBooks.com

CLARKSON POTTER is a trademark and POTTER with colophon is a registered trademark of Penguin Random House LLC.

This edition originally published in hardcover by BBC Books, an imprint of Ebury Books, a division of Penguin Random House LLC, in 2022.

Library of Congress Cataloging-in-Publication Data is available upon request.

ISBN 978-0-593-57815-5

Ebook ISBN 978-0-593-57816-2

Printed in China

Photographer: Ant Duncan
Food stylist: Isla Murray
Prop stylist: Hannah Wilkinson
Editor: Susan Roxborough
Editorial assistant: Bianca Cruz
Designer: Smith & Gilmour
Production editor: Patricia Shaw
Production manager: Kim Tyner
Compositors: dix! and Hannah Hunt
Project editor and copy editor: Jo Roberts-Miller
US project editor: Maria Zizka
Marketer: Brianne Sperber
Publicist: Erica Gelbard
Front cover and photograph on page 9 by Georgia Glynn Smith

10 9 8 7 6 5 4 3 2 1

First Potter Edition

CONTENTS

INTRODUCTION
AND
TECHNIQUES

INTRODUCTION

When I published my first major baking book, *Ultimate Cake Book*, in 1994, it was with the hope that it would encourage more people to take up homebaking, and show inexperienced cooks that cake making isn't as complicated as it might first appear. The success of that book has been tremendous and I have been touched by how many people still rely on it even now, nearly thirty years later!

In 2003, as I wrote the introduction for the revised edition of the *Ultimate Cake Book*, I remember marveling at the continuing demand for cake-making instruction. Now, it seems, people are turning to homebaking even more since the success of *The Great British Bake Off*!

In light of this increased interest in homebaking, I felt it was time to create a new complete book of baking—my Baking Bible. This is a new edition of *The Baking Bible* to include right up-to-date favorites—such as a glorious **Red Velvet Cake**, **Rainbow Cake**, **Quick Sourdough Loaf,** and **Herb and Garlic Flatbread**. I hope this book will inspire a new generation of cooks, as well as prove useful to seasoned bakers.

The aim was to produce an easy-to-use baking collection to satisfy all your baking needs. I have included a bread section, containing my new bread recipes. There are some unusual cakes to try, like **Zucchini Loaves**, and recipes for favorites, such as **Cupcakes**. But as this is a "baking bible," I have tried to include as many classic recipes as possible. There are lots of traditional celebration cakes for occasions such as Easter, Christmas and christenings, birthdays and weddings, and some well-known favorites like **Victoria sponge** and **Chocolate Chip Cookies**.

I've included lots of simple recipes for children to make (with supervision), and some more challenging recipes that require careful timing, and more skill, including pâtisserie-style desserts, such as **Gâteau Saint Honoré**. Cooks of all levels of experience should find something to make and to challenge them here. Since I first started writing recipes, the equipment available has evolved and improved enormously. Now we have reliable ovens, food processors and electric mixers, nonstick pans and baking sheets, and bread-makers. With the help of these aids, baking has become quick, easy, and stress-free. All you need is to weigh and measure your ingredients very carefully and follow the tested step-by-step instructions.

I have tried to include recipes for all occasions and I hope you will find plenty of bakes to suit your tastes. But, most of all, I hope that this new collection of my favorite and trusted recipes will help you enjoy homebaking. Cakes are made to be shared, so once you have mastered a recipe, invite your friends and family to enjoy the fruits of your labor with a good pot of tea—happy baking!

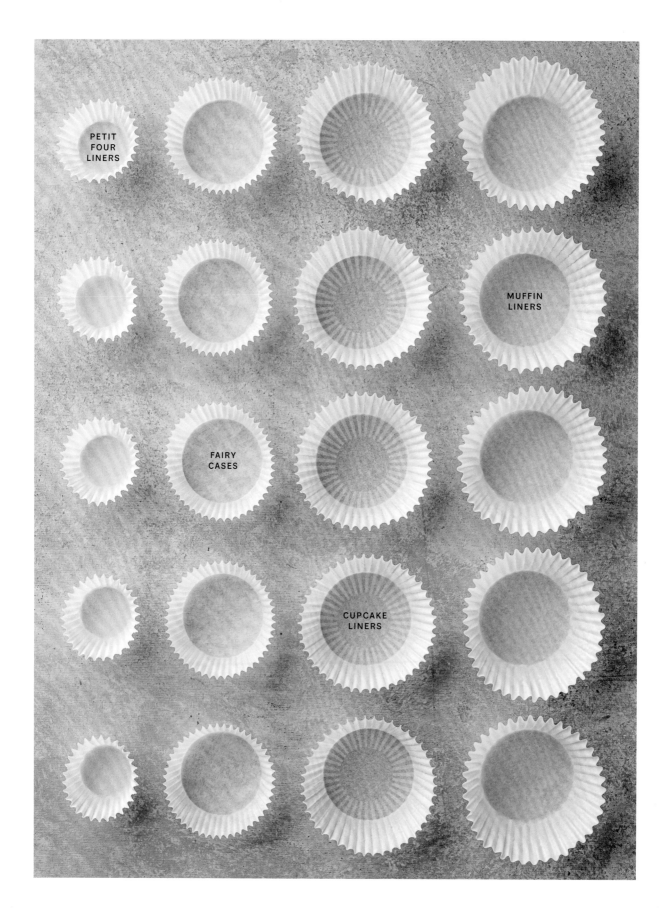

PETIT
FOUR
LINERS

MUFFIN
LINERS

FAIRY
CASES

CUPCAKE
LINERS

BAKING EQUIPMENT

Some people may be put off from baking because they think it requires lots of expensive utensils, but this really isn't the case. Although electric-powered equipment saves time and effort, it's not essential, and many of the recipes in this book, such as the sheet cakes, Victoria sponges, cookies, and crackers, require little more than a set of scales, a wooden spoon to beat the ingredients, a mixing bowl, and a cake pan or baking sheet, as they use the "all-in-one" technique. A lot of the equipment you will probably have already, and some you can improvise. If you are buying new equipment, do buy the best you can afford; good-quality baking equipment will last a long time so it will be a worthwhile investment.

MEASURES
You will need a set of measuring spoons including 1 teaspoon, ½ teaspoon, ¼ teaspoon, and 1 tablespoon. All the amounts given in these recipes are for level spoonfuls unless otherwise stated. To measure liquids, use a transparent heatproof jug that shows both metric and Imperial measures.

SCALES
One piece of equipment that is critical to achieving the perfect bake is measuring scales. Some people prefer old-fashioned balance scales with weights, but they take up a lot of space. Spring balance scales are fine for large amounts but are not accurate for small quantities. There are now a number of very reliable electric and battery-operated digital scales that can measure weights and volumes in metric, Imperial, and liquids. Test the scales for accuracy by putting something on them that has the weight printed on it, such as an unopened bag of flour or sugar.

SPOONS
A wooden spoon is vital, but it should have a rounded edge to get into all the bends of the bowl. A large metal spoon for mixing egg whites into a mixture is useful, as its sharper edges flatten the egg foam much less than a wooden spoon does. Use a bendy, rubber or silicone spatula to get all the cake mixture off the sides of the bowl.

WHISKS
Use a balloon whisk or a handheld electric mixer. It's useful to have two sizes of balloon whisk: a large one for whisking eggs and a small spiral one for small amounts of mixture.

MIXING BOWLS
I have a range of different-size bowls that fit inside each other for easy storage. If you are baking for the first time, invest in one large and one small, preferably Pyrex, mixing bowl with a rounded base so you can get to every bit of mixture with your whisk, spoon, or spatula. For all-in-one cakes you will need only one bowl, but it's useful to have at least two as some recipes require you, for example, to whisk egg white separately, then add it to the rest of the mixed cake ingredients.

FOOD MIXERS

A stand mixer is not essential but saves time and effort! Choose one that comes with a range of attachments so you can use it to beat and cream cake mixture, knead bread dough, whisk egg white, and whip cream. Stand mixers are good for large cakes and are easy to clean but do take up a lot of room. Alternatively, you can use a handheld electric mixer. I find that I only use the beating and whisking attachments. The great advantage is that hand mixers are inexpensive and they save time, too.

FOOD PROCESSORS

These useful time-saving machines can easily overmix a mixture so take care — if you don't keep a careful eye on them, they can chop nuts and fruit to nothing. It is best to fold in such ingredients by hand. Processors don't get air into the mixture in the same way as food mixers do, as they combine ingredients rather than beat them, thus are not suitable for making meringues and fatless sponges.

PANS

Good-quality, solid cake pans will last you a lifetime. Cheap cake pans can be very thin, may warp with use, and do not conduct heat evenly. Choosing the right-sized pan for the recipe is crucial to successful baking and particularly critical in sponge-making; if the pan is too shallow the cake will spill over the top of the pan as it rises, whereas a pan that is too large will produce a pale, flat-looking cake. I've included a list of all the pans used in this book (right). If you are a first-time baker, don't be put off by the long list! Start off by buying two 8-inch or 9-inch round cake pans to make a variety of round cakes; a 9 x 13-inch baking pan (if your roasting pan is not the right size); a 8½ x 4½-inch (450g) loaf pan; a 9 x 5-inch (900g) loaf pan; and a 12-cup muffin pan. As you

bake more frequently, add the other pans listed to your collection. Nonstick pans are easier to clean, but it is safer to follow the greasing and lining instructions in the recipes and not to rely solely on their nonstick properties. Choose black-lined pans as they conduct heat more effectively. Avoid pans with thick, insulated bases. They're designed to prevent cakes from burning on the bottom, but they prevent the cake from cooking evenly in most modern ovens.

SHEET PANS

Ideally have at least three sheet pans. They should be flat, rigid, and heavy. Check that they fit inside your oven!

CAKE PANS FOR KEEN BAKERS

round cake pans: 6-inch, 8-inch, 9-inch
springform pans: 7-inch, 8-inch, 9-inch, 10-inch
square cake pan: 8-inch, 9-inch
baking pan: 9 x 13-inch
square ovenproof baking dish: 9-inch
loaf pans: 8½ x 4½-inch (450g), 9 x 5-inch (900g)
deep fluted tart pan with removable bottom: 10-inch
shallow fluted tart pan with removable bottom:
    8-inch, 9½-inch, 10½-inch, 11-inch
ovenproof dish: 7 x 10½-inch
12-cup muffin pan
12-cup fairy cake pan
12-cup mini muffin pan
Bundt pan: 10-inch
1 French madeleine pan
ramekins
pie dish: 9-inch
4 heatproof bowls: 6 fl ounces
4 individual soufflé dishes or 1 large soufflé dish:
    8 ounces or 2 quarts

PARCHMENT PAPER

A useful cake-making aid that has evolved over time is parchment paper. The parchment paper used in this book is nonstick silicone, which doesn't require greasing. It comes in a variety of sizes and shapes to make lining pans and sheet pans easy.

If you're using greaseproof paper, you must grease the pan and then the paper (after you've lined the pan). Also available are pan-liner sheets. They are reusable, tough, and come in a variety of pan sizes. They lift off easily and just need to be washed, dried, and kept flat when stored.

Most recipes require only the bottom of the pan to be lined with parchment paper, some the sides and bottom, so I include here instructions for lining the most frequently used pan shapes in this cookbook.

To line the bottom of a round cake pan, using parchment paper from a roll, place the bottom of the pan on the parchment paper, draw around it in pencil, then cut out just inside the pencil line. Or you can buy circles of parchment in sizes to fit cake pans.

To line the sides of a round cake pan, cut a strip (or two strips if necessary) of parchment paper to reach around the pan and a little extra to overlap the ends. The strip(s) should be about 2 inches wider than the depth of the pan. Fold the bottom edge of the strip up by about 1 inch, creasing it firmly. Open out the fold and cut slanting lines into the folded paper at about 1-inch intervals. Fit the strip(s) around the greased pan (greasing the pan helps to make the lining stick to it). The snipped edge will help the paper fit snugly around the bottom of any shape pan. Fit the bottom paper over the cut-part of the side strips, then grease well with a pastry brush.

To line a rectangular pan, place the pan on the parchment paper and cut a rectangle about 2 inches bigger than the pan. Snip each corner then press the paper onto the greased pan, folding up the edges to create a paper basket.

To line a loaf pan, cut a piece of parchment paper to fit the widest sides and cover the bottom of the pan with about a 2-inch overhang. Press the paper into the greased pan. You do not need to line the ends of the pan, just loosen the cake with an offset spatula before turning out.

To line a sheet pan, follow the method for lining a rectangular pan, or mold aluminum foil into the pan and grease well.

GRIDDLE

Used in this book to make pancakes and Singin' Hinny. If you don't have a griddle pan, use a heavy-bottomed, nonstick frying pan instead.

WIRE COOLING RACKS

To cool cakes once they have been baked; they allow air to pass under the cakes or cookies as they cool. If you don't have a wire rack, you can use the rack from a broiler pan.

KNIVES

An offset spatula has a flexible blade with a rounded end, making it the best tool for spreading and smoothing cake mixture into pans or icing onto cakes. Use one to lift cookies off sheet pans or loosen a cake from the sides of the pan before turning it out onto the wire rack. A fish spatula is also good for lifting out sheet cakes and lifting cookies off sheet pans. For recipes in which the cake is cut into layers, use a long, sharp serrated knife for the cleanest finish.

SIEVE

For sifting flour and confectioners' sugar, and pressing through jam glazes to remove the seeds and solid fruit. Strong stainless steel sieves are good as they come in a variety of sizes and can be put in the dishwasher (wire sieves can become misshapen).

CAKE SKEWER

A long, thin metal skewer is indispensable for testing cooked cakes. Insert it into the center of the cake, where the mixture is at its most dense. If it comes out clean, the cake is ready. Use a skewer that has flat sides.

CONFECTIONERS' SUGAR SHAKER

A canister that has either a fine mesh sieve lid or a lid with tiny holes. A shaker is ideal for finishing the top of a sponge or tart with a dusting of confectioners' sugar.

ROLLING PIN

For making pastry I find a long wooden rolling pin with no handles is best.

FLEXIBLE SILICONE SPATULAS

For getting the last of the cake mixture out of the bowl.

PASTRY BRUSH

Use a pastry brush for greasing pans and glazing tarts with jam or uncooked scones with milk.

PIE WEIGHTS

Use ceramic or metal pie weights when a recipe calls for pastry to be blind-baked (see page 16 for definition). You can also use uncooked dried rice or beans.

CAKE SMOOTHER

To make the icing on top and the sides of cakes smooth.

COOKIE CUTTERS

For crackers, cookies, and scones. Keep a set of plain and fluted round cookie cutters in a range of sizes, and some fun-shaped cookie cutters to make novelty cookies such as gingerbread men. The most useful sizes of round cookie cutters are 2-inch and 3-inch. Metal cookie cutters are best, but make sure they are thoroughly dry before storing them. If you don't have cookie cutters, use the rim of an appropriately sized glass.

CAKE TURNTABLE

Will help to give a smoother and more even finish when icing cakes.

ICING NOZZLES

I have a box of metal icing nozzles of all sizes, but for the recipes in this book you only need ¼-inch and ½-inch plain nozzles and a large and medium star nozzle. Nozzles can be plastic or metal, and are fitted to a piping bag.

PIPING BAG

Used for decorating cakes with icing and whipped cream. A nylon piping bag is good as it is easily washable. You can make your own piping bag by slotting one small plastic food bag inside another, then snipping off the corners at one point. You can also buy disposable piping bags from kitchen stores.

DIGITAL THERMOMETER

For sugar syrups and tempering chocolate.

BAKING TERMINOLOGY

Cooking techniques can be confusing as the invention of new technology means that old baking techniques like creaming and beating can be done in more than one way. You will find the following terminology in the book, so I include some short explanations of what they mean.

ALL-IN-ONE METHOD
The easiest cake-making method, suitable for most cakes and sheet cakes. Measure all the ingredients into a mixing bowl and beat with a free-standing or handheld mixer or food processor. I find buttery spread in a tub, straight from the fridge, gives very good results. (Do not use low-fat spreads as they contain added liquid, which gives a poor result.) If using butter, make sure it is softened.

BLIND-BAKING
A method of cooking pastry before the filling is added, it results in the pastry being really crisp. To blind-bake, preheat the oven to 400°F. Line the pie pan with the pastry, cover with parchment paper, and fill with ceramic or metal pie weights (or old dried rice or beans). Bake for 10–15 minutes. Remove the paper and weights and bake for an additional 5 minutes to dry the pastry completely. Remove from the oven and add the chosen filling.

BEAT
In cake-making, this can be done either with a wooden spoon or with a free-standing or handheld electric mixer. Beat cake ingredients until they are well-blended, but be careful not to overbeat in a machine. It should take a couple of minutes to beat cake mixture until smooth. Beat an egg with a metal fork, breaking up the yolk and blending it into the egg white.

COMBINE (OR MIX)
Mixing ingredients that don't require as much air to be added, such as cookies. Use a wooden spoon or food processor to do this.

CREAMING METHOD
The beating of butter and sugar together until the mixture turns light and creamy. Cream with either a wooden spoon or food mixer until the color of the butter and sugar lightens and the texture is fluffy. This is not needed for cakes that can be made with the all-in-one method.

CRIMP
Used in pastry and pie making, it means to press the moistened pastry edges together to seal. You can do this with a finger, the handle of a knife, or a fork.

DUST
To sprinkle a fine coating of confectioners' sugar, cocoa powder, or flour over a cake or bread using a sieve or sugar shaker.

FOLD
A technique used to keep plenty of air in a cake mixture when adding ingredients such as sifted flour or whisked egg whites. Use a metal spoon or spatula to carefully mix the

ingredients, folding the mixture at the edges over into the center of the bowl and cutting through the middle until the mixture is evenly combined.

GREASE

Using a paper towel, cover the insides of the cake pan with a layer of butter or buttery spread to prevent the cake mixture from sticking as it cooks. You don't need to grease and line a pan if you are baking pastry as there is enough fat in the dough to prevent it from sticking.

KNEAD

Essential in most bread-making, this can be done by hand or with a stand mixer fitted with a dough hook. It is the act of mixing together the ingredients to form a smooth, elastic dough. It warms and stretches the dough so that, as the bread bakes, it retains air pockets. If the dough is not kneaded enough, the bread will be dense and heavy.

PUNCH DOWN (OR KNOCK BACK)

Similar to kneading, this is done after proofing to get rid of any large air pockets in the dough before it is baked.

LINE

Lining a pan with parchment paper to prevent the cake from sticking and ease its removal from the pan after baking. Some cakes require both the base and sides of the pan to be lined, others just the base. Due to the high-fat and low-sugar content in pastry, it does not require the pan to be lined (see note on parchment paper on page 12 for instructions on lining pans).

MELTING

Usually golden syrup or light corn syrup, or molasses, is melted with sugar and fat in a saucepan, then the other ingredients are added and combined. The mixture is then poured into the baking pan.

PROOF

After bread dough has been kneaded, it is covered in oiled plastic wrap and left in a warm place to allow the yeast to convert the glucose and other carbohydrates into carbon dioxide, causing the dough to rise. It also creates alcohol, giving the dough its flavor. The dough should double in size.

RUBBING IN

I use this method for scones and pastry. Dice the fat and then rub into the flour with your fingertips, or with an electric mixer or food processor, until the mixture resembles fine breadcrumbs.

WHISK (OR WHIP)

This can be done by hand with a balloon whisk, with a handheld electric mixer, or with a food processor. Most often used to describe the whipping of heavy cream or egg whites to a stiff consistency.

KEY INGREDIENTS

The ingredients listed here are those used most frequently in the book. I think it's useful to know what role each has in the baking process, to help you choose the right type of ingredients for the recipe you are following.

BUTTER AND BUTTERY SPREAD

For many of the recipes in this book, such as biscuits, shortbread, and genoise sponges, I have used butter. I tend to use salted or lightly salted butter, but you can use whichever you prefer—unsalted works just as well. It's important for the butter to be at the right temperature and consistency before adding it to the mixture.

In cake making, I have followed the all-in-one method using chilled buttery spread. If you use butter instead, it needs to be softened but not melted before creaming. If you have time, leave the butter at room temperature for at least 30 minutes before using. Even then, it is better to cream the butter on its own to soften it before adding the sugar.

My own trick to bring refrigerated butter to the right temperature is to cut it into cubes and put them into a bowl of cool/lukewarm tap water (approx. 82°F). Leave for 10 minutes or until a butter cube can be easily compressed. Drain off the water, then the soft butter is ready to use.

If rubbing into pastry, cut cold butter into pieces or grate it into the flour.

It is not always necessary to use butter in baking, unless you specifically require a buttery flavor. Buttery spreads have replaced margarines on the domestic market and are more economical than butter. You can use them in any of the recipes here if you prefer; however, I would advise that recipes without heavy flavorings, such as **Fork Cookies** (page 218) and **The Very Best Shortbread** (page 210) should be made with butter, as the buttery flavor is important.

Be careful that you do buy buttery spreads that specify they are suitable for baking. Low-fat spreads are not suitable because of their high water content. Buttery spreads should be used straight from the fridge.

Some recipes call for lard, vegetable shortening, or oil. Cakes made with oil are very easy to bake, and tend to be very moist, but they do need a little extra rising agent in the form of either baking powder or whisked egg whites to prevent heaviness. Choose an oil with as little flavor as possible, such as sunflower or vegetable oil.

FLOURS AND RISING AGENTS

There are a variety of different flours with different properties for baking. The main distinction is the amount of gluten each contains, and some also have an added rising agent. It's important to use the type of flour stated in the recipe, as the wrong flour will drastically affect the texture and appearance of the cake, pastry, or bread. Keep an eye on the use-by date on flours; they do deteriorate over time. Flours, rolled oats, and semolina should all be used within four months once the bags or packets have been opened.

In theory, you should always sift flour when baking, particularly cakes, to lighten the flour by incorporating air. Although I have to admit that I rarely sift flour! The only time I do is when I am folding it into a whisked, fatless sponge, when the sifting helps to combine the flour evenly into the mix.

ALL-PURPOSE FLOUR

For making cakes, you need to use flour with a low gluten content. It is more starchy and so absorbs the fat well, giving a lighter texture.

You can also buy whole wheat flour, which I have used in fruit recipes like **Jane's Fruit Cake** (page 72) and my **Classic Sticky Gingerbread** (page 70).

Whole wheat flour has not had the bran and germ extracted, which gives it a coarser texture that complements dense fruit like currants and raisins, and cooked stone fruits, like peaches, plums, and apricots, very well.

BREAD FLOURS

When making bread, it is important to use the correct flour. The two main bread flours used in this book are bread flour and whole wheat bread flour. These are all-purpose flours that have a higher proportion of the protein that forms gluten when mixed with water. This creates air pockets that cause the bread to rise.

I have also used a barley flour to make **Quick Malt Rolls** (page 286). The name of these flours does vary between brands and they are not always clearly labeled as bread-making flours, so double check that you are buying the right flour!

OTHER FLOURS

I have used other types of flour, including semolina, corn starch, and rice flour. These give a crunchier texture that works well in shortbread. I have also used potato starch and buckwheat flour, which has a stronger flavor that is delicious in my **Zucchini Loaves** (page 318).

BAKING POWDER

This rising agent is most commonly added to cake mixture. It consists of an acid (usually cream of tartar) and an alkali (baking soda) mixed with a dried starch or flour. When liquid is added the chemicals react, producing carbon dioxide that expands during baking, making the cake rise. Beware: If you add too much baking powder, the cake will rise at first and then collapse! Baking powders these days are slow acting, which means it is not a disaster if you make a cake but can't put it in the oven straightaway. When making scones or rock cakes, I add extra baking powder for a good rise.

YEAST

The rising agent used in bread making. I use fast-acting dried yeast, which is a dried yeast that comes in helpful ¼-ounce (7g) packets. It's easy to use—simply mix it with the flour and then add the liquid. If you use ordinary dried yeast, follow the manufacturer's instructions when adding liquid. It will require a more lengthy process.

CREAM OF TARTAR

Cream of tartar is not used as a rising agent on its own, but it can be mixed with baking soda as the acid ingredient in baking powder.

BAKING SODA

This rising agent has a bitter flavor so is best used in recipes with strong flavors, such as gingerbread. It is most effective in recipes where there are natural acids present in the ingredients such as molasses, lemon juice, or buttermilk.

PREMADE PASTRY

Don't feel guilty about using bought pastry, if you're short on time. There are a number of very good, butter-based pastries to buy now. They can be found in either the refrigerated or the frozen sections in the supermarket.

SUGARS

In my cakes, I prefer to use unrefined sugars, such as raw turbinado and granulated sugar, as they have more flavor, but do experiment with the wide range of sugars and sweeteners now available. The only time I would use fine white sugar is for meringues as it makes them really white.

GRANULATED SUGAR

Most commonly used in cake-making, especially for whisked sponges, creamed mixtures, and meringues, as its small, regular grains ensure that it blends smoothly, giving an even texture. You can make vanilla sugar by adding two or three vanilla pods to a jar of sugar. Leave for two weeks to allow the vanilla to infuse. You can refill the jar as you use the sugar.

SANDING SUGAR

This has a coarser texture than granulated sugar and is best used in melting and rubbed-in methods. If used in a creamed mixture, it will give a slightly gritty texture and speckled appearance, and will reduce the volume of the cake.

CONFECTIONERS' SUGAR

Not generally used in cake mixtures as it will create a hard crust and reduce the volume of the cake. It's most frequently used to make glacé icing and to dust baked goods before serving.

MUSCOVADO SUGAR

Made from raw cane sugar, the color and flavor vary with the molasses content. Light muscovado sugar can be used to make many cakes as it creams well. It is natural, so I prefer it to soft brown sugar. Use it for brown sugar meringues, using half light muscovado and half fine sugar. Dark muscovado sugar can be overpowering but works well in gingerbreads and rich fruit cakes. To prevent muscovado sugar from going damp, put a paper towel in the bag or jar and seal.

DEMERARA SUGAR

This is traditionally unrefined, but it has a lower molasses content than muscovado sugar. It is best suited to cakes made with the melting method to dissolve its large crystals, and to being sprinkled on top of cakes or added to cheesecake bases for extra crunch.

NIBBED SUGAR

"Nibbed" is an old-fashioned term meaning coarsely chopped. Nibs are the rough-shaped "shavings" formed when sugar cubes are cut. I use it to top cakes before baking, but you can use crushed sugar cubes instead, as nibbed sugar is difficult to get hold of.

GOLDEN SYRUP OR LIGHT CORN SYRUP, MOLASSES, AND HONEY

Light, sweet golden syrup (or light corn syrup) and darker, strong molasses are both made from crystallized refined sugar. Nature's equivalent, honey, is the oldest sweetener in the world. Use clear or runny honey in recipes as it dissolves more quickly.

BARLEY MALT SYRUP

Made from powdered malt that has been reduced into a syrup, this is added to breads to add a sweet flavor and to aid the action of carbon dioxide.

CONDENSED MILK

Milk that has had half the water content removed and sugar added, sold in cans. I have used it as a sweetener in some recipes to give a fudgey flavor.

When heated with butter and muscovado sugar it turns to a thick caramel, used in **Millionaires' Shortbread** (page 253).

MILK, CREAM, AND CHEESE

MILK

Recipes use reduced-fat milk, unless otherwise stated. Whole milk will obviously add a richness to baking, but non-fat milk works just as well, if you prefer it.

CREAM

Cream is best whipped from cold.

You have the option of using whipping cream for filling cakes, as it is healthier and cheaper than heavy cream, but you can use either. Heavy cream is best for piping because it holds its shape longer than whipping cream. Use whipped heavy cream if you are adding other flavorings, like brandy. Whipping cream gives a lighter texture to mousses.

As a more economical and healthier filling for a cake, I often use a mix of half whipped cream and half low-fat yogurt. Remember that yogurt is wetter than cream, so use a full-fat yogurt if you want a firmer filling.

CHEESE

For cheesecakes, use full-fat cream cheese. Cottage cheese is useful too, and has a slightly tart flavor, or you can use ricotta instead. This book does use hard cheese too, mainly Cheddar and Parmesan, in savory scones and crackers, including **Puff Pastry Cheese Straws** (page 232) and **Dorchester Crackers** (page 228).

EGGS

I use extra-large eggs throughout, unless otherwise stated, and always free-range or organic. Allow eggs to come to room temperature before using. Store leftover egg whites in the fridge in a container covered in plastic wrap. Spoon a little cold water over leftover yolks to prevent a skin from forming, then cover with plastic wrap. Keep for up to one week.

CHOCOLATE

DARK CHOCOLATE

There are a number of brands of dark chocolate that contain a high proportion of cocoa solids. Although they are delicious to eat, their high percentage of cocoa solids does not make them ideal for baking as the flavor can be too bitter. The finest-quality block chocolate always contains a high proportion of cocoa butter. The more cocoa butter the chocolate contains, the softer and creamier it will be. Some cheaper brands replace cocoa butter with palm or vegetable oils.

The cocoa-solids and cocoa-butter content will affect the consistency of your cake or icing. The cake might not rise properly, the icing might separate or not set, or heavier ingredients such as chocolate chips might sink to the bottom if there is not enough fat to hold them in place as the cake cooks. The cocoa flavor might also be too overpowering. I recommend using a dark chocolate that

contains about 39 percent cocoa solids, such as Bournville. This will ensure a ratio of cocoa solids to cocoa butter that will produce a cake or icing with the correct consistency and flavor. There is no need to buy an expensive brand for baking unless the recipe specifies.

MILK CHOCOLATE

This has the addition of whole milk and sugar, so is much sweeter and has a milder cocoa flavor. Milk chocolate is only ideal for decorating as the chocolate flavor is lost in baking.

WHITE CHOCOLATE

Contains cocoa butter but not the dark cocoa solids. The amounts of cocoa butter used varies between brands, and some cheaper ones replace the cocoa butter with vegetable oil. When buying milk and white chocolate for cooking, choose Belgian chocolate and check that it does not contain vegetable oil.

COCOA POWDER

This is a very good and inexpensive ingredient in baking, but always sift it with the dry ingredients or mix with a little boiling water before using. Don't use drinking chocolate instead, as the added sugar gives it a mild, sweet flavor not suitable for baking.

MELTING, CHOPPING, AND GRATING

When melting chocolate, it is essential that you do not let it overheat. Break the chocolate into small pieces in a heatproof bowl that fits snugly over a pan of hot, but not boiling, water. If the water boils, the chocolate can become solid and lose its shine. Also, make sure the bottom of the bowl does not touch the water. Heat liquids with the melting chocolate, do not add them to the chocolate once it has melted as this may cause the chocolate to "seize." White chocolate is more likely to separate on heating, so keep the heat low. You can melt chocolate in the microwave, but again heat gently on a defrost or low setting to avoid burning.

If a recipe calls for chopped or grated chocolate, put the bar in the fridge to chill first and make sure the grater or knife is cold and completely dry. You can chop chocolate in a food processor, but be careful not to overwork it, as the chocolate might melt or stick together.

BAKING TIPS

All the recipes in the book include individual cake-making instructions and for certain recipes I have given specific tips that are useful to know. However, there is some general advice that can be applied.

Always read the recipe carefully, checking that you have enough time and all the ingredients before you begin.

—

Weigh ingredients using accurate measures and scales and follow the order of the recipe, making sure nothing is missed—ticking off ingredients and instructions as you complete them helps prevent you from missing anything.

—

Mix ingredients by hand or in the food processor until the mixture is the specified color and texture. Make sure you follow a recipe using the right utensils when it instructs you to beat, whisk, or fold ingredients; these are different techniques and have specific effects on the cake mixture consistency—the success of the cake depends on this!

—

Always preheat the oven before starting to make a cake. It must be at the correct temperature by the time the cake is ready to go in. Make sure the oven shelves are in the right position beforehand—unless specified otherwise, cook cakes in the center of the oven.

—

Be patient and don't open the oven door or move the cake in the first stages of baking, as this can cause the cake to sink in the middle.

—

Don't overload your oven with sheet pans of cookies, as they will cook unevenly—cookies on a high shelf or at the edges of a pan can brown too quickly, while the others are still uncooked. There needs to be a good circulation of air as they bake. If you put more than one cake in the oven at a time, they will take a little longer to cook.

—

Most cakes are cooked when they begin to shrink away from the sides of the cake pan, and when the center of the cake springs back after being pressed lightly with a finger.

—

Check the recipe to see what color the cooked cake or cookies should be. Test fruit cakes by inserting a skewer into the center of the cake; it should come out clean. If there is any cake mixture stuck to the skewer, it needs a little longer in the oven. Cookies and scones are cooked when they are lightly and evenly colored on top; underneath, cookies should be lightly colored and scones golden.

—

Cover cakes with foil if they are browning too quickly, and perhaps reduce the oven temperature a little. Oven temperature settings do vary.

—

Follow each recipe for individual cooling instructions. Generally, sponge cakes should be allowed to cool for a few minutes before turning out onto a wire rack. The sides of the cake will shrink away from the pan, making them easier to remove. For sponge cakes, turn the cake the right side up on the wire rack and then cover with the cake pan. This prevents the moisture from evaporating while the cake cools, but doesn't make it soggy. Let fruit cakes cool completely in their pans.

—

Don't leave cookies on their sheet pans to cool completely, as they can stick. Remove them with an offset spatula while still warm.

—

To turn cakes out of a springform cake pan, stand the bottom on something like a large can so that the sides can slip down, leaving the cake still standing on the pan's bottom.

—

Make sure a cake, baked good, or cookie is completely cold before decorating, unless the recipe specifies otherwise. Fill when you are ready to serve. I like to keep the decoration simple, but there are so many options available now that you can get creative and experiment with lots of different toppings.

—

For many cakes, if you have time, it is good to brush it with an apricot glaze before icing. Make the glaze by pushing warmed apricot jam through a sieve. The glaze will prevent crumbs getting into the icing, and the icing will remain glossy as the cake won't absorb its moisture. Apricot glaze is also useful when covering a cake with almond paste: when spread over the cake before the paste is applied, it acts as "glue."

—

Most cakes should be eaten soon after making but they can be kept fresh for a short time in an airtight container, or wrapped in foil or plastic wrap. Sponges that have a low fat content or no fat (such as Swiss roll) do not keep well and should be eaten on the day or wrapped well and then filled and eaten the following day. Baked goods with a fresh cream filling or frosting should be kept in the fridge. Cookies, squares, and bars made with the melting method do keep well but should be stored in an airtight container to prevent them from going soggy.

—

Freeze undecorated cakes and cookies wrapped tightly in foil, plastic wrap, or freezer-proof bags, as soon as they are cold, to preserve their freshness. Keep them frozen for no longer than 3 months.

—

Open-freeze (freeze unwrapped) iced or decorated cakes until hard, then wrap well. Refresh small cakes such as scones by warming them in a 350°F oven after thawing.

—

Don't store cakes and cookies in the same container, as the moisture from the cake will make the cookies soggy. If cookies do go soggy, refresh them in a 350°F oven for 5–10 minutes, then cool and eat.

—

If fruit sinks to the bottom of the cake, it means that either the mixture was too runny to support the fruit, the fruit was too wet, or the wrong fat was used (see page 19 for information on baking fats). If not enough fat is added, the cake may be dry.

—

If cakes crack on top during baking, it means that the oven was too hot or the cakes were placed on too high a shelf.

—

A cake may sink if too much baking powder was used, the cake was taken out of the oven before it was cooked, or the oven door was opened before the cake mixture had time to set. It may also not rise properly if the mixture was overbeaten (so that the air was beaten out), or if not enough rising agent was added.

—

Make pastry either by hand in a mixing bowl or in a food processor, but be careful not to over-whiz; otherwise the dough will be tough.

—

Once a pastry case is lined the dough freezes very well, making it perfect to have in the freezer ready for a special occasion.

—

When proofing and rising bread, do not proof in too hot a place; otherwise the yeast will be killed and the rising process will stop.

—

CONVERSION TABLES

WEIGHT

METRIC	IMPERIAL
5g	⅛oz
10g	¼oz
15g	½oz
20g	¾oz
30g	1oz
35g	1¼oz
40g	1½oz
55g	2oz
65g	2½oz
75g	3oz
80g	3¼oz
90g	3½oz
115g	4oz
125g	4½oz
150g	5oz
175g	6oz
180g	6¼oz
200g	7oz
225g	8oz
250g	9oz
275g	10oz
300g	10½oz
325g	11½oz
350g	12oz
375g	13oz
400g	14oz
425g	15oz
450g	1lb
500g	1lb 2oz
550g	1¼lb
600g	1lb 5oz
650g	1lb 7oz
675g	1½lb
700g	1lb 9oz
750g	1lb 10oz
800g	1¾oz
850g	1lb 14oz
900g	2lb
1.3kg	3lb
1.8kg	4lb
2.25kg	5lb

LENGTH

METRIC	IMPERIAL
5mm	¼in
1cm	½in
2cm	¾in
2.5cm	1in
3cm	1¼in
4cm	1½in
5cm	2in
6.5cm	2½in
7cm	2¾in
7.5cm	3in
9cm	3½in
10cm	4in
11cm	4½in
12.5cm	5in
15cm	6in
18cm	7in
20cm	8in
23cm	9in
25cm	10in
28cm	11in
30cm	12in
33cm	13in
35cm	14in

VOLUME

METRIC	IMPERIAL
30ml	2 tbsps
50ml	¼ cup
75ml	⅓ cup
85ml	6 tbsps
100ml	7 tbsps
125ml	½ cup
150ml	⅔ cup
175ml	¾ cup
200ml	¾ cup + 2 tbsps
225ml	1 cup
240ml	1 cup + 1 tbsp
250ml	1 cup + 2 tbsps
300ml	1¼ cups
350ml	1½ cups
400ml	1¾ cups
450ml	1¾ cups + 2 tbsps
500ml	2¼ cups
600ml	2½ cups
700ml	3 cups
900ml	3¾ cups
1 liter	4¼ cups
1.2 liters	5 cups
1.25 liters	5¼ cups
1.5 liters	6⅓ cups
1.75 liters	7⅓ cups
2 liters	8½ cups
2.25 liters	9½ cups
2.5 liters	10½ cups
2.75 liters	11⅔ cups
3.4 liters	14⅓ cups
3.9 liters	16½ cups
4.5 liters	19 cups

OVEN TEMPERATURES

°C	°F
120	250
140	275
150	300
160	325
180	350
190	375
200	400
220	425
230	450
240	475

CHAPTER ONE

CLASSIC CAKES

This must be the best known and loved of all family cakes. The all-in-one method takes away the hassle of creaming, and ensures success every time. Buttery spreads give an excellent result, but the cake won't keep as long.

LARGE ALL-IN-ONE VICTORIA SANDWICH

CUTS INTO 6 GENEROUS SLICES

1 cup + 1 tbsp (225g) buttery spread, straight from the fridge
1 cup + 2 tbsps (225g) sugar
4 extra-large eggs
1¾ cups (225g) all-purpose flour
3½ tsps baking powder
½ tsp salt

For the filling and topping
about 4 tbsps strawberry jam
½ cup + 2 tbsps (150ml) heavy cream, whipped
a little sugar, for sprinkling

Preheat the oven to 350°F. Lightly grease two 8-inch round cake pans and line the bottom of each with parchment paper.

—

Measure all the cake ingredients into a large bowl and beat for about 2 minutes with an electric mixer until beautifully smooth and lighter in color. The time will vary depending on the efficiency of the mixer. Divide the mixture evenly between the pans and level the surfaces.

—

Bake for about 25 minutes, or until well-risen, golden, and the cakes are shrinking away from the sides of the pan. Let cool in the pans for a few minutes, then turn out, peel off the parchment paper, and finish cooling on a wire rack.

—

When completely cold, sandwich the cakes together with the jam and whipped cream. Sprinkle with sugar to serve.

TIP

Here are the ingredients and baking times for smaller cakes so that you don't have to calculate the quantities. Follow the instructions for the Large All-in-One Victoria Sandwich.

For a 7-inch Victoria Sandwich, use 3 extra-large eggs, ¾ cup + 1 tbsp (175g) buttery spread, ¾ cup + 2 tbsps (175g) sugar, 1⅓ cup (175g) all-purpose flour, 2¼ tsps baking powder, and ¼ tsp salt. Bake in two 7-inch greased and lined cake pans for about 25 minutes.

For a 6-inch Victoria Sandwich, use 2 extra-large eggs, ½ cup + 1 tbsp (115g) buttery spread, ½ cup + 1 tbsp (115g) sugar, 1 cup (115g) all-purpose flour, 2 tsps baking powder, and ¼ tsp salt. Bake in two 6-inch greased and lined cake pans for about 20 minutes.

This is a simple but delicious alternative to the classic Victoria Sandwich that's perfect for coffee time.

COFFEE VICTORIA SANDWICH

CUTS INTO 6 GENEROUS SLICES

4 extra-large eggs
2 heaped tsps instant coffee
granules
1 cup + 1 tbsp (225g) buttery
spread, straight from the
fridge
1 cup + 2 tbsps (225g)
granulated sugar
1¾ cups (225g) all-purpose
flour
1 tbsp baking powder
½ tsp salt

For the filling and topping
¼ cup (55g) butter, softened
1 cup + 6 tbsps (175g)
confectioners' sugar, sifted
1 tbsp strong coffee
1 tbsp milk (optional)

Preheat the oven to 350°F. Lightly grease two 8-inch round cake pans and line the bottom of each with parchment paper.

Break the eggs into a large bowl and beat with a fork. Stir in the instant coffee until dissolved. Add all the remaining cake ingredients and beat for about 2 minutes with an electric mixer until beautifully smooth and lighter in color. The time will vary depending on the efficiency of the mixer. Divide the mixture evenly between the pans and level the surfaces.

Bake for about 25 minutes or until well-risen and the cakes are shrinking away from the sides of the pan. Let cool in the pans for a few minutes, then turn out, peel off the parchment paper, and finish cooling on a wire rack.

To make the buttercream filling and topping, blend together the butter, confectioners' sugar, and coffee until smooth, adding the milk, if necessary. When the cakes are completely cold, use half the buttercream to sandwich the cakes together. Spread the remaining buttercream on top.

TIP
To make strong coffee, you can dissolve 1 heaped teaspoon instant coffee granules in 1 tablespoon hot water.

This light chocolate cake is sandwiched together with a white buttercream and looks as good as it tastes.

CHOCOLATE VICTORIA SANDWICH

CUTS INTO 6 GENEROUS SLICES

2 tbsps cocoa powder
3 tbsps boiling water
1 cup + 1 tbsp (225g) buttery spread, straight from the fridge
1 cup + 2 tbsps (225g) granulated sugar
4 extra-large eggs
1¾ cups (225g) all-purpose flour
1 tbsp baking powder
½ tsp salt

For the filling and topping
¼ cup (55g) butter, softened
1 cup + 6 tbsps (175g) confectioners' sugar, sifted
1 tbsp milk
coarsely grated dark chocolate, to decorate

Preheat the oven to 350°F. Lightly grease two 8-inch cake pans with removable bottoms and line the bottom of each with parchment paper.

—

Blend the cocoa and water in a large bowl then let cool slightly. Measure all the remaining cake ingredients into the bowl and beat for about 2 minutes with an electric mixer until beautifully smooth and lighter in color. The time will vary depending on the efficiency of the mixer. Divide the mixture evenly between the pans and level the surfaces.

—

Bake for about 25 minutes or until well risen and the cakes are shrinking away from the sides of the pan. Let cool in the pans for a few minutes, then turn out, peel off the parchment paper, and finish cooling on a wire rack.

—

To make the buttercream filling and topping, blend together the butter, confectioners' sugar, and milk until smooth. When the cake is completely cold, use half the buttercream to sandwich the cakes together, then spread the remaining buttercream on top and decorate with the grated chocolate.

To make an Orange or Lemon Victoria Sandwich, follow the recipe for a Large All-in-One Victoria Sandwich (page 34), adding the grated zest of an orange or lemon to the cake mixture. Sandwich the cooked cakes together with whipped cream and either orange marmalade or lemon curd, instead of the strawberry jam, and sprinkle the top with a little granulated sugar.

A family classic. You could decorate this roll with buttercream and use it for a Christmas log.

CHOCOLATE ROULADE

SERVES 8

4 extra-large eggs
1 cup + 1 tbsp (115g) granulated sugar, plus extra for sprinkling
½ cup (65g) all-purpose flour
½ cup (40g) cocoa powder, plus extra for dusting
¾ tsp baking powder
¼ tsp salt

For the filling
4 ounces (115g) dark chocolate, broken into pieces
3 tbsps raspberry jam
1¼ cups (300ml) heavy cream, whipped

Preheat the oven to 425°F. Grease a 9 x 13-inch baking pan and line with parchment paper.

—

Whisk the eggs and sugar in a large bowl until the mixture is light and frothy and the whisk leaves a trail when lifted out. Sift the flour, cocoa, baking powder, and salt into the mixture, carefully folding them in at the same time. Turn the mixture into the prepared pan and give it a gentle shake so that the mixture finds its own level, making sure that it spreads evenly into the corners.

—

Bake for about 10 minutes, or until the sponge begins to shrink from the sides of the pan.

—

While the cake is cooking, place a piece of parchment paper a little bigger than the size of the pan on a work surface and sprinkle it with granulated sugar. Invert the cake straight from the oven onto the sugared paper. Quickly loosen the paper on the bottom of the cake and peel it off. Trim the edges of the sponge with a sharp knife and make a score mark 1 inch in from one shorter edge, being careful not to cut right through. Roll the cake firmly from the scored end, with the paper inside, and let cool.

—

Place the chocolate in a small heatproof bowl. Place the bowl over a saucepan of simmering water, making sure the base of the bowl is not touching the water, until melted. Warm the jam gently in a small saucepan until easily spreadable. If it is too warm it will soak straight into the sponge.

—

Carefully unroll the cooled cake. Remove the paper and spread the sponge with jam, then the whipped cream. Drizzle half the melted chocolate over the cream and swirl into it. Re-roll the sponge, then drizzle the remaining chocolate over the top and dust with cocoa powder to serve.

This is a rich, densely textured sponge cake. It is essential that the butter is a creamy spreadable consistency before mixing the ingredients together.

MADEIRA CAKE

SERVES 6

¾ cup (175g) salted butter, softened
¾ cup + 2 tbsps (175g) sugar
1¾ cups (225g) all-purpose flour
2½ tsps baking powder
½ tsp salt
½ cup (55g) almond flour
4 extra-large eggs
finely grated zest of 1 lemon
a thin slice of candied lemon peel

Preheat the oven to 350°F. Line the bottom of an 8-inch round cake pan with parchment paper.

—

Measure all the ingredients except the candied peel into a large mixing bowl. Whisk with an electric mixer until thoroughly mixed.

—

Spoon into the prepared pan and level the surface. Place the slice of candied peel in the center. Bake for about 50 minutes, until well-risen and lightly golden. A skewer inserted into the center should come out clean. Let cool in the pan for 10 minutes, then turn out, peel off the parchment paper, and finish cooling on a wire rack.

TIP
If a fruit or Madeira cake has a slight dip in the center when it comes out of the oven, turn it upside down onto parchment paper on a wire rack. The action of gravity and the weight of the cake will level the top while it cools.

This fatless sponge is a nice alternative to a round cake at teatime.
The filling can be easily jazzed up to serve the Swiss Roll as a dessert.

SWISS ROLL

SERVES 8

4 extra-large eggs
1 cup + 1 tbsp (115g) sugar,
    plus extra for sprinkling
1 cup (115g) all-purpose flour
1½ tsps baking powder
¼ tsp salt

For the filling
4 tbsps strawberry or
    raspberry jam

Preheat the oven to 425°F. Grease a 9 x 13-inch baking pan and line with parchment paper.

—

Whisk the eggs and sugar together in a large bowl until the mixture is light and frothy and the whisk leaves a trail when lifted out. Sift the flour, baking powder, and salt into the mixture, carefully folding it in at the same time. Turn the mixture into the prepared pan and give it a gentle shake so that the mixture finds its own level, making sure that it spreads evenly into the corners.

—

Bake for about 10 minutes, or until the sponge is golden brown and begins to shrink from the sides of the pan. While the cake is cooking, place a piece of parchment paper a little bigger than the size of the pan on a work surface and sprinkle it with sugar.

—

Invert the cake onto the sugared paper. Quickly loosen the paper on the bottom of the cake and peel it off. Trim the edges of the sponge with a sharp knife and make a score mark 1 inch in from one shorter edge, being careful not to cut right through.

—

Let cool slightly, then spread with the jam. If the cake is too hot, the jam will soak straight into the sponge. Roll up the cake firmly from the scored end.

To make a smaller Swiss Roll, use 3 extra-large eggs, 6 tbsps (75g) sugar, ⅔ cup (75g) flour, 1 tsp baking powder, and ⅛ tsp salt. Bake in a greased and lined 11 x 7-inch baking pan.

To make a Coffee Swiss Roll, fill the basic Swiss Roll with coffee buttercream made with ⅓ cup (75g) softened butter, 1¾ cups (225g) sifted confectioners' sugar, 2 tsps milk, and 2 tsps strong coffee.

To make a Raspberry or Strawberry Swiss Roll, fill the basic Swiss Roll with 1¼ cups (300ml) cream, whipped, and sliced strawberries or whole raspberries, or both!

This recipe is delicious flavored with orange too. Substitute an orange for the lemon and orange marmalade for the lemon curd.

LEMON SWISS ROLL

SERVES 8

4 extra-large eggs
1 cup + 1 tbsp (115g) sugar,
    plus extra for sprinkling
finely grated zest of 1 lemon
1 cup (115g) all-purpose flour
1½ tsps baking powder
¼ tsp salt

For the filling
4 tbsps lemon curd

Preheat the oven to 425°F. Grease a 9 x 13-inch baking pan and line with parchment paper.

—

Whisk the eggs, sugar, and lemon zest in a large bowl until the mixture is light and frothy and the whisk leaves a trail when lifted out. Sift the flour, baking powder, and salt into the mixture, carefully folding it in at the same time. Turn the mixture into the prepared pan and give it a gentle shake so that the mixture finds its own level, making sure that it spreads evenly into the corners.

—

Bake for about 10 minutes, or until the sponge is golden brown and begins to shrink from the sides of the pan. While the cake is cooking, place a piece of parchment paper a little bigger than the size of the pan on a work surface and sprinkle it with sugar.

—

Invert the cake onto the sugared paper. Quickly loosen the paper on the bottom of the cake and peel it off. Trim the edges of the sponge with a sharp knife and make a score mark 1 inch in from one shorter edge, being careful not to cut right through.

—

Let cool slightly, then spread with the lemon curd. If the cake is too hot, the lemon curd will soak straight into the sponge. Roll up the cake firmly from the scored end.

This is a version of a cake that has been a favorite with my family for many years. Expect it to dip slightly in the center. It can be served with coffee or as a dessert with cream and is best eaten warm.

APPLE AND APRICOT CAKE

SERVES 8

2 cups (250g) all-purpose flour

1⅓ tbsps baking powder

½ tsp salt

1 cup + 2 tbsps (225g) sugar

2 extra-large eggs

½ tsp almond extract

⅔ cup (150g) salted butter, melted

1–2 large (325g total) tart cooking apples, peeled, cored, and thickly sliced

¾ cup + 2 tbsps (115g) dried apricots, snipped into pieces

⅓ cup (30g) sliced almonds

Preheat the oven to 325°F. Grease an 8-inch round cake pan and line the bottom with parchment paper.

—

Measure the flour, baking powder, salt, sugar, eggs, almond extract, and melted butter into a large bowl. Mix well to combine, then beat well for 1 minute. Add the apples and apricots and gently mix them in with a spoon.

—

Spoon the mixture into the prepared pan, gently level the surface and sprinkle with the sliced almonds. Bake for 1–1½ hours, until the cake is golden, firm to the touch, and beginning to shrink away from the side of the pan. Let cool in the pan for a few minutes, then turn out, peel off the parchment paper, and put onto a plate to serve warm.

This Canadian-inspired cake is a real treat for a special gathering.
Fill and cover ahead of time, so that the cake keeps moist.

MAPLE SYRUP CAKE

CUTS INTO 6-8 GENEROUS SLICES

1 cup (225g) salted butter, softened
1 cup + 3 tbsps (225g) light muscovado sugar
finely grated zest of 1 orange
4 extra-large eggs
⅓ cup (100ml) maple syrup
2¾ cups (350g) all-purpose flour
1½ tbsps baking powder
¾ tsp salt
½ tsp ground ginger
½ cup (55g) pecans, chopped

For the filling and topping
~2 cups (450ml) heavy cream
2 tbsps maple syrup
zest of 1 orange, to decorate

Preheat the oven to 325°F. Grease an 8-inch round cake pan and line the bottom with parchment paper.

——

Measure all the cake ingredients except the pecans into a large bowl and beat until evenly blended. Stir in the chopped pecans.

——

Spoon the mixture into the prepared pan and level the surface. Bake for about 1½ hours, until well-risen, golden, and springy to the touch. Let cool in the pan for a few minutes, then turn out, peel off the parchment paper, and finish cooling on a wire rack.

——

To make the filling and topping, whip the cream until it just holds its shape, then fold in the maple syrup.

——

Cut the cake into three pieces horizontally using a serrated or bread knife. Sit one piece on a plate and spread with some of the cream, right to the edge. Continue stacking the pieces and spreading with the cream. Finally, smooth the cream evenly over the top and sides of the whole cake and decorate the top with the orange zest. Keep chilled in the fridge.

The walnuts in this cake really complement the coffee flavor and provide extra bite to contrast the moist cake and the smooth buttercream.

COFFEE AND WALNUT SPONGE CAKE

SERVES 6

½ cup (115g) salted butter, softened
½ cup + 1 tbsp (115g) granulated sugar
2 extra-large eggs
1 cup (115g) all-purpose flour
2 tsps baking powder
¼ tsp salt
½ cup (55g) chopped walnuts
1 tbsp strong coffee

For the filling and topping
⅓ cup (75g) salted butter, softened
1¾ cups (225g) confectioners' sugar, sifted
2 tsps milk
2 tsps strong coffee
6 walnut halves, to decorate

Preheat the oven to 350°F. Grease two 8-inch round cake pans and line the bottom of each pan with parchment paper.

—

Measure all the cake ingredients into a bowl and beat until thoroughly blended and smooth.

—

Divide the mixture between the cake pans and level the surfaces. Bake for 20–25 minutes, or until well-risen and the top of the cakes spring back when lightly pressed with a finger. Let cool in the pans for a few minutes, then turn out, peel off the parchment paper, and finish cooling on a wire rack.

—

To make the filling and topping, beat together the butter, confectioners' sugar, milk, and coffee in a bowl until smooth. When the cakes are completely cold, sandwich together with half of the filling and use the rest for the top of the cake. Decorate with the walnut halves.

TIP
To make strong coffee, use 2 teaspoons instant coffee granules mixed with 1 tablespoon hot water.

Make sure you use deep cake pans, as the shallower pans tend to overflow.

CAPPUCCINO CAKE

SERVES 8

⅔ cup (55g) cocoa powder
6 tbsps boiling water
3 extra-large eggs
3 tbsps (50ml) milk
1⅓ cups (175g) all-purpose
    flour
2¾ tsps baking powder
½ tsp salt
½ cup (115g) salted butter,
    softened
1 cup + 6 tbsps (275g) sugar

For the filling and topping
1¼ cups (300ml) heavy
    cream
1 tsp instant coffee granules,
    dissolved in 2 tsps hot
    water
a little cocoa powder
    or drinking chocolate,
    for dusting

Preheat the oven to 350°F. Grease two 8-inch round cake pans and line the bottom of each pan with parchment paper.

—

Measure the cocoa powder into a large mixing bowl, add the boiling water and mix well until it has a paste-like consistency. Add all the remaining ingredients to the bowl and beat until just combined. The mixture will be a fairly thick batter (be careful not to overbeat).

—

Divide the cake mixture between the prepared pans and gently level the surfaces. Bake for 25–30 minutes, until the cakes are well-risen and beginning to shrink away from the sides of the pans. Let cool in the pans for a few minutes, then turn out, peel off the parchment paper, and finish cooling on a wire rack.

—

To finish the cake, whip the cream until it just holds its shape, then stir in the dissolved coffee. Use half the cream to fill the cake, and spread the remainder over the top. Gently smooth the surface with an offset spatula and dust with sifted cocoa powder or drinking chocolate.

TIP
This cake is best eaten fresh. Store it in the fridge if necessary.

This is a lovely moist cake. Keep it in the fridge and eat within a week.

LEMON YOGURT CAKE

SERVES 8

1½ cups (300g) granulated
  sugar
¼ cup (55g) salted butter,
  softened
3 extra-large eggs, separated
¾ cup + 1 tbsp (225g) Greek
  yogurt
finely grated zest of 1 lemon
1⅓ cups (175g) all-purpose
  flour
2 tsps baking powder
½ tsp salt

For the icing
1 cup (115g) confectioners'
  sugar, sifted
about 1½ tbsps fresh lemon
  juice

Preheat the oven to 350°F. Grease an 8-inch round cake pan and line the bottom with parchment paper.

—

Beat together the sugar, butter, and egg yolks in a bowl. Add the yogurt and lemon zest, and beat until smooth. Gently fold in the flour, baking powder, and salt.

—

Whisk the egg whites to a soft peak, then carefully fold into the cake mixture.

—

Turn into the prepared pan and bake for 1–1¼ hours, or until the cake is well-risen and firm to the touch. Let cool in the pan for a few minutes, then turn out, peel off the parchment paper, and finish cooling on a wire rack.

—

For the icing, mix together the sifted confectioners' sugar and the lemon juice and pour over the cold cake. Smooth over with an offset spatula and let set.

You can use either marzipan or homemade or bought almond paste for this famous checkerboard cake.

BATTENBERG CAKE
SERVES 8

½ cup (115g) salted butter, softened
½ cup + 1 tbsp (115g) sugar
2 extra-large eggs
½ cup (55g) almond flour
1 cup (115g) all-purpose flour
2 tsps baking powder
¼ tsp salt
a few drops of almond extract
red food coloring

To finish
about 3–4 tbsps apricot jam
1 cup (225g) almond paste or marzipan (see page 398 for almond paste recipe)

TIP
If you haven't got a Battenberg pan, grease a 7-inch square cake pan. Cut out a piece of parchment paper that is 3 inches longer than one side of the pan. Fold the paper in half crosswise. Open out the paper and push up the center fold to a 1½-inch pleat. Line the bottom of the pan with this, making any adjustments to ensure the pleat runs down the center of the pan.

Preheat the oven to 325°F. Grease a 7-inch Battenberg pan and line the bottom with parchment paper.

Measure the butter, sugar, eggs, almond flour, flour, baking powder, salt, and almond extract into a large bowl and beat for about 2 minutes until smooth.

Spoon half the mixture into the right half of the prepared pan as neatly as possible. Add a few drops of red food coloring to the remaining mixture to turn it a deep pink color, then spoon this into the left half of the pan. Try to get the seam between the 2 mixtures as neat as possible. Smooth the surface of each half.

Bake for 35–40 minutes, or until the cake is well-risen, springy to the touch, and has shrunk slightly from the sides of the pan. Let cool in the pan for a few minutes, then turn out, peel off the parchment paper, and finish cooling on a wire rack.

Trim the edges of the cake and then cut into 4 equal strips— 2 pink and 2 plain.

Gently heat the apricot jam in a small saucepan. Use the warmed jam to stick the 4 strips of cake together to make a checkerboard effect. Brush the top of the assembled cake with apricot jam.

Roll out the almond paste or marzipan into an oblong the length of the cake and sufficiently wide to wrap around the cake. Invert the cake onto the almond paste or marzipan, then brush the remaining 3 sides with apricot jam. Press the almond paste or marzipan neatly around the cake, arranging the seam in one corner. Score the top of the cake with a crisscross pattern and crimp the edges with your fingers to decorate.

This cake is always popular and a great idea for charity events or family get-togethers. I'm afraid, though, that it sounds much healthier than it really is!

CARROT CAKE

SERVES 8

1¾ cups (225g) all-purpose flour

1 tbsp baking powder

½ tsp salt

¾ cup (150g) light muscovado sugar

½ cup (55g) chopped walnuts

1 cup + 1 tbsp (115g) carrots, coarsely grated

2 ripe bananas, mashed

2 extra-large eggs

⅔ cup (150ml) sunflower or vegetable oil

For the topping

¾ cup (175g) full-fat cream cheese

¼ cup (55g) salted butter, softened

1 cup (115g) confectioners' sugar, sifted

a few drops of vanilla extract

walnut halves, to decorate

Preheat the oven to 350°F. Grease an 8-inch round cake pan and line the bottom with parchment paper.

—

Measure all the cake ingredients into a large bowl and beat well until thoroughly blended and smooth.

—

Turn into the prepared pan and level the surface. Bake for 50–60 minutes, until the cake is well-risen and shrinking away from the sides of the pan. Let cool in the pan for a few minutes, then turn out, peel off the parchment paper, and finish cooling on a wire rack.

—

For the topping, measure all the ingredients, except the walnuts, into a bowl or food processor, and blitz until smooth. Spread over the top of the cake, swirling with a spatula for a decorative effect. Decorate with the walnut halves and chill a little before serving. Store in the fridge as the topping is soft.

This is a truly old-fashioned cake iced with a simple "American frosting." If you have a sugar thermometer, try the alternative American frosting recipe on page 401.

FROSTED WALNUT LAYER CAKE

SERVES 8

1 cup (225g) salted butter, softened
1 cup + 2 tbsps (225g) sugar
4 extra-large eggs
1¾ cups (225g) all-purpose flour
1 tbsp baking powder
½ tsp salt
1 cup (115g) finely chopped walnuts

For the frosting
2 extra-large egg whites
1¾ cups (350g) sugar
4 tbsps water
¼ tsp cream of tartar

To decorate
walnut halves

Preheat the oven to 325°F. Grease three 8-inch round cake pans and line the bottom of each pan with parchment paper.

—

Measure all the cake ingredients into a large bowl and beat until thoroughly blended.

—

Divide the mixture equally between the pans and level the surfaces. Bake for 25–30 minutes, until the cakes are golden and springy to the touch. Let cool in the pan for a few minutes, then turn out, peel off the parchment paper, and finish cooling on a wire rack.

—

For the frosting, measure all the ingredients into a heatproof bowl over a saucepan of hot water and whisk for 10–12 minutes until thick.

—

Sandwich the cake layers together with a little of the frosting, then use the remainder to cover the top and sides of the cake, swirling the frosting to form softened peaks. Work quickly as the frosting sets rapidly. Let it set in a cool place, but not in the fridge. Decorate with the walnut halves.

TIP

Don't be tempted to use more baking powder than specified or the cake will rise up, then sink back again. In this all-in-one method, baking powder is used to give the cake the necessary lift. The quickness of the method means that less air is whisked into the mixture than if making the cake the traditional way.

Wash and dry the quartered cherries thoroughly before adding them to the cake mixture. This prevents them from sinking to the bottom during baking.

ENGLISH CHERRY CAKE

SERVES 8

1 cup + 3 tbsps (200g) maraschino cherries
2¼ cups (275g) all-purpose flour, plus 1 tbsp
¾ cup (75g) almond flour
1½ tbsps baking powder
½ tsp salt
1 cup (225g) salted butter, softened
1 cup + 2 tbsps (225g) sugar
4 extra-large eggs

Preheat the oven to 325°F. Grease an 8-inch round cake pan, then line the bottom with parchment paper.

—

Cut the cherries into quarters, put in a sieve, and rinse under running water. Drain well and dry thoroughly on a paper towel. Toss in the 1 tablespoon of flour.

—

Measure all the remaining ingredients into a large bowl and beat for 1 minute to mix thoroughly. Lightly fold in the cherries.

—

Turn into the prepared pan and level the surface. Bake for 1½–1¾ hours, or until a skewer inserted into the center of the cake comes out clean. Let cool in the pan for 10 minutes, then turn out, peel off the parchment paper, and finish cooling on a wire rack.

The same crunchy topping can be used on sheet cakes and tea cakes. The secret is to pour the crunchy topping over the cake while it is still warm so that the lemon soaks in and the sugar stays on top.

CRUNCHY-TOP LEMON CAKE

SERVES 8

½ cup (115g) salted butter, softened
¾ cup + 2 tbsps (175g) sugar
1⅓ cups (175g) all-purpose flour
2¾ tsps baking powder
½ tsp salt
2 extra-large eggs, beaten
4 tbsps milk
finely grated zest of 1 lemon

For the topping
juice of 1 lemon
½ cup + 1 tbsp (115g) sugar

Preheat the oven to 350°F. Grease an 8-inch round cake pan and line the bottom with parchment paper.

—

Measure all the cake ingredients into a large bowl and beat for about 2 minutes until smooth and well-blended.

—

Turn the mixture into the prepared pan and level the surface. Bake for 35–40 minutes, or until the cake has shrunk slightly from the sides of the pan and springs back when lightly pressed with a finger.

—

While the cake is baking, make the crunchy topping. Measure the lemon juice and sugar into a bowl and stir until blended. When the cake comes out of the oven, spread the lemon paste over the top while the cake is still hot. Let cool completely in the pan, then turn out and peel off the parchment paper.

TIP
If a softened cake has sunk disastrously in the middle, cut this out, fill with softened fruits and whipped cream, and serve as a dessert.

A lovely light sponge cake, this is always popular and is especially good on the day it's made.

DOUBLE ORANGE CAKE

SERVES 8

¾ cup (175g) salted butter, softened
¾ cup + 2 tbsps (175g) granulated sugar
3 extra-large eggs, beaten
1⅓ cups (175g) all-purpose flour
2¾ tsps baking powder
½ tsp salt
finely grated zest and juice of 1 large orange

To finish
about 2 tbsps apricot jam
1 cup (115g) confectioners' sugar
finely grated zest and juice of ½ orange

Preheat the oven to 350°F. Grease an 8-inch round cake pan, then line the bottom with parchment paper.

—

Measure all the cake ingredients into a large bowl and beat until thoroughly blended.

—

Turn into the prepared pan and level the surface. Bake for about 35 minutes, until well-risen and springy to the touch. Let cool in the pan for a few minutes, then turn out, peel off the parchment paper, and finish cooling on a wire rack.

—

Measure the apricot jam into a small pan and gently warm through. Brush the jam over the top of the cake.

—

Sift the confectioners' sugar into a bowl and mix in the orange juice to a coating consistency. Pour over the top of the cake and gently spread out with a small offset spatula. Allow to set before decorating with the orange zest.

CHAPTER TWO

SPICED CAKES

Gingerbread is said to be one of the oldest forms of cake in the world. Most European countries have their own version. One of the major advantages of homemade gingerbread is that it improves with keeping.

ICED GINGERBREAD WITH CRYSTALLIZED GINGER

CUTS INTO 16 SQUARES

½ cup (115g) salted butter, softened

½ cup + 2 tbsps (115g) light muscovado sugar

2 extra-large eggs

⅓ cup + 2 tbsps (150g) molasses

⅓ cup + 2 tbsps (150g) golden syrup or light corn syrup

1¾ cups (225g) all-purpose flour

1 tsp ground ginger

1 tsp pumpkin pie spice

½ tsp baking soda

2 tbsps milk

For the icing

1⅓ cups (175g) confectioners' sugar

3 tbsps water

2 tbsps chopped crystallized ginger

Preheat the oven to 325°F. Grease an 8-inch square cake pan, then line the bottom with parchment paper.

—

Measure the butter, sugar, eggs, molasses, and golden syrup (or light corn syrup) into a bowl and beat until thoroughly mixed. Sift the flour with the spices and fold into the mixture. Add the baking soda to the milk, then stir this into the mixture.

—

Pour into the prepared pan and level the surface. Bake for 1 hour.

—

Lower the oven temperature to 300°F and bake for an additional 15–30 minutes, or until well-risen and firm to the touch. Let cool in the pan for 10 minutes, then turn out, peel off the parchment paper, and finish cooling on a wire rack.

—

For the icing, sift the confectioners' sugar into a bowl and add the water to make a spreading consistency. Mix to form a smooth icing. Add the chopped crystallized ginger and pour the icing over the cake. Allow to set before cutting into squares.

A favorite from the north of England, parkin definitely improves with keeping, so try to store it for at least a week before cutting.

TRADITIONAL PARKIN

CUTS INTO 16 SQUARES

½ cup (175g) molasses
⅔ cup (150g) salted butter
½ cup + 2 tbsps (115g) dark muscovado sugar
1⅓ cups (175g) all-purpose flour
2 tsps ground ginger
1 tsp ground cinnamon
1 tsp freshly grated nutmeg
3 cups (275g) rolled oats
1 extra-large egg
⅔ cup (150ml) milk
1 tsp baking soda

Preheat the oven to 350°F. Grease an 8-inch square cake pan, then line the base with parchment paper.

Measure the molasses, butter, and sugar into a medium saucepan and heat gently until the butter has melted and the sugar has dissolved. Allow to cool slightly.

Sift the flour and spices into a large bowl and add the rolled oats. Mix together the egg and milk and stir in the baking soda. Add to the dry ingredients, along with the molasses mixture, and stir well to mix.

Pour into the prepared pan and bake for about 1 hour, or until firm to the touch. Let cool in the pan for 10 minutes, then turn out, peel off the parchment paper, and finish cooling on a wire rack.

Wrap the cold parkin in parchment paper and store in a cake pan for a week before cutting into 16 squares.

A thin layer of sweet almond paste is baked through the center of this cake and works very well with the warming flavors of cinnamon and clove.

ALMOND SPICE CAKE

SERVES 8

½ cup (115g) almond paste or marzipan (see page 398 for almond paste recipe)
¾ cup (175g) salted butter, softened
¾ cup + 2 tbsps (175g) sugar
3 extra-large eggs
1¾ cups (225g) all-purpose flour
1 tbsp baking powder
½ tsp salt
½ tsp ground cinnamon
¼ tsp ground cloves
1⅓ cups (115g) sliced almonds, toasted

For the topping
¼ cup (55g) salted butter
½ cup + 2 tbsps (115g) light muscovado sugar
2 tbsps heavy cream

Preheat the oven to 350°F. Grease an 8-inch round cake pan, then line the bottom with parchment paper.

Roll out the almond paste or marzipan to an 8-inch circle, then set aside.

Measure the butter, sugar, eggs, flour, baking powder, salt, and spices into a bowl and beat until thoroughly blended. Fold in 1 cup of the toasted sliced almonds.

Spoon half of the cake mixture into the prepared pan and level the surface. Lightly place the circle of almond paste on top, then add the remaining cake mixture and level the surface.

Bake for 1–1¼ hours, or until well-risen, golden brown, and the surface springs back when lightly pressed with a finger. Let cool in the pan for 5 minutes, then turn out, peel off the parchment paper, and finish cooling on a wire rack.

For the topping, heat the butter, sugar, and cream in a saucepan until blended, then bring to a boil. Stand the wire rack on a sheet pan to catch any drips, and drizzle the icing over the cake. Sprinkle with the remaining toasted sliced almonds, then allow to set for 10–15 minutes.

If possible, store the cake for two days, wrapped in parchment paper and foil, before icing. This allows the cake to mature and become moist and sticky.

STICKY GINGER AND ORANGE CAKE

SERVES 8

⅓ cup (115g) golden syrup or
    light corn syrup
⅓ cup (115g) molasses
1 cup (250ml) water
½ cup (115g) salted butter,
    softened
½ cup + 1 tbsp (115g)
    granulated sugar
finely grated zest of 1 orange
1 extra-large egg, beaten
2¼ cups (275g) all-purpose
    flour
1½ tsps baking soda
1 tsp ground cinnamon
1 tsp ground ginger

For the icing
1 cup (115g) confectioners'
    sugar
juice of 1 orange

Preheat the oven to 350°F. Grease a 9-inch round cake pan, then line the bottom and sides with parchment paper.

—

Measure the golden syrup (or light corn syrup) and molasses into a saucepan along with the water and bring to a boil.

—

Meanwhile, put the remaining cake ingredients into a mixing bowl and beat well until thoroughly blended. Add the syrup and molasses mixture and beat again until smooth.

—

Pour the mixture into the prepared pan and level the surface. Bake for about 50 minutes, or until a skewer inserted into the center comes out clean. Let cool in the pan for 10 minutes, then turn out, peel off the parchment paper, and finish cooling on a wire rack.

—

To make the icing, sift the confectioners' sugar into a bowl and add enough orange juice to make a smooth, fairly thick mixture. Stand the wire rack on a sheet pan to catch any drips, then spoon the icing over the top of the cake and allow to set for about 1 hour.

This keeps and freezes extremely well. Sometimes you get a dip in the middle of the gingerbread, which indicates that you have been a bit heavy-handed with the syrup and molasses. It just means it tastes even more scrumptious!

CLASSIC STICKY GINGERBREAD

CUTS INTO 16 PIECES

1 cup (225g) salted butter
1 cup + 3 tbsps (225g) light muscovado sugar
⅔ cup (225g) golden syrup or light corn syrup
⅔ cup (225g) molasses
1¾ cups (225g) all-purpose flour
2 cups (225g) whole wheat flour
2½ tsps baking powder
½ tsp salt
4 tsps ground ginger
2 extra-large eggs
1¼ cups (300ml) milk

Preheat the oven to 325°F. Grease a 9 x 13-inch baking pan, then line the bottom and sides with parchment paper.

—

Measure the butter, sugar, golden syrup or light corn syrup, and molasses into a medium saucepan and heat gently until the mixture has melted evenly. Allow to cool slightly.

—

Put the flours, baking powder, salt, and ground ginger into a large bowl and stir together lightly. Beat the eggs into the milk. Pour the cooled butter and syrup mixture into the flour, along with the egg and milk mixture, and beat until smooth.

—

Pour the mixture into the prepared pan and tilt gently to level the surface. Bake for 50 minutes, until well-risen, golden, and springy to the touch. Let cool in the pan for a few minutes, then turn out, peel off the parchment paper, and finish cooling on a wire rack.

—

When cold, cut into 16 squares.

This is a good family cake. It goes quite dark when baked because of the whole wheat flour.

JANE'S FRUIT CAKE

SERVES 8

¾ cup + 2 tbsps (200g) salted butter, softened
1¾ cups + 2 tbsps (350g) light muscovado sugar
3 extra-large eggs
4 cups (450g) whole wheat flour
2 tbsps baking powder
1 tsp salt
1 tsp ground ginger
½ cup + 2 tbsps (150ml) buttermilk
2½ cups (350g) golden raisins
2½ cups (350g) currants
⅔ cup (55g) sliced almonds, for sprinkling

Preheat the oven to 275°F. Grease a 9-inch round cake pan and line the bottom and sides with a double layer of parchment paper.

—

Measure all the cake ingredients, except the sliced almonds, into a large bowl and mix thoroughly. Beat the mixture for 2–3 minutes until smooth and glossy.

—

Spoon into the prepared pan and level the surface. Sprinkle with the sliced almonds. Bake for 3–3½ hours, or until a skewer inserted into the center comes out clean. Let cool in the pan, then turn out but leave the parchment paper on as this helps to keep the cake moist.

—

Wrap the cake in more parchment paper and then some foil to store, and keep in a cool place.

Excellent if you are short on time, this cake is quick to make and needs no maturing.

BOOZY FRUIT CAKE

SERVES 8

⅔ cup (150g) salted butter, softened
½ cup (175g) golden syrup or light corn syrup
¾ cup (175ml) milk
⅔ cup (115g) dried pitted dates, roughly chopped
1 cup (150g) golden raisins
1 cup (150g) raisins
⅓ cup (55g) currants
⅔ cup (55g) candied orange or lemon peel, finely chopped
1 cup (115g) walnuts, roughly chopped
1¾ cups (225g) all-purpose flour
2 tsps pumpkin pie spice
½ tsp baking soda
2 extra-large eggs
4 tbsps brandy, rum, or sherry, to feed the cake

Preheat the oven to 300°F. Grease an 8-inch round cake pan, then line the bottom and sides with a double layer of parchment paper.

—

Measure the butter, syrup, milk, dried fruit, chopped orange or lemon peel, and nuts into a saucepan and gently heat, stirring occasionally, until the butter has melted. Simmer very gently for 5 minutes. Allow to cool slightly.

—

Sift the flour, spices, and baking soda into a bowl, add the fruit mixture and the eggs, and beat until thoroughly combined.

—

Pour into the prepared pan and level the surface. Bake for 1½–1¾ hours, or until firm to the touch and a skewer inserted into the center comes out clean. Allow the cake to cool in the pan for 10 minutes.

—

Remove the cake from the pan, peel off the parchment paper, and pierce the top of the cake in several places with a skewer. Spoon in a little brandy, rum, or sherry. Replace the parchment paper on the bottom of the cake, as this helps to keep the cake moist. Wrap in more parchment paper and then some foil, and store in a cool place.

—

Feed the cake at intervals with the alcohol, alternating feeding the top and then the bottom of the cake. To give as a gift, wrap in cellophane with a generous bow on top.

This is a traditional name for a cake that is so delicious that everyone will come back for another slice. Good for a hungry family, this is not a rich cake, so it is best eaten as fresh as possible.

CUT AND COME AGAIN CAKE

SERVES 8

2¾ cups (350g) all-purpose flour
4 tsps baking powder
¾ tsp salt
1 tsp pumpkin pie spice
¾ cup (175g) salted butter, softened
¾ cup + 2 tbsps (175g) sugar
3 extra-large eggs, beaten
1¼ cup (175g) currants
¾ cup (115g) golden raisins
¾ cup (115g) raisins
3 tbsps milk

Preheat the oven to 350°F. Grease an 8-inch round cake pan, then line the bottom with parchment paper.

—

Measure all the ingredients into a large bowl and beat until thoroughly mixed.

—

Turn into the prepared pan and level the surface. Bake for 1¼–1½ hours, or until a skewer inserted into the center of the cake comes out clean. Let cool in the pan for 10 minutes, then turn out, peel off the parchment paper, and finish cooling on a wire rack.

In Victorian times, cakes were made larger than they are now, and so one-pound quantities—hence the name—would have been used. In this version, the ingredients are in half-pound quantities.

POUND CAKE

SERVES 8

⅔ cup (115g) maraschino cherries, quartered
1 cup (225g) salted butter, softened
1 cup + 3 tbsps (225g) light muscovado sugar
4 extra-large eggs
1¾ cups (225g) all-purpose flour
2½ tsps baking powder
½ tsp salt
1½ cups (225g) raisins
1½ cups (225g) golden raisins
1 tsp pumpkin pie spice
1 tbsp brandy

Preheat the oven to 300°F. Grease an 8-inch round cake pan, then line the bottom with parchment paper.

—

Place the cherries in a sieve and rinse under running water. Drain well, then dry thoroughly on a paper towel. Measure all the ingredients into a large bowl and beat together until thoroughly combined.

—

Turn the mixture into the prepared pan and level the surface. Bake for 2–2¼ hours, covering the top with parchment paper after an hour to prevent the cake from becoming too brown. When cooked, the cake should be firm to the touch and a skewer inserted into the center should come out clean. Let cool in the pan for 30 minutes, then turn out, peel off the parchment paper, and finish cooling on a wire rack.

CHAPTER THREE

CHOCOLATE TREATS

These small loaves are great to take on a picnic. You can vary the thickness of the slices, depending on how much of a sweet tooth your guests have!

BROWNIE LOAVES WITH WHITE CHOCOLATE CHIPS

MAKES 2 LOAVES

½ cup (55g) almond flour
1 cup + 1 tbsp (225g) buttery
 spread, straight from the
 fridge
1⅓ cups (175g) all-purpose
 flour
1 cup + 3 tbsps (225g) light
 muscovado sugar
⅔ cup (55g) cocoa powder
5 extra-large eggs
3 tsps baking powder
½ tsp salt
¾ cup (150g) white
 chocolate chips

For the frosting
6 ounces (175g) dark
 chocolate, broken into
 pieces
¼ cup (50g) salted butter

Preheat the oven to 350°F. Grease and line two 8½ x 4½-inch loaf pans with parchment paper.

Measure all the brownie loaf ingredients, except the white chocolate chips, into a large bowl. Whisk together using an electric mixer until light and fluffy. Stir in ⅔ cup (125g) of the chocolate chips.

Spoon into the prepared pans and level the surfaces. Bake for about 1 hour, or until well-risen and the top of the loaves spring back when lightly pressed. Let cool in the pan for a few minutes, then turn out onto a wire rack and peel off the parchment paper.

To make the frosting, melt the dark chocolate and butter in a heatproof bowl over a saucepan of simmering water. Let cool slightly. Fold in the remaining white chocolate chips before spreading over the tops of the loaves to make a ripple effect.

Cut each loaf into slices to serve.

TIP
The loaves freeze well.

A really simple brownie recipe—just measure all the ingredients into a bowl and give it a good mix! Be careful not to overcook your brownies: they should have a slightly gooey texture. The outside crust should be on the crisp side, though, thanks to the high proportion of sugar.

CHOCOLATE CHIP BROWNIES

CUTS INTO 24 PIECES

1¼ cups (275g) salted butter, softened
1¾ cups + 2 tbsps (375g) sugar
4 extra-large eggs
¾ cup (75g) cocoa powder
1 cup (115g) all-purpose flour
1½ tsps baking powder
¼ tsp salt
⅔ cup (115g) dark chocolate chips

Preheat the oven to 350°F. Grease a 9 x 13-inch baking pan, then line the bottom and sides with parchment paper.

—

Measure all the ingredients into a large bowl and beat until evenly blended.

—

Spoon the mixture into the prepared pan, scraping the sides of the bowl with a silicone spatula. Gently spread the mixture to the corners of the pan and level the surface. Bake for 40–45 minutes, or until the brownies have a crusty top and a skewer inserted into the center comes out clean. (Cover loosely with foil for the last 10 minutes if the mixture is browning too much.) Let cool in the pan.

—

Cut into 24 pieces and store in an airtight container.

With a little coffee, some chopped walnuts, and the addition of dark chocolate chips, these brownies have a rich, "grown-up" flavor. Cooked brownie mixture, like gingerbread, is likely to dip in the middle, but this all adds to the charm.

DARK INDULGENT CHOCOLATE AND WALNUT BROWNIES

CUTS INTO 24 PIECES

12 ounces (350g) dark chocolate, broken into pieces
1 cup (225g) salted butter
2 tsps instant coffee granules
2 tbsps hot water
3 extra-large eggs
1 cup + 2 tbsps (225g) sugar
1 tsp vanilla extract
⅔ cup (75g) all-purpose flour
1 tsp baking powder
¼ tsp salt
1⅓ cups (175g) walnuts, chopped
1¼ cups (225g) dark chocolate chips

Preheat the oven to 375°F. Grease a 9 x 13-inch baking pan, then line the bottom with parchment paper.

Place the chocolate and butter in a large heatproof bowl set over a saucepan of simmering water until melted, stirring occasionally. Let cool.

Dissolve the coffee in the hot water in a large bowl and allow to cool for 5 minutes. Add the eggs, sugar, and vanilla extract and mix together.

Gradually beat the chocolate mixture into the coffee mixture, then fold in the flour, baking powder, salt, walnuts, and chocolate chips.

Pour the mixture into the prepared pan and level the surface. Bake for 40–45 minutes, or until the brownies have a crusty top and a skewer inserted into the center comes out clean. Allow the brownies to cool in the pan.

Cut into 24 pieces. Store in an airtight container.

I have included a generous amount of frosting to fill and ice this cake, as death by chocolate should be sheer luxury and a complete indulgence! The frosting is very easy to make, but take care not to overheat it or it will lose its shine.

DEATH BY CHOCOLATE CAKE

SERVES 8

2¼ cups (275g) all-purpose flour
3 tbsps cocoa powder
1½ tsps baking soda
1½ tsps baking powder
1 cup (200g) sugar
3 tbsps golden syrup or light corn syrup
3 extra-large eggs, beaten
¾ cup + 3 tbsps (225ml) sunflower oil
¾ cup + 3 tbsps (225ml) milk

For the frosting
1 lb (450g) dark chocolate, broken into pieces
¾ cup + 2 tbsps (200g) unsalted butter

To finish
2 ounces (55g) Belgian white chocolate, coarsely grated
2 ounces (55g) dark chocolate, coarsely grated

TIP
Don't store the cake in the fridge, or the frosting will lose its shine—a cool place is fine.

Preheat the oven to 325°F. Grease two 8-inch cake pans, then line the bottom of each with parchment paper.

Sift the flour, cocoa powder, baking soda, and baking powder into a large bowl. Add the sugar and mix well. Make a well in the center of the dry ingredients and add the golden syrup or light corn syrup, eggs, oil, and milk. Beat well, using a wooden spoon, until smooth.

Pour into the prepared pans and level the surfaces. Bake for about 35 minutes, or until well-risen and the tops of the cakes spring back when lightly pressed with a finger. Let cool in the pans for a few minutes, then turn out, peel off the parchment paper, and finish cooling on a wire rack. When cold, cut each cake in half horizontally using a serrated or bread knife.

To make the frosting, place the chocolate in a large heatproof bowl. Place the bowl over a saucepan of simmering water until the chocolate has melted, making sure that the bottom of the bowl is not touching the water and you do not overheat the chocolate. Remove from the heat, add the butter, and allow it to melt into the chocolate.

Stand the wire rack on a sheet pan to catch any drips, then sandwich the cake layers together with the frosting. Pour the remaining frosting over the top of the cake and use a small offset spatula to smooth it evenly over the top and around the sides. Allow it to set.

Decorate with the grated white and dark chocolates.

There are quite a few stages to this cake, so it's not one to tackle if you're in a hurry, but you can make the cake in advance and freeze it. Be very light-handed when folding in the flour and melted butter, or the butter will sink and result in a heavy cake. Eat as a dessert, with a fork.

CHOCOLATE MOUSSE CAKE

SERVES 8

2 tbsps (30g) salted butter
6 extra-large eggs
¾ cup + 2 tbsps (175g) sugar
1 cup (115g) all-purpose flour
⅓ cup (30g) cocoa powder
2 tbsps cornstarch
1½ tsps baking powder
¼ tsp salt

For the mousse filling
1¼ tsps powdered gelatin
6 ounces (175g) dark
    chocolate, broken into
    pieces
2 tbsps brandy
2 tbsps warm water
2 extra-large eggs, separated
1¼ cups (300ml) heavy
    cream, whipped
    to soft peaks

For the decoration
7 ounces (200g) dark
    chocolate
5 ounces (150g) Belgian
    white chocolate

To finish
⅔ cup (150ml) heavy cream,
    whipped
confectioners' sugar, for
    dusting

Preheat the oven to 350°F. Grease a 9-inch springform pan, then line the bottom with parchment paper.

—

Put the butter in a small saucepan and heat gently until melted, then let cool slightly.

—

Beat the eggs and sugar together at full speed until the mixture is pale, creamy, and thick enough to leave a trail when the whisk is lifted from the mixture.

—

Sift the flour, cocoa, cornstarch, baking powder, and salt together.

—

Carefully fold half the dry ingredients into the egg mixture. Pour half the cooled butter around the edge of the mixture and carefully fold in. Gradually fold in the remaining dry ingredients, then the remaining butter.

—

Pour the mixture into the prepared pan and level the surface. Bake for 35–40 minutes, or until well-risen and the top of the cake springs back when lightly pressed with a finger. Let cool in the pan for a few minutes, then turn out, peel off the parchment paper, and finish cooling on a wire rack. Wash the cake pan and, when the cake is cold, cut it in half horizontally using a serrated or bread knife and put the bottom half back in the pan.

—

Recipe continued on the next page

To make the mousse filling, place the powdered gelatin in a small bowl and add 2 tablespoons of warm water. Stir for a few minutes until dissolved. Make sure never to boil any gelatin mixture as it will lose its thickening quality.

Meanwhile, melt the chocolate with the brandy in a heatproof bowl set over a pan of simmering water, making sure the bottom of the bowl is not touching the water, stirring occasionally. Once the melted chocolate has cooled slightly, dissolve the gelatin, along with the egg yolks. Fold in the whipped cream.

Whisk the egg whites until stiff but not dry, then gently fold into the chocolate mixture. Pour the mousse on top of the cake in the pan. Gently level the surface and top with the remaining cake. Cover and allow to set in the fridge for a minimum of 4 hours.

While the mousse is setting, shave the dark chocolate and white chocolate with a vegetable peeler for the decoration and keep them separate.

When the mousse is set, ease around the sides of the mousse with a small offset spatula, then stand the bottom of the cake pan on a large can. Ease the sides of the pan down, then slip the cake off the cake pan bottom and onto a serving plate.

Cover the top and sides of the cake with whipped cream and arrange the dark and white chocolate shavings to cover the cake completely, in any pattern you'd like! Finish with a little dusting of sifted confectioners' sugar.

The origin of this pie is rather uncertain, but it has become a very popular dessert in cafés and bistros. Like many American recipes, it is rich, so serve in small slices.

MISSISSIPPI MUD PIE

SERVES 6-8

For the crust
¾ cup (115g) graham crackers, crushed
¼ cup (55g) salted butter, melted
2 tbsps (30g) demerara sugar

For the filling
7 ounces (200g) dark chocolate, broken into pieces
½ cup (115g) salted butter
1 heaped tsp instant coffee granules
1 tbsp boiling water
1¼ cups (300ml) half-and-half
¾ cup + 3 tbsps (175g) dark muscovado sugar
6 extra-large eggs, beaten

To finish
⅔ cup (150ml) heavy cream, whipped

Preheat the oven to 350°F. Grease a 9-inch springform pan.

—

To make the crust, mix together the crushed graham crackers, melted butter, and sugar. Spoon into the prepared pan and press the biscuit mixture into an even layer, using the back of a metal spoon.

—

To make the filling, place the chocolate, butter, instant coffee granules, and water in a large saucepan over a gentle heat until the butter and chocolate have melted, stirring occasionally. Remove from the heat and beat in the half-and-half, sugar, and eggs.

—

Pour the mixture onto the graham cracker crust and bake for about 1¼ hours, or until set. Let cool completely in the pan, then turn out and decorate the top with whipped cream.

*This will become your favorite chocolate cake recipe—it is the best!
It is speedy to make, and the easy filling doubles as a frosting. The cake
is moist and has a "grown-up" chocolate flavor.*

VERY BEST CHOCOLATE FUDGE CAKE

SERVES 8

⅔ cup (55g) sifted cocoa
    powder
6 tbsps boiling water
3 extra-large eggs
3 tbsps (50ml) milk
1⅓ cups (175g) all-purpose
    flour
1 tbsp baking powder
½ tsp salt
½ cup (115g) salted butter,
    softened
1 cup + 6 tbsps (275g) sugar

For the frosting and filling
3 tbsps apricot jam
5 ounces (150g) dark
    chocolate, broken into
    pieces
⅔ cup (150ml) heavy cream

Preheat the oven to 350°F. Grease two 8-inch round cake pans, then line the bottom of each pan with parchment paper.

Blend the cocoa and boiling water in a large bowl, then add the remaining cake ingredients and beat until the mixture is a smooth, thickish batter.

Divide the cake mix equally between the prepared pans and level the surfaces. Bake for 25–30 minutes, or until well-risen and the tops of the cakes spring back when lightly pressed with a finger. Let cool in the pans for a few minutes, then turn out, peel off the parchment paper, and finish cooling on a wire rack.

Warm the apricot jam in a very small saucepan, then spread a little over the base of one cake and the top of the other.

To make the frosting, melt the chocolate with the cream in a heatproof bowl set over a saucepan of simmering water, stirring occasionally. Remove the bowl from the heat and let cool until it is on the point of setting, then spread on top of both cakes. Sandwich the cakes together and use an offset spatula to spread the frosting on the top. Keep in a cool place until ready to serve.

TIP
The cake can be frozen (iced or un-iced) for up to 1 month. Store in a round freezer-safe container about 1 inch bigger than the diameter of the cake. Sit the cake on the inside of the lid and place the container over the top. Seal, label, and freeze. If the cake is frozen iced, the frosting will not be quite as shiny once thawed. To defrost, release the lid but leave in position and thaw for 4 hours at room temperature.

This moist chocolate cake is laced with rum, then filled and covered with a glossy chocolate frosting that melts in the mouth. It is irresistible to chocoholics and can be served as an afternoon cake, or as a pudding with half-and-half.

CHOCOLATE RUM CAKE

SERVES 8

7 ounces (200g) dark chocolate, broken into pieces
½ cup (115g) salted butter, cubed
3 extra-large eggs, separated
½ cup + 2 tbsps (115g) dark muscovado sugar
3 tbsps (50ml) dark rum
⅔ cup (75g) all-purpose flour, sifted
½ cup (55g) almond flour
1 tsp baking powder
¼ tsp salt

For the filling and frosting
8 ounces (225g) dark chocolate, broken into pieces
½ cup (115g) salted butter, cubed
4 tbsps apricot jam

For the chocolate ganache (optional)
6 ounces (175g) dark chocolate, broken into pieces
4 tbsps half-and-half
¼ cup (55g) salted butter, cubed
2 extra-large egg yolks
1 tbsp dark rum

Preheat the oven to 350°F. Grease an 8-inch round cake pan, then line the bottom with parchment paper.

—

Melt the chocolate and butter in a heatproof bowl set over a saucepan of simmering water, stirring occasionally, then allow to cool slightly.

—

Place the egg yolks and sugar in a large bowl and whisk until pale and creamy. Add the cooled chocolate mixture and the rum and mix well. Gently fold in the flours, baking powder, and salt.

—

In a separate bowl, whisk the egg whites until stiff but not dry, then lightly fold into the cake mixture.

—

Turn into the prepared pan and gently level the surface. Bake for about 45 minutes, or until well-risen and the top of the cake springs back when lightly pressed with a finger. Let cool in the pan for a few minutes, then turn out, peel off the parchment paper, and finish cooling on a wire rack.

—

When cold, slice the cake in half horizontally using a serrated or bread knife.

—

To make the filling and frosting, melt the chocolate in a heatproof bowl set over a saucepan of simmering water, making sure the base of the bowl is not touching the water, stirring occasionally. Add the cubed butter and stir until the mixture has the consistency of thick heavy cream. Use a little of the frosting to fill the sliced cakes.

—

Warm the apricot jam, then push through a sieve. Brush this over the cake top and sides and allow to set. Smooth the frosting over the cake and allow to set.

—

To make the chocolate ganache, if using, melt the chocolate with the half-and-half in a heatproof bowl set over a saucepan of simmering water, stirring occasionally. Cool slightly, then beat in the butter a little at a time. Beat in the egg yolks and rum, then let sit until cool and firm, stirring occasionally. When firm enough to hold its shape, spoon into a piping bag fitted with a star nozzle and pipe rosettes of ganache to decorate the cake.

TIP
If you don't have a piping bag, use two plastic food bags, which have been put inside each other for strength, and snip off one corner.

Chocolate and orange are a favorite combination, and this is a light sponge that everyone will enjoy.

ORANGE CHOCOLATE CAKE

SERVES 6-8

1⅓ cups (175g) all-purpose flour

¾ cup + 1 tbsp (175g) buttery spread, straight from the fridge

¼ cup (20g) cocoa powder

¾ cup + 2 tbsps (175g) granulated sugar

2 tsps baking powder

½ tsp salt

3 extra-large eggs

finely grated zest of 1 orange

For the frosting

8½ ounces (240g) orange chocolate, broken into pieces

½ cup + 1 tbsp (125g) salted butter, softened

1¾ cups (225g) confectioners' sugar

1.2 ounces (35g) orange chocolate, roughly chopped

Preheat the oven to 350°F. Grease and line two 8-inch round cake pans with parchment paper.

—

Measure all the cake ingredients into a large bowl. Whisk with an electric mixer until light and fluffy.

—

Spoon into the pans and level the surfaces. Bake for 25 minutes, or until well-risen and the top of the cakes spring back when lightly pressed with a finger. Let cool in the pan for 10 minutes, then turn out onto a wire rack and peel off the parchment paper.

—

To make the frosting, melt 7 ounces (200g) of the orange chocolate in a heatproof bowl set over a saucepan of simmering water, making sure the base of the bowl is not touching the water, stirring occasionally. Remove the bowl from the heat.

—

Whisk the butter and confectioners' sugar together in a large bowl with an electric mixer until light and fluffy. Whisk in the melted chocolate.

—

Spread half the frosting over one cake and sandwich the two cakes together. Spread the remaining frosting on top. Roughly chop the remaining orange chocolate and scatter over the top of the cake.

A golden vanilla cake that is a bit different. The white chocolate frosting is sweet, and with three layers you won't need a big slice.

WHITE CHOCOLATE
AND VANILLA CAKE

1¾ cups (350g) granulated sugar
2¾ cups (350g) all-purpose flour
1⅔ cups (350g) buttery spread, straight from the fridge
6 extra-large eggs
3 tsps vanilla extract
2 tbsps baking powder
¾ tsp salt

For the frosting
10½ ounces (300g) white chocolate
¾ cup + 2 tbsps (200g) salted butter, softened
1½ cups + 2 tbsps (360g) full-fat cream cheese
2 cups + 3 tbsps (275g) confectioners' sugar
2 tbsps freeze-dried raspberries

Preheat the oven to 350°F. Line three 8-inch round cake pans with parchment paper.

—

Measure all the cake ingredients into a large bowl. Whisk with an electric mixer until light and fluffy.

—

Spoon into the pans and level the surfaces. Bake for 30–35 minutes, or until well-risen and pale golden. Let cool in the pan for 5 minutes, then turn out onto a wire rack and peel off the baking paper.

—

To make the frosting, melt the chocolate in a heatproof bowl set over a saucepan of simmering water, making sure the base of the bowl is not touching the water, stirring occasionally. Remove the bowl from the heat and set aside to cool.

—

Meanwhile, whisk the butter, cream cheese, and confectioners' sugar together in a large bowl until light and fluffy. Add the cooled melted chocolate and mix well.

—

Place one of the cakes on a large plate and pipe a third of the frosting over the surface. Top with the second cake and pipe another third of frosting over the surface. Top with the final cake and the remaining frosting.

—

Scatter with freeze-dried raspberries to decorate.

This family weekend cake has a nice texture and looks spectacular, marbled with white and brown. It must be eaten fresh.

MARBLED CHOCOLATE RING CAKE

SERVES 8

1 cup (225g) salted butter, softened

1 cup + 2 tbsps (225g) sugar

4 extra-large eggs

1¾ cups (225g) all-purpose flour

1 tbsp baking powder

½ tsp salt

1½ tbsps cocoa powder

1½ tbsps boiling water

For the frosting

5 ounces (150g) dark chocolate, broken into pieces

½ cup (115g) salted butter

2 ounces (55g) Belgian milk chocolate, broken into pieces

Preheat the oven to 350°F. Generously butter a 9-inch Bundt pan, then sprinkle with flour to prevent sticking.

Measure all the cake ingredients, except the cocoa and boiling water, into a large bowl. Beat until thoroughly blended. Dot about half of this mixture, in small spoonfuls, into the bottom of the prepared pan.

Mix the cocoa powder and boiling water together in a small bowl, then mix into the remaining cake mixture. Dot this mixture over and between the plain mixture in the pan until all is used up.

Swirl a little with a knife, then carefully level the surface. Bake for about 40 minutes, or until well-risen and the top of the cake springs back when lightly pressed with a finger. Let cool in the pan for a few minutes, then turn out, peel off the parchment paper, and finish cooling on a wire rack.

To make the frosting, melt the dark chocolate with 2 tablespoons water and the butter in a heatproof bowl set over a saucepan of simmering water, stirring occasionally. Pour the frosting over the cake, then allow to set for about 1 hour.

Melt the milk chocolate in a small heatproof bowl set over a saucepan of simmering water, making sure the bottom of the bowl is not touching the water, stirring occasionally. Spoon into a paper piping bag, cut off the tip of the bag, and drizzle the chocolate over the top of the dark chocolate frosting. Allow to set.

Achieving a lovely shine to your mirror cake will make this an impressive cake to behold. It is worth trying! The cake will keep well in the fridge without losing its shine.

CHOCOLATE MIRROR CAKE

SERVES 8

4 extra-large eggs
⅔ cup (125g) sugar
1 cup (125g) all-purpose
   flour, sifted
1½ tsps baking powder
¼ tsp salt
¼ cup (55g) salted butter,
   melted and cooled

For the icing
2 (¼-ounce/7g) envelopes
   powdered gelatin
1 cup + 2 tbsps (225g) sugar
¾ cup (75g) cocoa powder
⅓ cup (75ml) heavy cream
1 cup (240ml) warm water
2 ounces (55g) dark
   chocolate, broken into
   pieces

Preheat the oven to 350°F. Grease a 9-inch springform pan and line the bottom with parchment paper.

Place the eggs and sugar in a large mixing bowl. Whisk together using an electric mixer until thick ribbon stage. Gently fold the flour, baking powder, and salt into the egg mixture until well-combined. Pour the butter around the edge of the bowl, then carefully fold into the mixture.

Pour into the prepared pan and level the surface. Bake for about 30 minutes, or until pale golden and coming away from the sides of the pan. Let cool in the pan for a few minutes, then turn out, peel off the parchment paper, and finish cooling on a wire rack.

To make the icing, place the powdered gelatin in a small bowl and add ½ cup (120ml) warm water. Stir and let rest for a few minutes until dissolved. Make sure never to boil any gelatin mixture, as it will lose its thickening quality. Measure the sugar, cocoa, cream, and remaining warm water into a saucepan. Place over a gentle heat until melted, then bring up to a boil, stirring until smooth. Remove from the heat and add the chocolate, stirring to melt and incorporate. Let cool for 5 minutes.

Add the dissolved gelatin to the warm chocolate mixture and stir until dissolved. Pour the icing through a sieve into a bowl and allow to thicken at room temperature for about 15 minutes, or until it's a thick pouring consistency. Depending on the heat of your kitchen, you may need to pop it in the fridge.

Place a sheet pan under the cooled sponge on the wire rack and pour the icing all over the surface and sides until completely covered. Let sit for 30 minutes for the icing to set before transferring to a serving plate.

CHAPTER FOUR

CUPCAKES
AND OTHER
SMALL GOODIES

Cupcakes are great for teatime, or arranged stacked on a cake stand instead of a large traditional birthday cake or even a wedding cake. Cupcakes are a different shape than fairy cakes—the liners are deeper and have less angular sides.

CUPCAKES

MAKES 12 CAKES

7 tbsps (100g) salted butter, softened
1¼ cups (150g) all-purpose flour
1¾ tsps baking powder
½ tsp salt
¾ cup (150g) granulated sugar
3 tbsps milk
2 extra-large eggs
½ tsp vanilla extract

For the icing/frosting
(choose one type of icing or frosting, or halve the ingredients and make a mixture of both)

Buttercream frosting
7 tbsps (100g) salted butter, softened
1¾ cups (225g) confectioners' sugar, sifted
½ tsp vanilla extract

Glacé icing
juice of 1 lemon, warmed
1¾ cups (225g) confectioners' sugar, sifted

To decorate
combination of plain or white chocolate curls or shavings, chocolate hearts, sprinkles, marshmallows, and silver balls

Preheat the oven to 350°F. Put muffin liners into a 12-cup muffin pan.

—

Measure all the cupcake ingredients into a large bowl and beat until the mixture is well blended and smooth.

—

Fill each muffin liner with the mixture and bake for 20–25 minutes, until risen and golden brown. Lift the paper liners out of the pan and cool them on a wire rack until completely cold before icing.

—

To make the buttercream frosting, beat together all the ingredients to give a creamy, thick frosting, then smooth it over the cold cupcakes. To make the glacé icing, gradually add the warmed lemon juice to the confectioners' sugar to give a glossy icing.

—

Decorate the cupcakes with chocolate curls or shavings, chocolate hearts, sprinklers, marshmallows, or silver balls.

To make Fruity Celebration Cupcakes, follow the ingredients and method for Rich Fruit Cake (page 133) and cook at 325°F for about 1 hour. Ice with fondant icing (page 400).

TIPS

If you are making a double quantity of cupcakes or using a smaller pan, you can prepare the cupcake mixture in one go and spoon it into the paper liners ready to go into the oven. They will come to no harm, as rising agents react more slowly nowadays. Bake one pan of cupcakes at a time.

Try adding 2 tablespoons cocoa powder or 1 teaspoon strong coffee to the buttercream frosting to make chocolate or coffee frosting. When making the glacé icing, warming the lemon juice before mixing with the confectioners' sugar helps it set better.

Butterfly cakes are quick and easy to make, they look pretty, and they are very popular at children's parties.

BUTTERFLY CAKES

MAKES 12 CAKES

½ cup (115g) salted butter, softened
½ cup + 1 tbsp (115g) granulated sugar
2 extra-large eggs
1 cup (115g) all-purpose flour
2 tsps baking powder
¼ tsp salt

For the frosting
¾ cup (175g) salted butter, softened
2¾ cups (350g) confectioners' sugar, sifted, plus extra for dusting

Preheat the oven to 400°F. Place fairy cake liners in a 12-cup fairy cake pan.

Measure all the cake ingredients into a large bowl and beat well for 2–3 minutes until the mixture is well-blended and smooth.

Fill each paper liner with the mixture and bake for 15–20 minutes, until the cakes are well-risen and golden brown. Lift the paper liners out of the pan and cool them on a wire rack.

To make the frosting, beat the butter and confectioners' sugar together until well-blended. Cut a slice from the top of each cake and cut this slice in half. Pipe a swirl of buttercream into the center of each cake and place the half slices of cake on top to resemble butterfly wings. Dust the cakes with confectioners' sugar to finish.

To make Chocolate Butterfly Cakes, follow the recipe above but make chocolate frosting by mixing 2 tbsps cocoa powder with 3 tbsps boiling water. Allow to cool slightly, then beat in ¾ cup (175g) softened salted butter and 2¾ cups (350g) sifted confectioners' sugar until well-blended. To make them really chocolatey, you can replace ¼ cup (30g) of all-purpose flour from the cake ingredients with ⅓ cup (30g) cocoa powder.

To make Orange or Lemon Butterfly Cakes, add the grated zest of 1 orange or lemon to the cake mixture in step 2. Ice them with a buttercream made from butter, confectioners' sugar, and a little orange or lemon juice, then dust with confectioners' sugar.

For this recipe, you will need dariole molds, which are available from specialty kitchen stones and department stores.

ENGLISH MADELEINES
MAKES 10 MADELEINES

½ cup (115g) salted butter, softened
½ cup + 1 tbsp (115g) sugar
2 extra-large eggs
1 cup (115g) all-purpose flour
2 tsps baking powder
¼ tsp salt
2–3 drops of vanilla extract

To finish
4 tbsps raspberry or strawberry jam
½ cup (55g) shredded coconut
5 maraschino cherries, halved

Preheat the oven to 350°F. Grease ten dariole molds and line the bottom of each with parchment paper. Stand the pans on a baking sheet.

Measure the cake ingredients into a large bowl and beat until the mixture is well-blended and smooth.

Spoon the mixture into the dariole molds, filling them about half full. Bake for about 20 minutes, until well-risen and firm to the touch. Let cool in the molds for 5 minutes, then turn out, peel off the parchment paper, and finish cooling on a wire rack.

When the cakes are cool, trim the bottoms so that they stand firmly. Push the raspberry or strawberry jam through a sieve, then warm in a small saucepan. Spread the coconut out on a large plate. Use a fork to spear the bases of the cakes to hold them. Brush them with the warm jam, then roll in the coconut to coat. Decorate each madeleine with half a maraschino cherry.

These shell-shaped cakes are made using a madeleine pan, available from specialty kitchen stores and department stores. It is worth greasing and flouring the pans well so that the cakes come out cleanly. They are best on the day of making and, in France, are traditionally dipped into tea to eat.

FRENCH MADELEINES

MAKES ABOUT 30 MADELEINES

1¼ cups (150g) all-purpose flour, plus extra for dusting
⅔ cup (150g) salted butter
3 extra-large eggs
¾ cup (150g) sugar
2¼ tsps baking powder
½ tsp salt
finely grated zest of 1 lemon
confectioners' sugar, to dust (optional)

Preheat the oven to 425°F. Grease a madeleine pan, dust with flour, and shake off any excess.

Melt the butter in a small saucepan and allow to cool slightly.

Measure the eggs and sugar into a large bowl and whisk until pale and thick.

Sift in half the flour with the baking powder, salt, and lemon zest and fold in gently. Pour in half the melted butter around the edge of the bowl and fold in. Repeat the process with the remaining flour and butter.

Spoon the mixture into the prepared molds so that they are just below the rim. Bake for 8–10 minutes, until well-risen, golden, and springy to the touch. Ease out of the pans with a small offset spatula and cool on a wire rack.

Grease and flour the pans again and repeat until all the mixture has been used up.

Dust with confectioners' sugar to serve, if you like.

These large muffins look quite impressive. They're best eaten on the day of baking.

CHOCOLATE CHIP
AMERICAN MUFFINS

2 cups (250g) all-purpose flour
4 level tsps baking powder
½ tsp salt
¼ cup (55g) salted butter, softened
6 tbsps (75g) sugar
1 cup (175g) dark chocolate chips
2 extra-large eggs
1 tsp vanilla extract
1 cup + 1 tbsp (250ml) milk

Preheat the oven to 400°F. Place muffin liners in a 12-cup muffin pan.

—

Measure the flour, baking powder, and salt into a large bowl. Add the butter and rub into the flour, using your fingertips, until the mixture resembles fine breadcrumbs. Stir in the sugar and chocolate chips.

—

Mix together the eggs, vanilla extract, and milk, then pour all in one go into the dry ingredients. Mix quickly with a wooden spoon to blend. The mixture should have a lumpy consistency.

—

Spoon the mixture into the paper liners, filling almost to the top. Bake for 20–25 minutes, or until well-risen and firm to the touch. Let cool for a few minutes in the pan, then lift out and cool for a little longer on a wire rack.

This makes special little cakes, ideal for children's parties.

ICED FAIRY CAKES

MAKES 24 CAKES

½ cup (115g) salted butter, softened
½ cup + 1 tbsp (115g) granulated sugar
2 extra-large eggs
1 cup (115g) all-purpose flour
2 tsps baking powder
¼ tsp salt

For the icing
1¾ cups (225g) confectioners' sugar, sifted
2–3 tbsps warm water
sweets, to decorate

Preheat the oven to 400°F. Place fairy cake liners in two 12-cup fairy cake pans.

___

Measure all the cake ingredients into a large bowl and beat for 2–3 minutes until the mixture is well blended and smooth.

___

Fill each paper liner with the mixture and bake for 15–20 minutes, until the cakes are well-risen and golden brown. Lift the paper liners out of the pan and cool them on a wire rack.

___

Place the confectioners' sugar in a bowl and gradually blend in the warm water until you have a fairly stiff icing. Spoon over the top of the cakes and decorate with sweets.

To make Orange Fairy Cakes, follow the recipe above and add the grated zest of 1 orange with the other ingredients. To make the icing, gradually blend the confectioners' sugar with the juice of 1 orange until you have a fairly stiff icing.

These spicy little currant cakes, enclosed in a flaky pastry, come from the north of England. You can use premade puff pastry, if you wish.

ECCLES CAKES

MAKES ABOUT 8 CAKES

For the flaky pastry
1¾ cups (225g) all-purpose
    flour
¾ cup (175g) salted butter
a squeeze of lemon juice
8 tbsps cold water

For the filling
¼ cup (55g) salted butter,
    softened
¼ cup (55g) light muscovado
    sugar
½ tsp pumpkin pie spice
¾ cup (55g) candied orange
    or lemon peel, chopped
¾ cup + 1 tbsp (115g)
    currants

To finish
1 egg white, beaten
a little granulated sugar

First make the flaky pastry. Measure the flour into a bowl. Divide the butter into 4 equal portions and rub one portion of it into the flour, using your fingertips, until the mixture resembles fine breadcrumbs. Add the lemon juice and water and mix to form a soft dough.

On a lightly floured work surface, gently knead the dough until smooth. Roll out into an oblong three times as long as it is wide. Dot a second portion of the butter in small pieces over the top two-thirds of the pastry. Fold the bottom third of the pastry up over the middle third and the top third down, then seal the edges well with the edge of your hand. Wrap the pastry in plastic wrap and put in the fridge to relax for about 15 minutes.

Re-roll the pastry as before, always starting with the folds of the dough to the left, until the remaining portions of butter have been used up. Wrap the pastry again in plastic wrap and leave in the fridge for at least 30 minutes before using.

Preheat the oven to 425°F.

To make the filling, mix the butter, sugar, spice, chopped orange or lemon peel, and currants in a bowl. Roll out the pastry thinly and cut into eight rounds about 6 inches in diameter (use a small plate as a guide). If using premade puff pastry, remember to roll it out very thinly—otherwise it will be too thick when cooked.

Place a generous tablespoon of the filling into the center of each round, dampen the pastry edges with water, then draw together to enclose the filling. Turn the pastry over and flatten gently with the rolling pin so that the currants just show through. Re-shape to a round with your hands, if necessary. Make 3 small cuts in the top of each cake, brush with the beaten egg white, and sprinkle with granulated sugar.

—

Transfer the cakes to a baking sheet and bake for 10–15 minutes until golden. Let cool on the baking sheet for a few minutes before lifting onto a wire rack to cool completely.

TIP

For light pastry, incorporate as much air as possible by sifting flour from a height, cutting butter in small pieces with a knife, and lifting your hands well above the bowl when rubbing-in.

Traditionally a red jam is used for the center of these cakes, which are buttery and very delicious.

APRICOT SWISS CAKES

MAKES 18 CAKES

1 cup (225g) salted butter, softened

⅔ cup (75g) confectioners' sugar, sifted, plus extra for dusting

1⅔ cups (200g) all-purpose flour

½ cup (55g) cornstarch

2½ tsps baking powder

½ tsp salt

To finish
a little apricot jam

Preheat the oven to 350°F. Place liners in a 12-cup fairy cake pan.

—

Place the butter in a large bowl. Add the confectioners' sugar and beat well until really soft and fluffy. Stir in the flour, cornstarch, baking powder, and salt and mix until smooth. Spoon the mixture into a large piping bag fitted with a large star nozzle.

—

Pipe circles of the mixture into the bottom of each paper liner and bake for 15–20 minutes, or until pale golden brown. Remove the paper liners from the pan and cool them on a wire rack.

—

Put a small amount of apricot jam on the center of each cake. Dust lightly with sifted confectioners' sugar.

American muffins (very different from English muffins) are hugely popular. These are best served warm.

BLUEBERRY MUFFINS

MAKES 12 MUFFINS

2 cups (250g) all-purpose
flour
4 tsps baking powder
+ ½ tsp salt
¼ cup (55g) salted butter,
softened
6 tbsps (75g) sugar
1 cup (175g) blueberries
finely grated zest of 1 lemon
2 extra-large eggs
1 cup + 1 tbsp (250ml) milk

Preheat the oven to 400°F. Place muffin liners in a 12-cup muffin pan.

Measure the flour, baking powder, and salt into a large bowl. Add the butter and rub into the flour, using your fingertips, until the mixture resembles fine breadcrumbs. Stir in the sugar, blueberries, and lemon zest.

Mix together the eggs and milk, then pour all in one go into the dry ingredients. Mix quickly to blend. The mixture should have a lumpy consistency.

Spoon the mixture into the paper liners, filling almost to the top. Bake for 20–25 minutes, until well-risen, golden, and firm to the touch. Let cool for a few minutes in the pan, then lift out the paper liners and cool for a few minutes on a wire rack. Serve warm.

CHAPTER FIVE

CELEBRATION CAKES

This is a wonderful, rich, traditional fruit cake. It can be made up to three months in advance. Make sure you allow plenty of time to "feed" the cake with brandy and let it mature. I've included a table on the next page to show the different ingredient quantities needed to make variously sized cakes.

CLASSIC RICH CHRISTMAS CAKE

SERVES 12

⅔ cup (115g) maraschino cherries, quartered

¾ cup + 3 tbsps (115g) dried apricots, snipped into pieces

2 cups (275g) currants

1¼ cups (175g) golden raisins

1¼ cups (175g) raisins

¾ cup (55g) candied orange or lemon peel, finely chopped

3 tbsps brandy

1¾ cups (225g) all-purpose flour

¼ tsp freshly grated nutmeg

½ tsp pumpkin pie spice

1 cup (225g) salted butter, softened

1 cup + 3 tbsps (225g) dark muscovado sugar

4 extra-large eggs

⅓ cup (55g) chopped almonds

scant 1 tbsp molasses

finely grated zest of 1 lemon

finely grated zest of 1 orange

To finish

brandy, to feed the cake

3 cups (675g) almond paste or marzipan (see page 398 for almond paste recipe)

1 × 24-ounce box (675g) fondant or ready-to-roll icing (page 400)

Begin this cake the night before you want to bake it. Place the cherries in a sieve and rinse under running water. Drain well, then dry thoroughly on a paper towel. Measure all the fruits and chopped peel into a large bowl. Mix in the brandy, cover, and let sit in a cool place overnight.

—

Preheat the oven to 275°F. Grease an 8-inch round cake pan, then line the bottom and sides with a double layer of parchment paper.

—

Measure the flour, spices, butter, sugar, eggs, almonds, molasses, and lemon and orange zests into a large bowl. Beat well, then fold in the soaked fruits.

—

Spoon the mixture into the prepared pan and spread out evenly with the back of a spoon. Cover the top of the cake loosely with a double layer of parchment paper. Bake for 4½–4¾ hours, or until the cake feels firm to the touch and a skewer inserted into the center comes out clean. Allow the cake to cool in the pan.

—

When cool, pierce the cake at intervals with a fine skewer and feed with a little brandy. Wrap the completely cold cake in a double layer of parchment paper, and again in foil, and store in a cool place, feeding at intervals with more brandy. Don't remove the lining paper when storing as this helps to keep the cake moist. Cover the cake with almond paste or marzipan about a week before icing.

—

Recipe continued on the next page

To decorate
almond paste (left over from putting over the cake)
green food coloring
confectioners' sugar, sifted
ribbon, holly, or your favorite decorations

Cover the cake with fondant or ready-to-roll icing. Color the almond paste (left over from putting the almond paste onto the cake) dark green. Roll out on a board that has been lightly sprinkled with confectioners' sugar and cut into 1-inch-wide strips. Cut these into diamonds and then, with the tip of an icing nozzle, remove half circles from the sides of the diamonds to create holly-shaped leaves. Make vein marks on the leaves with a sharp knife, bend the leaves over the handles of wooden spoons, and leave to dry. Decorate the top of the cake with the almond paste holly leaves, dust lightly with confectioners' sugar, and finish by tying a ribbon around the sides of the cake.

	6-inch round 5-inch square	7-inch round 6-inch square	8-inch round 7-inch square	9-inch round 8-inch square	10-inch round 9-inch square	11-inch round 10-inch square	12-inch round 11-inch square	13-inch round 12-inch square
Maraschino cherries	⅓ cup (55g)	6 tbsps (75g)	⅔ cup (115g)	¾ cup (150g)	1 cup (175g)	1¼ cups (225g)	1½ cups (275g)	2 cups (350g)
Dried apricots	½ cup (55g)	⅔ cup (75g)	¾ cup + 3 tbsps (115g)	1 cup + 3 tbsps (150g)	1⅓ cup (175g)	1¾ cup (225g)	2 cups + 2 tbsps (275g)	2¾ cups (350g)
Currants	1 cup (150g)	1 cup + 6 tbsps (200g)	2 cups (275g)	2¾ cups (400g)	3 cups + 3 tbsps (450g)	3¾ cups + 3 tbsps (550g)	5⅓ cups (750g)	5⅔ cups (800g)
Golden raisins	½ cup (75g)	¾ cup (115g)	1¼ cups (175g)	1½ cups (225g)	1¾ cups + 3 tbsps (275g)	2 cups + 6 tbsps 350g (12oz)	3 cups + 2 tbsps (450g)	3¾ cups (550g)
Raisins	½ cup (75g)	¾ cup (115g)	1¼ cups (175g)	1½ cups (225g)	1¾ cups + 3 tbsps (275g)	2 cups + 6 tbsps 350g (12oz)	3 cups + 2 tbsps (450g)	3¾ cups (550g)
Candied orange or lemon peel	6 tbsps (30g)	½ cup (40g)	⅔ cup (55g)	¾ cup (65g)	1 cup (75g)	1½ cups (115g)	2 cups (150g)	2⅓ cups (175g)
Brandy	1½ tbsps	2 tbsps	3 tbsps	4 tbsps	5 tbsps	6 tbsps	7 tbsps	8 tbsps
All-purpose flour	1 cup (115g)	1⅓ cups (175g)	1¾ cups (225g)	2¼ cups (275g)	3¼ cup (400g)	3⅔ cups (450g)	4 cups (500g)	4⅓ cups (550g)
Grated nutmeg	⅛ tsp	scant ¼ tsp	¼ tsp	scant ½ tsp	½ tsp	½ tsp	¾ tsp	1 tsp
Pumpkin pie spice	¼ tsp	scant ½ tsp	½ tsp	¾ tsp	¾ tsp	1 tsp	1¼ tsps	1½ tsps
Softened butter	½ cup (115g)	¾ cup (175g)	1 cup (225g)	1¼ cups (275g)	1¾ cups (400g)	2 cups (450g)	2¼ cups (500g)	2 cups + 7 tbsps (550g)
Dark musc. sugar	½ cup + 2 tbsps (115g)	¾ cup + 3 tbsps (175g)	1 cup + 3 tbsps (225g)	1½ cups (275g)	2 cups + 2 tbsps (400g)	2⅓ cups (450g)	2⅔ cups (500g)	2¾ cups + 3 tbsps (550g)
Extra-large eggs	2	3	4	5	7	8	9	10
Chopped almonds	¼ cup (30g)	⅓ cup (40g)	½ cup (55g)	½ cup (65g)	⅔ cup (75g)	1 cup (115g)	1⅓ cups (150g)	1½ cups (175g)
Molasses	½ tbsp	rounded ½ tbsp	scant 1 tbsp	1 tbsp	1½ tbsps	2 tbsps	3 tbsps	4 tbsps
Zested lemon	½	½	1	1½	2	2	3	3
Zested orange	½	½	1	1½	2	2	3	3
Baking times (approx.)	3½ hrs	4 hrs	4½ hrs	4¾ hrs	5 hrs	5½ hrs	6 hrs	6½ hrs

Unlike traditional Christmas cakes, this mixture produces a light, yet succulent, cake. The pineapple makes it lovely and moist.

VICTORIAN CHRISTMAS CAKE

SERVES 14

2 cups (350g) maraschino cherries, quartered

1 × 8-ounce (227g) can pineapple in natural juice, drained and chopped

2¾ cups (350g) dried apricots, snipped into pieces

1 cup (115g) almonds, roughly chopped

finely grated zest of 2 lemons

2 cups + 6 tbsps (350g) golden raisins

2 cups (250g) all-purpose flour

1 tbsp baking powder

½ tsp salt

1¼ cups (250g) granulated sugar

1 cup + 2 tbsps (250g) salted butter, softened

¾ cup (75g) almond flour

5 extra-large eggs

To decorate
whole almonds
maraschino cherries
candied pineapple (available from natural food stores)
1 cup (115g) confectioners' sugar, sifted

Preheat the oven to 325°F. Grease a 9-inch round cake pan, then line the bottom and sides with a double layer of parchment paper.

—

Place the cherries in a sieve and rinse under running water, then drain well. Dry the drained cherries and the pineapple very thoroughly on a paper towel. Place in a bowl with the apricots, chopped almonds, lemon zest, and golden raisins and gently mix together.

—

Measure the remaining cake ingredients into a large bowl and beat well for 1 minute until smooth. Lightly fold in the fruit and nuts.

—

Turn the mixture into the prepared cake pan and level the surface. Decorate the top with the whole almonds, halved maraschino cherries, and pieces of candied pineapple. Bake for about 2¼ hours, or until golden brown. A skewer inserted into the center of the cake should come out clean. Cover the cake loosely with foil after 1 hour to prevent the top from becoming too dark. Allow to cool in the pan for about 30 minutes, then turn out, peel off the parchment paper, and finish cooling on a wire rack.

—

Mix the confectioners' sugar with a little water and drizzle over the cake to glaze.

Individual fruit cakes are particularly welcome gifts for those who live on their own or have small appetites.

TINY FRUIT CAKES

MAKES 3 CAKES

¼ cup (40g) maraschino
   cherries, quartered
⅓ cup (55g) raisins
⅓ cup (55g) golden raisins
⅓ cup (55g) currants
¼ cup (30g) dried apricots,
   snipped into pieces
¼ cup (15g) candied orange
   or lemon peel, chopped
2 tsps brandy, rum, or sherry,
   plus extra for feeding the
   cake
3 tbsps (15g) almonds,
   chopped
3 tbsps (15g) almond flour
finely grated zest of ¼ lemon
⅔ cup (75g) all-purpose
   flour
½ tsp pumpkin pie spice
¼ cup (55g) dark muscovado
   sugar
¼ cup (55g) salted butter,
   softened
2 tsps molasses
1 extra-large egg
1 tbsp sliced almonds

For the icing
3 tbsps apricot jam
1 cup (225g) almond paste
   or marzipan (see page 398
   for almond paste recipe)
8 ounces (225g) fondant or
   ready-to-roll icing
   (page 400)

Place the cherries in a sieve and rinse under running water. Drain well, then dry thoroughly on a paper towel. Measure all the dried fruits and chopped peel into a large bowl, add the brandy, rum, or sherry, cover the bowl tightly, and leave overnight.

Preheat the oven to 325°F. Grease and line three (3-inch) mini cheesecake pans with parchment paper. Place them on a baking sheet lined with parchment paper.

Measure the chopped almonds and almond flour, lemon zest, flour, pumpkin pie spice, sugar, butter, molasses, and egg into a large bowl and mix together. Beat thoroughly for about 2 minutes until the mixture is smooth. Add the soaked fruit and any liquid and stir to mix in thoroughly. Spoon the mixture into the prepared pans. Level the surfaces, then sprinkle with the sliced almonds.

Bake for 1–1¼ hours, or until a fine skewer inserted into the center comes out clean. Allow the cakes to cool in the pans. Pierce the top of the cakes in several places with a skewer and spoon in a little brandy, rum, or sherry.

Remove the cakes from the rings but do not remove the parchment paper as this helps to keep the cakes moist. Wrap in more parchment paper and then some foil, and store in a cool place for a week.

Sieve the apricot jam and warm it slightly, then brush it over the surface of the cakes. Cover with almond paste or marzipan and icing in the usual way. Decorate as desired.

I've often been asked for this recipe, which doesn't have to be made in advance or fed with brandy. The cake is light and moist.

FAST MINCEMEAT CHRISTMAS CAKE

SERVES 12

⅔ cup (150g) salted butter, softened
¾ cup (150g) light muscovado sugar
2 extra-large eggs
1¾ cups (225g) all-purpose flour
2½ tsps baking powder
½ tsp salt
14 ounces (400g) high-quality mincemeat
1¼ cups (175g) currants
½ cup (55g) almonds, chopped

To decorate
3 cups (675g) almond paste or marzipan (see page 398 for almond paste recipe)
1 quantity of royal icing (page 399)

Preheat the oven to 325°F. Grease an 8-inch round cake pan, then line the bottom and sides with parchment paper.

—

Measure all the cake ingredients into a large bowl and beat well for 1 minute until thoroughly mixed.

—

Turn into the prepared pan and level the surface. Bake for about 1¾ hours, or until a skewer inserted into the center comes out clean and the cake is shrinking from the sides of the pan. Cover the cake with foil after 1 hour if beginning to brown too much. Let cool in the pan for 10 minutes, then turn out, peel off the parchment paper, and finish cooling on a wire rack.

—

Cover the cake with almond paste about a week before icing. Make the royal icing and spread some of the icing thickly over the sides of the cake, smoothing with an offset spatula. Spoon more royal icing on top of the cake. Smooth a strip in the center (this is where the ribbon will go), then pull the remainder into peaks with the back of a spoon. Allow the icing to harden for a few hours, then decorate the cake with ribbon.

I'm often asked for the boiled fruit cake with condensed milk that Granny used to make—here it is. Although I add fat to make it even tastier!

QUICK BOILED FRUIT CAKE

SERVES 10 TO 12

1 × 14-ounce (397g) can full-fat condensed milk
⅔ cup (150g) salted butter
1½ cups (225g) raisins
1½ cups (225g) golden raisins
1¼ cups (175g) currants
1 cup (175g) maraschino cherries, roughly chopped
1¾ cups (225g) all-purpose flour
2½ tsps baking powder
½ tsp salt
2 tsps pumpkin pie spice
1 tsp ground cinnamon
2 extra-large eggs

Preheat the oven to 300°F. Grease a 7-inch round cake pan, then line the bottom and sides with parchment paper.

—

Pour the condensed milk into a heavy-bottomed saucepan and add the butter, dried fruit, and maraschino cherries. Place over low heat until the butter has melted into the condensed milk. Stir well, then simmer gently for 5 minutes. Remove from the heat and set aside to cool for about 10 minutes, stirring occasionally.

—

Measure the flour, baking powder, salt, and spices into a large bowl and make a well in the center. Add the eggs and the cooled fruit mixture and quickly mix together until well-blended.

—

Turn into the prepared pan and level the surface. Bake for 1¾–2 hours, or until the cake is well-risen, golden brown, and the top feels firm. A skewer inserted into the center should come out clean. Let cool in the pan for 10 minutes, then turn out, peel off the parchment paper, and finish cooling on a wire rack.

This has become the traditional Easter cake, but originally it was given by servant girls to their mothers when they went home on Mother's Day. The almond paste balls represent the eleven apostles (excluding Judas).

EASTER SIMNEL CAKE

SERVES 12

⅔ cup (115g) maraschino cherries, quartered

1 cup + 1 tbsp (225g) buttery spread, straight from the fridge

1 cup + 3 tbsps (225g) light muscovado sugar

4 extra-large eggs

1¾ cups (225g) all-purpose flour

2½ tsps baking powder

½ tsp salt

1½ cups (225g) golden raisins

¾ cup (115g) currants

¾ cup + 2 tbsps (115g) dried apricots, snipped into pieces

¾ cup (55g) candied orange & lemon peel, chopped

finely grated zest of 2 lemons

2 tsps pumpkin pie spice

For the filling and topping

2¼ cups (500g) almond paste or marzipan (see page 398 for almond paste recipe)

2 tbsp apricot jam

1 extra-large egg, beaten, to glaze

Preheat the oven to 300°F. Grease an 8-inch round cake pan, then line the bottom and sides with parchment paper.

—

Place the cherries in a sieve and rinse under running water. Drain well, then dry thoroughly on a paper towel.

—

Measure all the cake ingredients into a large mixing bowl and beat well until thoroughly blended. Place half the mixture in the prepared pan and level the surface.

—

Take one-third of the almond paste or marzipan and roll it out to a circle the size of the pan and place on top of the cake mixture.

—

Spoon the remaining cake mixture on top and level the surface. Bake for about 2½ hours until well-risen, evenly brown, and firm to the touch. Cover with foil after 1 hour if the top is browning too quickly. Let cool in the pan for 10 minutes, then turn out, peel off the parchment paper, and finish cooling on a wire rack.

—

When the cake is cool, brush the top with a little warmed apricot jam. Roll half the remaining almond paste into a ball, then roll out to an 8-inch circle. Press firmly on the top and crimp the edges to decorate. Mark a crisscross pattern on the almond paste with a sharp knife. Form the remaining almond paste into 11 balls.

—

Brush the almond paste with the beaten egg and arrange the almond paste balls around the edge of the cake. Brush the tops of the balls with beaten egg, too, then place the cake under a hot broiler to turn the almond paste golden.

This cake is robust enough to pack for a picnic and also makes a good alternative Christmas cake. Instead of dried cranberries, you can use the same weight of maraschino cherries, but wash and dry them thoroughly.

CRANBERRY AND APRICOT FRUIT CAKE

SERVES 12 TO 14

1 × 8-ounce (227g) can pineapple in natural juice, drained and roughly chopped

2¾ cups (350g) dried apricots, snipped into pieces

¾ cup (115g) almonds, roughly chopped

3 cups (350g) dried cranberries

¾ cup (75g) almond flour

2⅓ cups (350g) golden raisins

finely grated zest of 2 lemons

2 cups (250g) all-purpose flour

1 tbsp baking powder

½ tsp salt

1¼ cups (250g) sugar

1 cup + 2 tbsps (250g) salted butter, softened

5 extra-large eggs

To decorate
⅓ cup (55g) whole almonds

Preheat the oven to 300°F. Grease a 9-inch round cake pan, then line the bottom and sides with parchment paper.

Dry the pineapple thoroughly on a paper towel. Combine all the fruits, chopped almonds, almond flour, and lemon zest in a large bowl and mix together well.

Measure the remaining ingredients into a large mixing bowl and beat until smooth. Fold in the fruit and nuts, then spoon the mixture into the prepared pan. Level the top with the back of a spoon and decorate with concentric circles of regularly spaced almonds.

Bake for about 2½ hours, or until the cake is nicely browned. If it shows signs of becoming too browned before it is cooked, cover the top loosely with foil. When cooked, the cake should show signs of shrinking away from the sides of the pan and a skewer inserted into the center of the cake should come out clean. Let cool in the pan for about 30 minutes, then turn out, leaving the parchment paper in place, and finish cooling on a wire rack.

TIPS

Like most fruit cakes, this improves after storing and can be made up to 1 week ahead. Leave the parchment paper in place, wrap the cake snugly in plastic wrap, and store in an airtight container.

To freeze the cake, wrap snugly in plastic wrap as above, seal inside a plastic bag (this takes up less space than a plastic freezer box), then label and freeze for up to 3 months. To defrost, put the cake, fully wrapped, in the fridge overnight or remove from the plastic bag and thaw for 8 hours at room temperature.

I use this for Christmas, birthdays, and all special occasions—it's a winner. Start preparing the cake the night before you want to bake it, as the dried fruits need to be soaked in brandy so that they become plump.

RICH FRUIT CAKE

SERVES 12 TO 14

1 cup (175g) maraschino cherries, quartered

2½ cups (350g) currants

1½ cups (225g) golden raisins

1½ cups (225g) raisins

1⅓ cups (175g) dried apricots, snipped into pieces

1 cup (75g) candied orange or lemon peel, finely chopped

4 tbsps brandy, plus extra to feed the cake

3¼ cups (400g) all-purpose flour

½ tsp grated nutmeg

½ tsp pumpkin pie spice

1¾ cups (400g) salted butter, softened

2 cups + 2 tbsps (400g) dark muscovado sugar

5 extra-large eggs

½ cup (65g) almonds, chopped

1 tbsp molasses

finely grated zest of 1 lemon

finely grated zest of 1 orange

To decorate

⅓ cup (55g) whole almonds

⅓ cup (55g) maraschino cherries, rinsed, dried, and halved

Place the cherries in a sieve and rinse under running water. Drain well, then dry thoroughly on a paper towel. Place the cherries, currants, golden raisins, raisins, apricots, and chopped orange or lemon peel in a large bowl, stir in the brandy, cover, and let sit in a cool place overnight.

—

The next day, preheat the oven to 275°F. Grease a 9-inch round cake pan, then line the bottom and sides with a double layer of parchment paper.

—

Measure the flour, grated nutmeg, pumpkin pie spice, butter, sugar, eggs, chopped almonds, molasses, and grated lemon and orange zests into a large bowl and beat to mix thoroughly. Fold in the soaked fruits, then spoon the mixture into the prepared cake pan and level the surface. Decorate the top with the whole almonds and halved maraschino cherries, pushing them lightly into the top of the cake mixture.

—

Cover the top of the cake loosely with a double layer of parchment paper and bake for 4–4½ hours, until the cake feels firm to the touch and a skewer inserted into the center comes out clean. Let cool in the pan, then, when the cake is almost cold, turn out, peel off the parchment paper, and finish cooling on a wire rack.

—

Pierce the base at intervals with a fine skewer and feed with a little brandy. Once the cake is completely cold, wrap it in a double layer of parchment paper and then in foil. Store in a cool place for up to 3 months, feeding at intervals with more brandy.

This is a version of a French Christmas log, which is suitable for serving as a dessert or with coffee.

BÛCHE DE NOËL

SERVES 10

1 unfilled Chocolate Roulade
   (see page 38)

For the filling
1 tbsp instant coffee
   granules
2 tbsps hot milk
8 ounces (225g)
   unsweetened chestnut
   purée
2 tbsps brandy
¼ cup (55g) sugar
⅔ cup (150ml) heavy cream,
   whipped

For the topping
1¼ cups (300ml) heavy
   cream, whipped
cocoa powder, for dusting

First make the Chocolate Roulade. Roll with parchment paper inside and let cool.

While it is cooling, make the filling. Dissolve the coffee in the hot milk. Sieve the chestnut purée into a bowl and beat in the coffee mixture, brandy, and sugar until the mixture is smooth. Fold the whipped cream into the chestnut purée mixture.

Carefully unroll the chocolate Swiss roll. Remove the paper and spread the chestnut filling all over the cake, then re-roll. Cut a small slice off at an angle from one of the ends of the roll, then place the roll on a serving plate or board and attach the slice to look like a branch.

Spread the whipped cream over the cake to cover completely, using a small offset spatula in long strokes to give the bark effect. Dust lightly with cocoa and decorate with Christmassy decorations of your choice.

A lemon cake is perfect for a christening. Color the icing pale pink or pale blue, if you like, or maybe a pale primrose yellow.

SPONGE CHRISTENING CAKE

SERVES 10 TO 12

⅓ cup (75g) salted butter
6 extra-large eggs
¾ cup + 2 tbsps (175g)
    granulated sugar
1¼ cups (150g) all-purpose
    flour
1¾ tsps baking powder
¼ tsp salt
2 tbsps cornstarch

For the filling
1¼ cups (300ml) heavy
    cream, whipped
4 tbsps lemon curd

To finish
confectioners' sugar, for
    dusting
1 pound, 9 ounces (700g)
    fondant or ready-to-roll
    icing (see page 400 for
    fondant recipe)
crystallized flowers
    (page 401)
ribbon, to decorate

Preheat the oven to 350°F. Grease a 9-inch round cake pan, then line the bottom with parchment paper.

Melt the butter in a small saucepan, then let cool slightly.

Measure the eggs and sugar into a large heatproof bowl and whisk over hot water with an electric mixer on high speed until the mixture becomes pale and creamy and leaves a trail on the surface when the whisk is lifted. Remove from the heat and continue to whisk until the mixture is cold.

Sift the flour, baking powder, salt, and cornstarch into a bowl. Fold half of the dry ingredients into the egg mixture, then carefully pour half the cooled butter around the edge of the mixture and lightly fold in. Repeat with the remaining dry ingredients and butter.

Pour into the prepared pan and level the surface. Bake for about 40 minutes, or until well-risen, firm to the touch, and beginning to shrink away from the sides of the pan. Let cool in the pan for a few minutes, then turn out, peel off the parchment paper, and finish cooling on a wire rack.

Cut the cake into three horizontally using a serrated or bread knife. Reserve 3–4 tablespoons of the whipped cream, then mix the remainder with the lemon curd and use to sandwich the slices together. Spread the reserved cream around the sides and over the top of the cake.

Dust the work surface with confectioners' sugar and roll out the fondant icing large enough to cover the cake completely. Fold the icing over the rolling pin and carefully lift onto the cake, gently smoothing the sides. Trim the extra icing from the base of the cake. Decorate with crystallized flowers and ribbon.

This cake serves about 100 people and makes a super dessert for a wedding breakfast served with raspberry coulis. You can make this recipe all in one go, but you will need huge bowls. The separate quantities needed to make each layer individually have also been included, which some might find an easier method—also useful if you want to make one of the layers for a practice run. The cakes can be frozen for up to 2 months, but the frosting should be made the day before the wedding.

AMERICAN CHOCOLATE
SERVES 100 WEDDING CAKE

Total ingredients needed

3 lbs, 9 ounces (1.6kg) dark chocolate, broken into pieces
30 extra-large eggs, separated
8 extra-large eggs, whole
6¼ cups (1.25kg) sugar
8¾ cups (840g) almond flour
7½ tsps freshly made black coffee

For the filling and frosting

⅔ cup + 1 tbsp (225g) apricot jam
2½ lbs (1.25kg) dark chocolate
2 cups (450g) unsalted butter

To decorate

edible foliage and flowers

To make each layer separately, see ingredient quantities on the next page

Preheat the oven to 375°F. Lightly grease a 6-inch, 9-inch, and 12-inch round cake pan, then line the bottom and sides of each pan with parchment paper.

———

To make the cakes, melt the chocolate in a bowl set over a saucepan of simmering water, making sure the bottom of the bowl is not touching the water, stirring occasionally. Remove from the heat and allow to cool slightly.

———

Measure the yolks, whole eggs, and sugar into a large bowl and beat until thick and light. Add the melted chocolate along with the almonds and coffee.

———

In a separate bowl, whisk the egg whites until stiff but not dry. Fold carefully into the chocolate mixture.

———

Divide the mixture between the prepared pans and bake (they can all go into the oven at once; put the large cake on the middle shelf and the two smaller cakes on the top shelf). The small cake will take about 45 minutes, the medium cake 1–1¼ hours, and the large cake 1½–1¾ hours (cover loosely with foil after 1 hour). Test the center of each with a skewer, which should come out just about clean. Let cool in the pans for a few minutes, then turn out, peel off the parchment paper, and finish cooling on a wire rack. At this point, the cakes can be frozen.

———

Recipe continued on the next page

6-inch cake

6 ounces (175g) dark
    chocolate, broken into pieces
3 extra-large eggs, separated
1 extra-large egg, whole
¾ cup (150g) sugar
¾ cup (75g) almond flour
½ tsp freshly made black coffee

For the filling and frosting
2 tbsps apricot jam
8 ounces (225g) dark
    chocolate, broken into pieces
⅓ cup (75g) unsalted butter

9-inch cake

1 lb, 3 ounces (525g) dark
    chocolate, broken into pieces
10 extra-large eggs, separated
2 extra-large eggs, whole
2 cups + 2 tbsps (425g) sugar
2¾ cups (275g) almond flour
2½ tsps freshly made black
    coffee

For the filling and frosting
¼ cup (75g) apricot jam
12 ounces (350g) dark
    chocolate, broken into pieces
⅔ cup (150g) unsalted butter

12-inch cake

2 lbs (900g) dark chocolate,
    broken into pieces
17 extra-large eggs, separated
5 extra-large eggs, whole
3½ cups (700g) sugar
5 cups (475g) almond flour
4½ tsps freshly made black
    coffee

For the filling and frosting
⅓ cup (115g) apricot jam
1¼ lbs (550g) dark chocolate,
    broken into pieces
1 cup (225g) unsalted butter

Turn the cold cakes upside down so that the flat side is facing up. Push the apricot jam through a sieve, then brush over the tops and sides of the cakes.

—

To make the frosting, melt the chocolate gently in a heatproof bowl over a saucepan of simmering water, making sure the bottom of the bowl is not touching the water, stirring occasionally. Add the butter and stir until the butter has melted.

—

Stand each cake on the wire rack on a sheet pan to catch any drips, then pour over the chocolate frosting. Smooth the top and sides with an offset spatula and then allow to set in a cool place.

—

Transport the cake as separate layers and assemble and decorate at the destination. Place the largest cake on a cake board or serving plate, then carefully stack the other two cakes on top. Decorate with fresh edible flowers and foliage to match the wedding bouquet. Serve with raspberry coulis.

TIPS

The cakes will freeze un-iced for up to a month or can be made up to 7 days ahead. It is normal for the cakes to have crusty tops when baked—trim if necessary. Use a good-quality chocolate for the frosting. I find better-quality chocolates give a smoother finish. The high chocolate and sugar content make the cakes susceptible to burning, so do keep an eye on them. You may need to cover them with foil or parchment paper. The cakes are firm enough to stack as they are, but use thin cake boards slightly smaller than each layer if you prefer. Don't ice the cake more than a day before the wedding to prevent it from losing its sheen. Once iced, keep the cake in a cool place, but not in the fridge.

This is a very rich, "fudgy" cake that needs no filling. There is no flour in this recipe; almond flour imparts the flavor and texture.

DIVINE CHOCOLATE BIRTHDAY CAKE

SERVES ABOUT 10

6 extra-large eggs, 5 of them
   separated
1 cup + 1 tbsp (215g) sugar
9½ ounces (265g) dark
   chocolate, broken into
   pieces
1 tsp instant coffee granules
1 tsp hot water
1 cup + 3 tbsps (150g)
   almond flour

For the frosting
4 tbsps apricot jam
8 ounces (225g) dark
   chocolate, broken into
   pieces
½ cup (115g) unsalted butter

Preheat the oven to 375°F. Grease a 9-inch round cake pan, then line the bottom with parchment paper.

Place the egg yolks and whole egg in a large bowl with the sugar and beat together until thick and light in color.

Melt the chocolate in a heatproof bowl set over a saucepan of simmering water, making sure the bottom of the bowl is not touching the water, stirring occasionally. Dissolve the coffee granules in the hot water and add to the melted chocolate. Cool slightly, then stir into the egg mixture along with the almond flour.

In a separate bowl, whisk the egg whites until stiff but not dry. Carefully fold into the egg and chocolate mixture.

Turn into the prepared pan and gently level the surface. Bake for about 50 minutes, or until well-risen and a skewer inserted into the center comes out clean. Let cool in the pan for 10 minutes, then turn out, peel off the parchment paper, and finish cooling on a wire rack. Measure the apricot jam into a small saucepan and allow to melt over low heat. Brush over the cake.

To make the frosting, melt the chocolate gently in a heatproof bowl set over a saucepan of simmering water, making sure the bottom of the bowl is not touching the water, stirring occasionally. Remove from the heat, add the butter, and stir until the frosting has the consistency of heavy cream.

Stand the wire rack on a sheet pan to catch any drips, then pour the frosting over the cake, smoothing it over the top and sides with an offset spatula. Allow to set, then decorate as you like.

A super and impressive, large celebration cake.

RED VELVET CAKE

SERVES 16

For the sponges
1¼ cups (300ml) sunflower oil
4 cups (500g) all-purpose flour
2 tbsps cocoa powder
4 tsps baking powder
2 tsps baking soda
2⅔ cups (500g) light muscovado sugar
1 tsp salt
1½ cups + 2 tbsps (400ml) buttermilk
4 tsps vanilla extract
2 tbsps (30ml) red food coloring gel or about ¼ tsp food coloring paste (use a professional food coloring paste if you can; a natural liquid coloring won't work and may turn the sponge green)
4 extra-large eggs

For the frosting
1 cup + 2 tbsps (250g) butter, softened
6 cups (750g) confectioners' sugar
1½ cups + 1 tbsp (350g) full-fat cream cheese
1 tsp vanilla extract

TIP
The sponge cakes can be made up to 3 days ahead and will stay moist if wrapped in plastic wrap, or you can wrap well and freeze for up to 2 months.

Preheat the oven to 350°F. Grease and line the bottoms of two 8-inch cake pans with parchment paper.

—

Measure half each of the flour, cocoa powder, baking powder, baking soda, sugar, and salt into a bowl and mix well.

—

Mix half each of the buttermilk, oil, vanilla, food coloring, and ⅓ cup + 1 tablespoon (100ml) water in a bowl. Add 2 eggs and whisk until smooth. Pour the wet ingredients into the dry ingredients and whisk until well-combined. The cake mixture should be bright red, and it will get a little darker as it cooks. If it's not as vivid as you'd like, add a touch more coloring.

—

Divide the cake mixture evenly between the two pans and level the surfaces. Bake for 25–30 minutes, or until well-risen and the cakes are shrinking away from the sides of the pan. Cool in the pans for 10 minutes, then turn out onto a wire rack, peel off the parchment paper, and let cool.

—

Repeat these steps with the remaining ingredients, until you have four cakes in total.

—

To make the frosting, place the butter in a large bowl and sift in half the confectioners' sugar. Roughly mash together with a spatula, then whiz with an electric mixer until smooth. Add the cream cheese and vanilla, sift in the remaining confectioners' sugar, mash together again, then blend once more with the electric mixer.

—

To assemble the cake, stick one of the sponges to a cake stand or board with a little of the soft frosting. Use roughly half the frosting to stack the remaining cakes on top, spreading a generous amount between each layer. Pile the remaining frosting on top of the assembled cake and use an offset spatula to ease it over the edges, covering the entire surface of the cake.

CHAPTER SIX

SPECIAL CAKES

This Hungarian cake is not quick to make, but it does look spectacular. The caramel topping will soften due to the moisture from the cake, so serve it within 12 hours.

DOBOS TORTE

SERVES 8

For the sponge
4 extra-large eggs
¾ cup + 2 tbsps (175g) granulated sugar
1¼ cups (150g) all-purpose flour, sifted
1¾ tsps baking powder
½ tsp salt

For the chocolate buttercream
2 extra-large egg whites
1 cup (115g) confectioners' sugar
1 cup (225g) unsalted butter, softened
4 ounces (115g) dark chocolate, broken into pieces

For the caramel
6 tbsps (75g) granulated sugar
3 tbsps water

Preheat the oven to 425°F. Mark six 8-inch circles on parchment paper and lay on baking sheets.

To make the sponge, whisk the eggs and sugar in a large bowl until the mixture is light and foamy and leaves a trail. Lightly fold in the flour, baking powder, and salt, a little at a time.

Divide the mixture between the 6 marked circles, spreading the mixture out evenly. Bake for 6–8 minutes, until pale golden and springy to the touch. With a sharp knife, trim the circles. Peel off the paper and let cool on a wire rack.

To make the chocolate buttercream, whisk the egg whites and confectioners' sugar in a heatproof bowl set over a saucepan of simmering water until the mixture holds its shape. Cream the butter until really soft, then add the egg white mixture to it a little at a time. Melt the chocolate gently in a heatproof bowl set over a saucepan of hot water, making sure the bottom of the bowl is not touching the water, stirring occasionally. Cool slightly, then add to the buttercream and mix well until evenly blended.

Take one of the sponge circles and place on a sheet of parchment paper, ready to be topped with caramel. To make the caramel, dissolve the sugar in the water over a low heat, then increase the heat and boil the syrup until it reaches a deep straw color. Allow it to cool slightly then pour over the sponge circle. When the caramel on top of the sponge is just beginning to set, mark it and cut into 16 portions with an oiled knife.

Sandwich the remaining five circles of sponge together with the buttercream. Spread buttercream around the sides, and pipe buttercream rosettes on the top. Place a caramel-topped wedge of cake at an angle on each rosette to form the top layer.

Nusskuchen comes in many forms, but always contains hazelnuts. This one is filled with a delicious apple mixture and topped with melted chocolate.

NUSSKUCHEN

SERVES 6

¼ cup (40g) shelled
   hazelnuts
½ cup (115g) salted butter,
   softened
½ cup + 1 tbsp (115g) sugar
2 extra-large eggs, separated
1 tsp instant coffee granules
1 tbsp warm milk
1 cup (115g) all-purpose flour
1½ tsps baking powder
¼ tsp salt

For the filling
2 medium (450g) dessert
   apples, peeled, cored, and
   sliced
2 tbsps apricot jam
grated zest and juice of
   ½ lemon

To finish
2 ounces (55g) dark
   chocolate, broken into
   pieces

Preheat the oven to 375°F. Grease and line the bottom of an 8-inch round cake pan with parchment paper.

Place the hazelnuts on a baking sheet and put in the oven for about 10 minutes. Tip onto a tea towel and rub them together to remove the skins. (Some stubborn ones may need to go back into the oven, but don't worry about getting every last bit of skin off—it's not necessary.) Place the nuts in a food processor and grind.

Measure the butter and sugar into a bowl and beat together until light and fluffy. Gradually beat in the egg yolks and stir in the prepared nuts. Dissolve the coffee in the warm milk, then stir into the nut mixture. Carefully fold in the flour, baking powder, and salt.

In a separate bowl, whisk the egg whites until they form soft peaks, then gently fold into the cake mixture.

Turn into the prepared pan and level the surface. Bake for 25 minutes, or until well-risen and the top of the cake springs back when lightly pressed with a finger. Let cool in the pan for a few minutes, then turn out, peel off the parchment paper, and finish cooling on a wire rack.

Meanwhile, prepare the filling. Place the apples in a saucepan with the apricot jam and lemon zest and juice. Cover and cook very gently until the apples are soft but still retain their shape. Let cool.

Cut the cake in half horizontally using a serrated or bread knife, then sandwich the slices together with the cooled apple mixture.

Melt the chocolate gently in a heatproof bowl set over a saucepan of simmering water, making sure the bottom of the bowl is not touching the water. Spread over the top of the cake and allow to set.

This chocolate cake is said to have been invented in Vienna by the chef Franz Sacher in 1832. It is quite dense and rich, so serve in small wedges.

SACHERTORTE

SERVES 12

5 ounces (150g) dark chocolate, broken into pieces
⅔ cup (150g) unsalted butter, softened
½ cup + 1 tbsp (115g) sugar
½ tsp vanilla extract
5 extra-large eggs, separated
¾ cup (75g) almond flour
⅓ cup (40g) all-purpose flour

For the topping and frosting
6 tbsps apricot jam
5 ounces (150g) dark chocolate, broken into pieces
¾ cup + 1 tbsp (200ml) heavy cream
1 ounce (30g) milk chocolate, broken into pieces

Preheat the oven to 350°F. Grease and line the bottom of a 9-inch round cake pan with parchment paper.

Melt the chocolate for the cake gently in a heatproof bowl set over a saucepan of simmering water, making sure the bottom of the bowl is not touching the water, stirring occasionally, then cool slightly.

Beat the butter until really soft in a large bowl, then gradually beat in the sugar until the mixture is light and fluffy. Add the cooled chocolate and the vanilla extract and beat again. Add the egg yolks, one at a time, beating between each addition, then fold in the almond flour and all-purpose flour.

In a separate bowl, whisk the egg whites until stiff but not dry. Add about one-third to the chocolate mixture and stir in vigorously. Gently fold in the remaining egg whites. Pour into the prepared pan and level the surface. Bake for 45–50 minutes, until well-risen and the top springs back when lightly pressed with a finger. Let cool in the pan for a few minutes, then turn out, peel off the parchment paper, and finish cooling on a wire rack.

Heat the apricot jam in a small saucepan, then brush evenly over the top and sides of the cold cake. Allow to set.

To make the topping, melt the dark chocolate gently with the cream in a small saucepan. Stir occasionally. Allow to cool for 1–2 minutes to thicken slightly, then pour onto the cake. Spread it gently over the top and down the sides, and allow to set.

For the frosting, melt the milk chocolate gently in a heatproof bowl set over a saucepan of hot water. Spoon into a small frosting bag and snip off the corner. Pipe "Sacher" across the cake and allow to set.

A Parisian speciality, this gâteau was named in honor of Saint Honoré, the patron saint of bakers. It's an absolute classic but does take time and skill to make.

GÂTEAU SAINT HONORÉ
SERVES 8

For the pâté sucrée
1 cup (115g) all-purpose flour
¼ cup (55g) salted butter, softened
¼ cup (55g) sugar
2 extra-large egg yolks

For the choux pastry
¼ cup (55g) salted butter
½ cup + 2 tbsps (150ml) water
½ cup (65g) all-purpose flour
2 extra-large eggs, beaten

For the crème pâtissière
6 egg yolks
½ cup + 1 tbsp (115g) sugar
½ cup (55g) all-purpose flour
1 tbsp cornstarch
2 cups + 2 tbsps (500ml) whole milk
1 tsp vanilla extract
⅔ cup (150ml) heavy cream, lightly whipped

For the caramel and spun sugar
1 cup + 2 tbsps (225g) sugar
⅓ cup (75ml) water

Grease 3 baking sheets.

To make the pâté sucrée, measure the flour, butter, and sugar into a food processor and whiz briefly until the mixture resembles fine breadcrumbs. Add the egg yolks and pulse until just blended to form a dough. Knead the mixture gently until smooth. Wrap in plastic wrap and let rest in the fridge for about 30 minutes.

Preheat the oven to 375°F.

Roll out the pâté sucrée on a lightly floured work surface to a 7-inch round. Place on one of the prepared baking sheets, crimp the edges, and prick all over with a fork.

Bake for 15–20 minutes, or until the pastry is a pale golden brown. Let cool on the baking sheet for a few minutes, then turn out and finish cooling on a wire rack. Increase the oven temperature to 425°F.

Next make the choux pastry. Measure the butter and water into a medium saucepan, heat gently until the butter has melted, then bring slowly to a boil. Remove the saucepan from the heat, add the flour all at once and beat until the mixture forms a soft ball. Allow the flour mixture to cool slightly, then gradually beat in the eggs, beating well between each addition to give a smooth, shiny paste.Spoon the dough into a piping bag fitted with a ½-inch plain nozzle. Pipe a 7-inch ring of choux pastry onto the second baking sheet and pipe 16 pieces about the size of a walnut on the third baking sheet. Bake for about 10 minutes, then lower the temperature to 375°F and cook for an additional 20 minutes until well-risen, golden brown, and crisp.

Recipe continued on the next page

The sugar syrup used to make the caramel and spun sugar can easily burn skin. Please take extra care when handling, particularly if there are children in the house at the time.

To make the spun sugar, cover your working area with sheets of oiled foil, and cover a rolling pin with foil and oil it lightly. Have ready 2 forks taped together back to back. Dip the prongs of the forks in the caramel and, holding the covered rolling pin in the other hand, flick the forks back and forth over the rolling pin, to form long strands of sugar. Repeat with the remaining caramel, then place on an oiled baking sheet until needed.

Remove the baking sheet from the oven and pierce the choux ring and the buns at intervals underneath, to allow the steam to escape. Return to the oven for about 5 minutes to dry out completely. Cool on a wire rack.

To make the crème pâtissière, place the yolks, sugar, cornstarch, and flour in a large bowl. Whisk, using an electric mixer, until the mixture is thick and has become paler. Heat the milk in a medium-sized saucepan until scalding, then add the vanilla extract. Slowly pour this milk into the egg mixture and continue whisking until smooth. Pour back into the saucepan and stir constantly over a medium heat. Cook until the mixture is very thick and smooth. Spoon into a bowl, cover the surface with parchment paper to stop a skin from forming, and let cool.

Whisk the cooled crème pâtissière until smooth, then fold in the cream. Cover tightly with plastic wrap and chill thoroughly.

Pipe a little of the crème pâtissière into the choux ring and buns, using the holes made in the bases to allow the steam to escape. Let sit in a cool place while making the caramel.

To make the caramel, measure the sugar and water into a heavy-bottomed saucepan. Heat gently until the sugar has dissolved, brushing down the sides of the saucepan with hot water from time to time. Bring to a boil and boil the syrup until it turns a golden color. Immediately plunge the base of the saucepan into cold water to stop the caramel from darkening further. Place the saucepan in a large bowl and fill the bowl with boiling water, to keep the caramel fluid.

Put the pâté sucrée on a plate and position the choux ring on top. One by one, dip the base of each choux bun in the caramel and place on the choux ring, holding it in place for a few seconds to secure. Continue with the remaining buns. Spoon a little caramel over the top of each bun.

Spoon the remaining crème pâtissière into the choux case and, if you like, decorate with spun sugar (see Tip). If you have decorated the gâteau with spun sugar, serve it within the hour, as the sugar will gradually start to disintegrate due to the moisture.

This cake is perfect not just for Wimbledon, but for all summer occasions. It uses no flour, and the semolina used instead gives it a slightly crunchy, dense texture. The cake must be eaten on the day of filling.

WIMBLEDON CAKE

SERVES 6-8

6 extra-large eggs, separated
1 cup (200g) granulated
　sugar
finely grated zest and juice
　of 2 oranges
¾ cup + 3 tbsps (150g)
　semolina

For the filling and topping
¾ cup (115g) strawberries
1 passion fruit
⅔ cup (150ml) heavy cream,
　whipped
confectioners' sugar, to
　finish

Preheat the oven to 350°F. Grease an 8-inch round cake pan, then line the bottom with parchment paper.

Measure the egg yolks, sugar, orange zest and juice, and the semolina into a bowl and beat until pale and thick using an electric mixer. In a separate clean bowl, whisk the egg whites until they are stiff but not dry, then gently fold into the orange and semolina mixture. Turn into the prepared pan and level the surface.

Bake for about 40 minutes, or until well-risen and the top of the cake springs back when lightly pressed with a finger. Let cool in the pan for a few minutes, then turn out, peel off the parchment paper, and finish cooling on a wire rack.

Reserve a few strawberries to decorate the top of the cake, then slice the remainder. Halve the passion fruit and scoop out the pulp.

Cut the cake in half horizontally using a serrated or bread knife, then sandwich the halves together with the sliced strawberries, passion fruit pulp, and whipped cream.

Just before serving, decorate with the reserved strawberries, sliced or left whole, and sift some confectioners' sugar over the top.

Made with semolina and almond flour instead of all-purpose flour, this cake has a lovely light but crumbly texture. It keeps better than an ordinary sponge cake and is delicious with different fruits. For an even more luscious cake, double the quantities of cream and lemon curd to smooth over the top of the cake as well as fill it.

LEMON GRIESTORTE

SERVES 6-8

3 extra-large eggs, separated
½ cup + 1 tbsp (115g)
    granulated sugar
finely grated zest and juice
    of ½ lemon
⅓ cup (55g) fine semolina
3 tbsps (15g) almond flour

For the filling
⅔ cup (150ml) heavy cream
4 tbsps lemon curd
1 cup (115g) raspberries
    (optional)

To finish
confectioners' sugar

Preheat the oven to 350°F. Grease an 8-inch round cake pan and line the bottom and sides with parchment paper.

Measure the egg yolks and sugar into a bowl and whisk until pale and light in texture. Add the lemon juice and continue to whisk until the mixture is thick. Fold in the grated lemon zest, semolina, and almond flour. In a separate bowl, whisk the egg whites until they form soft peaks, then fold into the mixture until evenly blended.

Turn into the prepared pan and bake for 30–35 minutes, or until well-risen and a pale golden brown. Let cool in the pan for a few minutes, then turn out, peel off the parchment paper, and finish cooling on a wire rack.

Whisk the cream until it holds its shape, then fold in the lemon curd.

Cut the cake in half horizontally using a serrated or bread knife, then sandwich the halves together with the lemon cream and raspberries, if using. Dust the top with confectioners' sugar to serve.

These small cakes can be fiddly to make, but are delicious and have a sponge that is moist and light. They are the sort of cake that would be sold in the very best French pâtisseries.

CHOCOLATINES

MAKES 9 CHOCOLATINES

For the genoise sponge
3 tbsps (40g) salted butter
3 extra-large eggs
6 tbsps (75g) sugar
½ cup (65g) all-purpose
   flour
1 tbsp cornstarch
¾ tsp baking powder
¼ tsp salt

*For the crème au
   beurre chocolat*
4 ounces (115g) dark
   chocolate, broken into
   pieces
¼ cup (55g) sugar
4 tbsps water
2 extra-large egg yolks
¾ cup (175g) salted
   butter, softened

To finish
½ cup (75g) mixed nuts,
   toasted and finely
   chopped

Preheat the oven to 350°F. Grease a 7-inch square cake pan, then line the bottom with parchment paper.

To make the sponge, gently melt the butter in a saucepan, then set aside to cool slightly.

Measure the eggs and sugar into a large bowl and whisk at full speed until the mixture is pale, mousse-like, and thick enough that a trail is left when the whisk is lifted from the mixture.

Sift the flour, cornstarch, baking powder, and salt together into a bowl. Carefully fold half the flour mixture into the egg mixture, then gently pour half the cooled butter around the edge of the mixture and fold in. Repeat with the remaining flour and butter.

Pour the mixture into the prepared pan and level the surface. Bake for 35–40 minutes, or until well-risen and the top of the cake springs back when lightly pressed with a finger. Let cool in the pan for a few minutes, then turn out, peel off the parchment paper, and finish cooling on a wire rack.

To make the crème au beurre chocolat (chocolate buttercream), place the chocolate in a large heatproof bowl. Place the bowl over a saucepan of simmering water until melted, making sure that the bottom of the bowl is not touching the water.

Measure the sugar and water into a small heavy-bottomed saucepan. Heat very gently until the sugar has dissolved. Bring to a boil, then boil steadily for about 5 minutes until the syrup is clear and forms a slim thread when pulled apart between 2 teaspoons.

Put the egg yolks into a bowl and give them a quick stir to break them up. Pour the syrup in a thin stream onto the egg yolks, whisking all the time. Continue to whisk until the mixture is thick and cold. In another bowl, cream the butter until very soft and gradually beat in the egg yolk mixture. Stir in the cooled, melted chocolate to flavor.

Cut the cold sponge in half horizontally using a serrated or bread knife, then sandwich the halves together with a thin layer of the chocolate buttercream. Trim the cake edges and cut neatly into 2¼-inch squares. Spread the top and sides of each cake with most of the remaining buttercream and press the chopped, toasted nuts around the sides. Finish by piping the tops of the squares with tiny rosettes of the remaining buttercream.

TIP
Leftover egg whites can be stored in a covered container in the fridge for up to three weeks, or frozen for up to six months.

These are a coffee-flavored variation of the chocolatines on page 156.
I've often seen them in fashionable Parisian pâtisseries.

MOKATINES

MAKES 8 MOKATINES

For the genoise sponge
3 tbsps (40g) salted butter
3 extra-large eggs
6 tbsps (75g) granulated
    sugar
½ cup (65g) all-purpose
    flour
1 tbsp cornstarch
¾ tsp baking powder
¼ tsp salt

**For the crème au
    beurre moka**
3 tbsps (40g) granulated
    sugar
2 tbsps water
1 extra-large egg yolk
⅓ cup (75g) salted butter,
    softened
1 tbsp strong coffee

For the soft coffee frosting
3 tbsps apricot jam
¼ cup (55g) salted butter
3 tbsps milk
1 tbsp instant coffee
    granules
1¾ cups (225g)
    confectioners' sugar,
    sifted

Preheat the oven to 350°F. Grease a 7-inch square cake pan, then line the bottom with parchment paper.

To make the sponge, gently melt the butter in a saucepan, then set to one side to cool slightly. Measure the eggs and sugar into a large bowl and whisk at full speed until the mixture is pale and mousse-like, and thick enough so that a trail is left when the whisk is lifted from the mixture.

Sift the flour, cornstarch, baking powder, and salt together into a bowl. Carefully fold half the flour mixture into the egg mixture, gently pour half the cooled butter around the edge of the mixture, and then fold in. Repeat with the remaining flour and butter.

Pour the mixture into the prepared pan and level the surface. Bake for 35–40 minutes, or until well-risen and the top of the cake springs back when lightly pressed with a finger. Let cool in the pan for a few minutes, then turn out, peel off the parchment paper, and finish cooling on a wire rack.

To make the crème au beurre moka (coffee buttercream), measure the sugar and water into a small heavy-bottomed saucepan. Heat very gently until the sugar has dissolved. Bring to a boil, then boil steadily for about 5 minutes until the syrup is still clear and forms a slim thread when pulled apart between 2 teaspoons.

Recipe continued on the next page

Put the egg yolk into a bowl and give it a quick stir to break it up. Pour the syrup in a thin stream over the yolk, whisking all the time. Continue to whisk until the mixture is thick and cold. In another bowl, cream the butter until very soft and gradually beat in the egg yolk mixture. Stir in the coffee to flavor.

Cut the cold cake in half horizontally using a serrated or bread knife, then sandwich the halves together with a thin layer of the coffee buttercream. Trim the cake edges and neatly cut in half, then cut each half into 4 to make 8 oblongs. Sieve the apricot jam into a small saucepan and warm gently. Brush the tops and sides of the cakes with the hot apricot jam.

To make the soft coffee frosting, measure the butter, milk, and coffee into a small saucepan and heat gently until the butter has melted. Add the sifted confectioners' sugar and beat until smooth and glossy. Let thicken slightly, then use most of the soft frosting to pour over each cake, smoothing the sides quickly if necessary. Let set, then decorate with the remaining piped soft coffee frosting.

TIP

Store eggs in a cool place, like a fridge, pointed end down, and away from strong-smelling foods such as fish. Bring them to room temperature before using.

This is one of my favorite coffee cakes, and it looks spectacular, too.

GÂTEAU MOKA AUX AMANDES

SERVES 8

3 extra-large eggs
½ cup + 1 tbsp (115g) granulated sugar
⅔ cup (75g) all-purpose flour
1 tsp baking powder
¼ tsp salt

For the crème au beurre moka
6 tbsps (75g) granulated sugar
4 tbsps water
2 extra-large egg yolks
¾ cup (175g) salted butter, softened
1–2 tbsps strong coffee

To finish
1¾ cups (175g) slivered or sliced almonds, toasted
confectioners' sugar, for dusting (optional)

Preheat the oven to 375°F. Grease a 9-inch round cake pan, then line the bottom with parchment paper.

Measure the eggs and sugar into a large bowl and whisk at full speed until the mixture is pale in color and thick enough to just leave a trail when the whisk is lifted. Sift the flour, baking powder, and salt over the surface of the mixture and gently fold in with a metal spoon or spatula.

Turn into the prepared pan and level the surface. Bake for about 30 minutes, or until well-risen and the top of the cake springs back when lightly pressed with a finger. Let cool in the pan for a few minutes, then turn out, peel off the parchment paper, and finish cooling on a wire rack.

To make the crème au beurre moka (coffee buttercream), measure the sugar and water into a small, heavy-bottomed saucepan. Heat very gently until the sugar has dissolved. Bring to a boil, then boil steadily for about 5 minutes until it has reached a temperature of 224°F on a sugar thermometer, or until the syrup forms a slim thread when pulled apart between 2 teaspoons. Place the egg yolks in a bowl and give them a quick stir to break them up. Pour the syrup in a thin stream onto the egg yolks, whisking all the time. Continue to whisk until the mixture is thick and cold. In another bowl, cream the butter until very soft and gradually beat in the egg yolk mixture. Stir in the coffee to flavor.

Cut the cake in half horizontally using a serrated or bread knife, then sandwich the halves together with a thin layer of the coffee buttercream. Spread buttercream over the top and sides of the cake, retaining some for decoration, then press the toasted almonds all over the cake. Dust lightly with confectioners' sugar and finish by piping rosettes of buttercream around the top.

This is a light walnut sponge filled with strawberries and cream, often served in broader Europe as a dessert. For a lighter filling, you could use full-fat crème fraîche, and you could use wild strawberries when they are in season.

SWISS STRAWBERRY
SERVES 8 AND WALNUT CAKE

3 extra-large eggs
½ cup + 1 tbsp (115g) sugar
⅔ cup (75g) all-purpose flour
1 tsp baking powder
¼ tsp salt
½ cup (55g) walnuts, finely chopped

For the filling and topping
1¼ cups (300ml) heavy cream, whipped
3¼ cups (450g) strawberries, roughly chopped, plus extra kept whole for decoration

Preheat the oven to 350°F. Grease an 8-inch round cake pan, then line the bottom with parchment paper.

Measure the eggs and sugar into a large bowl and beat until the mixture is thick and mousse-like and leaves a trail when the whisk is lifted out of the mixture. Sift the flour onto the mixture and lightly fold in along with the baking powder, salt, and chopped walnuts.

Turn into the prepared cake pan and level the surface. Bake for 40–45 minutes, or until well-risen and the top of the cake springs back when lightly pressed with a finger. Let cool in the pan for a few minutes, then turn out, peel off the parchment paper, and finish cooling on a wire rack.

When cold, cut the cake into three layers horizontally using a serrated or bread knife, then sandwich the slices together with a good amount of whipped cream and strawberries. Spread the remaining cream over the top and the sides of the cake and decorate with the reserved strawberries.

CHAPTER SEVEN

SHEET CAKES

This is the simplest of cakes to make. When it is cooked and cold, sift a little confectioners' sugar over the top to finish, if you would like.

BASIC ALL-IN-ONE SHEET CAKE

CUTS INTO 16 PIECES

1 cup + 1 tbsp (225g) buttery spread, straight from the fridge

1 cup + 2 tbsps (225g) granulated sugar

2¼ cups (275g) all-purpose flour

4¼ tsps baking powder

½ tsp salt

4 extra-large eggs

4 tbsps milk

To finish
a little sifted confectioners' sugar (optional)

Preheat the oven to 350°F. Grease a 9 x 13-inch baking pan then line the bottom with parchment paper.

—

Measure all the ingredients into a large bowl and mix with an electric mixer until well-blended.

—

Turn the mixture into the prepared pan and level the surface. Bake for 35–40 minutes, or until the cake has shrunk from the sides of the pan and springs back when pressed in the center with your fingertips. Let cool in the pan.

—

Cut into 16 pieces and peel off the parchment paper.

To make a larger sheet cake, follow the method above. Grease a 13½ x 10½-inch lasagna pan and line the bottom with parchment paper. Measure 1½ cups (350g) buttery spread, 1¾ cups (350g) granulated sugar, 3⅔ cups (450g) all-purpose flour, 6½ tsps baking powder, 1 tsp salt, 6 extra-large eggs, and 6 tbsps milk into a large bowl and beat until well-blended. Bake for 40–45 minutes, or until the cake has shrunk from the sides of the pan and springs back when pressed in the center with your fingertips. Let cool in the pan before cutting into 24 pieces and removing the parchment paper.

You can vary a basic sheet cake quite simply—in this case by adding a subtle lemon flavor and a lemon glacé icing.

ICED LEMON SHEET CAKE
CUTS INTO 16 PIECES

1 cup + 1 tbsp (225g) buttery spread, straight from the fridge
1 cup + 2 tbsps (225g) granulated sugar
2¼ cups (275g) all-purpose flour
4¼ tsps baking powder
½ tsp salt
4 extra-large eggs
4 tbsps milk
grated zest of 2 lemons

For the icing
3 tbsps fresh lemon juice
1¾ cups (225g) confectioners' sugar, sifted

Preheat the oven to 350°F. Grease a 9 x 13-inch baking pan, then line the bottom with parchment paper.

—

Measure all the sponge ingredients into a large bowl and mix with an electric mixer until well-blended.

—

Turn the mixture into the prepared pan and level the surface. Bake for 35–40 minutes, or until the cake has shrunk from the sides of the pan and springs back when pressed in the center with your fingertips. Let cool in the pan, then turn out and peel off the parchment paper.

—

To make the icing, mix together the lemon juice and confectioners' sugar to give a runny consistency. Spread out evenly over the cake and allow to set before cutting into 16 pieces.

Chocolate cakes are always popular, and this is a particularly simple version that's great for family teas or lunch boxes.

ICED CHOCOLATE SHEET CAKE

CUTS INTO 16 PIECES

4 tbsps cocoa powder
4 tbsps boiling water
1 cup + 1 tbsp (225g) buttery spread, straight from the fridge
1 cup + 2 tbsps (225g) granulated sugar
1¾ cups (225g) all-purpose flour
1 tbsp baking powder
½ tsp salt
4 extra-large eggs
1 tbsp milk

For the icing and decoration
4 tbsps apricot jam
5 ounces (150g) dark chocolate, broken into pieces
6 tbsps water
2¾ cups (350g) confectioners' sugar, sifted
1 tsp sunflower oil
chocolate curls (page 402)

Preheat the oven to 350°F. Grease a 9 x 13-inch baking pan, then line the bottom with parchment paper.

—

Blend the cocoa and boiling water together in a large bowl, then allow to cool slightly. Add all the remaining sponge ingredients and mix with an electric mixer until well-blended.

—

Turn the mixture into the prepared pan and level the surface. Bake for 35–40 minutes, or until the cake has shrunk from the sides of the pan and springs back when pressed in the center with your fingertips. Let cool in the pan, then turn out and peel off the parchment paper.

—

Warm the apricot jam in a saucepan and brush all over the cake.

—

To make the icing, melt the chocolate in a saucepan with the water, heating gently until melted and smooth. Allow to cool slightly, then beat in the confectioners' sugar and oil. Pour over the cake and smooth gently with an offset spatula. Let set for 30 minutes, then decorate with chocolate curls before cutting into 16 pieces.

TIP
Brushing the cold cake with apricot jam before icing it gives the cake a lovely flavor and prevents cake crumbs from getting into the icing.

Bought mixtures of chopped nuts might include a high proportion of peanuts. I always prefer to make up my own mix from shelled nuts.

AMERICAN SPICED CARROT SHEET CAKE

CUTS INTO 16 PIECES

2¼ cups (275g) all-purpose flour
1¾ cups (350g) sugar
4¼ tsps baking powder
½ tsp salt
⅔ cup (75g) unsalted mixed nuts, chopped
3 tsps ground cinnamon
2 tsps ground ginger
1¼ cups (300ml) sunflower oil
2½ cups (275g) carrots, coarsely grated
4 extra-large eggs
1 tsp vanilla extract

For the topping
1¾ cups (400g) full-fat cream cheese
4 tsps clear honey
2 tsps fresh lemon juice
mixed unsalted nuts, chopped, to decorate

Preheat the oven to 350°F. Grease a 9 x 13-inch baking pan, then line the bottom with parchment paper.

—

Measure all the dry cake ingredients into a large bowl. Add the oil, grated carrots, eggs (one at a time), and vanilla extract, beating between each addition.

—

Pour into the prepared pan and level the surface. Bake for 50–60 minutes, or until the cake is well-risen, golden brown in color, and firm to the touch. Let cool in the pan for 10 minutes, then turn out, peel off the parchment paper, and finish cooling on a wire rack.

—

To make the topping, mix together the cream cheese, honey, and lemon juice. Add a little extra lemon juice, if necessary, to make a spreading consistency. Spread evenly over the cake with an offset spatula, then sprinkle with the chopped nuts to decorate.

TIP
You can store the iced cake in the fridge for up to 2 weeks.

Coffee and walnuts go particularly well together, but you can use other nuts for this recipe if you prefer.

COFFEE AND WALNUT SHEET CAKE

CUTS INTO 16 PIECES

1 cup + 1 tbsp (225g) buttery spread, straight from the fridge

1 cup + 3 tbsps (225g) light muscovado sugar

2¼ cups (275g) all-purpose flour

4¼ tsps baking powder

½ tsp salt

4 extra-large eggs

2 tbsps milk

2 tbsps strong coffee (see Tip)

⅔ cup (75g) walnuts, chopped

For the frosting

⅓ cup (75g) salted butter, softened

1¾ cups (225g) confectioners' sugar, sifted

2 tsps milk

2 tsps strong coffee

30g (1oz) walnuts, roughly chopped

Preheat the oven to 350°F. Grease a 9 x 13-inch baking pan, then line the bottom with parchment paper.

—

Measure all the sponge ingredients into a large bowl and mix with an electric mixer until well-blended.

—

Turn the mixture into the prepared pan and level the surface. Bake for 35–40 minutes or until the cake has shrunk from the sides of the pan and springs back when pressed in the center with your fingertips. Let cool in the pan, then turn out and peel off the parchment paper.

—

To make the frosting, beat together the butter with the confectioners' sugar, milk, and coffee. Spread evenly over the cold cake using an offset spatula, then decorate with the chopped walnuts.

TIP
To make strong coffee, you can mix 2 teaspoons coffee granules with 2 tablespoons water.

This really is a top favorite. It is always moist and crunchy. The cake needs to be still-warm when the topping is added so that it absorbs the lemon syrup easily, leaving the sugar on top. Do allow the cake to cool a little, though—if it is too hot, the syrup will tend to run straight through.

LEMON DRIZZLE SHEET CAKE
CUTS INTO 16 PIECES

1 cup + 1 tbsp (225g) buttery spread, straight from the fridge
1 cup + 2 tbsps (225g) granulated sugar
2¼ cups (275g) all-purpose flour
4¼ tsps baking powder
½ tsp salt
4 extra-large eggs
4 tbsps milk
finely grated zest of 2 lemons

For the crunchy topping
¾ cup + 2 tbsps (175g) sanding sugar
juice of 2 lemons

Preheat the oven to 350°F. Grease a 9 x 13-inch baking pan then line the bottom with parchment paper.

—

Measure all the sponge ingredients into a large bowl and mix with an electric mixer until well-blended.

—

Turn the mixture into the prepared pan and level the surface. Bake for 35–40 minutes, or until the cake has shrunk from the sides of the pan and springs back when pressed in the center with your fingertips.

—

Let cool in the pan for a few minutes, then turn out, carefully peel off the parchment paper, and let cool a little on a wire rack.

—

To make the crunchy topping, mix the sanding sugar and lemon juice in a small bowl to give a runny consistency. Stand the wire rack with the sheet cake on a sheet pan to catch any drips, and spoon the lemon syrup evenly over the sheet cake while it is still a little warm. Allow to finish cooling on the wire rack.

To make a Lemon Poppy Seed Sheet Cake, add ¼ cup (30g) poppy seeds with the other sheet cake ingredients.

Children will adore this sheet cake. Double chocolate and marshmallows, what could be better?

DOUBLE CHOCOLATE CHIP AND MARSHMALLOW SHEET CAKE

CUTS INTO 16 PIECES

4 tbsps cocoa powder
4 tbsps boiling water
4 extra-large eggs
1 cup + 1 tbsp (225g) buttery
  spread, straight from the
  fridge
1 cup + 2 tbsps (225g)
  granulated sugar
1¾ cups (225g) all-purpose
  flour
1 tbsp baking powder
½ tsp salt
⅔ cup (115g) dark chocolate
  chips

For the frosting
½ cup (40g) cocoa powder,
  sifted
¼ cup (55g) salted butter,
  softened
3–4 tbsps milk
1 cup (125g) confectioners'
  sugar, sifted

To decorate
⅔ cup (30g) mini
  marshmallows
⅔ cup (75g) chocolate malt
  balls, crushed or chopped

Preheat the oven to 350°F. Grease a 9 x 13-inch baking pan, then line the bottom with parchment paper.

—

To make the sponge, measure the cocoa powder and boiling water into a large bowl and mix until smooth. Add all the remaining sponge ingredients, except the chocolate chips, and mix with an electric mixer until light and fluffy. Stir in the chocolate chips.

—

Turn the mixture into the prepared pan and level the surface. Bake in the middle of the oven for about 35 minutes, or until the cake has shrunk from the sides of the pan and springs back when pressed in the center with your fingertips. Let cool in the pan, then turn out and peel off the parchment paper.

—

To make the frosting, measure the cocoa, butter, milk, and confectioners' sugar into a bowl. Beat well to a light, smooth consistency, then spread over the top of the cool cake.

—

Scatter the marshmallows and chocolate malt balls over the top to decorate.

CHAPTER EIGHT

BAKING
FOR
CHILDREN

Lovely little tarts for a kids' party. Children love to have small mouthfuls of food, and this is a great recipe for starting them off on pastry.

MINI JAM TARTS

MAKES 18 DEEP TARTS

1 cup (115g) all-purpose flour
¼ cup (55g) salted butter
1 tbsp confectioners' sugar
1 extra-large egg yolk
1 tbsp water
½ jar raspberry jam
   or lemon curd

Preheat the oven to 400°F. You will need 2 x 12-cup mini muffin pans or 1 x 24-cup mini muffin pan.

—

Measure the flour, butter, and confectioners' sugar into a food processor and whiz until the mixture resembles fine breadcrumbs. Add the egg yolk and water and whiz again until it forms a ball.

—

Roll the pastry out thinly onto a lightly floured work surface. Stamp out 18 rounds using a 2½-inch round cookie cutter. Line the mini muffin pan(s) with the pastry and prick the bottoms with a fork.

—

Spoon 1 heaped small teaspoon of jam or lemon curd into each of the crusts. Bake for about 15 minutes, or until the pastry is pale golden. Let sit for a few minutes, then transfer to a wire rack to cool.

Once these are made, keep them in a cool place during warm weather. When I was small, my mother made them on the waxed paper from inside the cornflakes box!

CHOCOLATE CRISPIES

MAKES 18 SMALL OR 12 LARGE CRISPIES

8 ounces (225g) dark
  chocolate, broken into
  pieces
1 tbsp golden syrup or light
  corn syrup
¼ cup (55g) salted butter
3 cups (75g) cornflakes

Place the chocolate in a large saucepan with the golden syrup or light corn syrup and butter. Melt over a low heat, stirring occasionally. Meanwhile, place 18 paper cupcake liners on a large baking sheet.

—

Add the cornflakes to the saucepan and stir gently until they are evenly coated. Spoon the mixture into the paper liners and chill in the fridge to set.

TIP
If you haven't any paper liners, you can spoon the mixture onto parchment paper in mounds and allow to set.

Young children can easily make these—under supervision, of course.
They're fun for Bonfire Night.

CHOCOLATE AND VANILLA
PINWHEEL COOKIES

For the vanilla
cookie mixture
¼ cup (55g) salted butter,
softened
3 tbsps (30g) sugar
¼ cup (30g) cornstarch
½ cup (55g) all-purpose
flour
½ extra-large beaten egg
a few drops of vanilla extract

For the chocolate
cookie mixture
¼ cup (55g) salted butter,
softened
3 tbsps (30g) sugar
¼ cup (30g) cornstarch
⅓ cup (40g) all-purpose
flour
½ extra-large beaten egg
1 tbsp cocoa powder

Measure all the ingredients for the vanilla cookie mixture into a bowl and mix to form a soft dough. Wrap in plastic wrap and chill in the fridge for about 30 minutes until firm. Meanwhile, make the chocolate cookie mixture in the same way, then wrap and chill.

Roll out both pieces of dough on a lightly floured work surface to oblongs about 7 x 10 inches. Place the vanilla biscuit dough on top of the chocolate dough, then roll up the two together from a narrow edge. Wrap in plastic wrap and chill again for about 30 minutes.

Preheat the oven to 350°F and lightly grease two baking sheets.

Using a sharp knife, cut the roll into about 20 slices and place on the prepared baking sheets.

Bake for about 20 minutes, or until the vanilla portion is golden in color. Lift onto a wire rack and let cool.

This is a popular sheet cake for parties, and children particularly enjoy the fun of making marble cakes.

CHOCOLATE CHIP AND VANILLA MARBLE CAKE

CUTS INTO 21 SMALL PIECES

1 cup + 1 tbsp (225g) buttery spread, straight from the fridge
1 cup + 2 tbsps (225g) sugar
2¼ cups (275g) all-purpose flour
4¼ tsps baking powder
½ tsp salt
4 extra-large eggs
2 tbsps milk
½ tsp vanilla extract
1½ tbsps cocoa powder
2 tbsps boiling water
⅓ cup (55g) dark chocolate chips

For the icing
2 ounces (55g) dark chocolate, broken into pieces
2 ounces (55g) Belgian white chocolate, broken into pieces

Preheat the oven to 350°F. Grease a 9 x 13-inch baking pan and line the bottom with parchment paper.

Measure the buttery spread, sugar, flour, baking powder, salt, eggs, milk, and vanilla extract into a large bowl and beat well for about 2 minutes until well-blended. Spoon half the mixture into the prepared pan, dotting the spoonfuls apart.

In a small bowl, blend the cocoa and boiling water. Cool slightly, then stir into the remaining cake mixture along with the chocolate chips. Spoon this chocolate mixture in between the plain cake mixture in the pan to fill the gaps.

Bake for 35–40 minutes, or until the cake has shrunk from the sides of the pan and springs back when pressed in the center with your fingertips. Let cool in the pan, then turn out and peel off the parchment paper.

To make the icing, melt the plain and white chocolate separately in small heatproof bowls set over pans of simmering water, making sure the bottoms of the bowls are not touching the water, stirring occasionally. Spoon into two separate small plastic bags, snip off a corner of each bag, and drizzle the chocolates all over the top of the cake to decorate.

Let set for about 30 minutes before cutting into pieces.

Excellent for hungry teenagers, these are best eaten as fresh as possible.

DOUGHNUTS

MAKES 16 DOUGHNUTS

4⅓ cups (550g) all-purpose
   flour, plus extra for dusting
1 x ¼-ounce (7g) packet
   fast-acting dried yeast
2 tbsps (30g) salted butter
6 tbsps (75g) sugar
2 extra-large eggs, beaten
6 tbsps tepid milk
6 tbsps tepid water
light vegetable oil, for
   deep-frying

For the filling
raspberry jam

For the coating
½ cup + 1 tbsp (115g) sugar
2 tsps ground cinnamon

Lightly grease and flour three baking sheets.

Measure the flour into a large bowl and stir in the yeast. Rub the butter in with your fingertips until the mixture resembles fine breadcrumbs, then stir in the sugar. Make a well in the center of the dry ingredients and pour in the eggs, milk, and water. Mix to a smooth dough.

Turn out onto a lightly floured work surface and knead for about 5 minutes until the dough is smooth and elastic. Return it to the bowl, cover with oiled plastic wrap, and let rise until doubled in size, about 1–1½ hours in a warm room.

Turn the dough out and knead to knock out the air until the dough is smooth and elastic once more. Divide into 16 equal pieces and shape each into a ball. Flatten each ball, then place a small teaspoon of jam in the center of each piece. Gather the edges together over the jam and pinch firmly to seal. Place well apart on the prepared baking sheets, then cover with oiled plastic wrap or put the baking sheets inside large plastic bags and allow to proof for about 30 minutes, until the balls have doubled in size.

Heat 2 inches of oil in a deep-fat fryer or heavy saucepan until a cube of bread dropped into the fat browns in 30 seconds. Fry the doughnuts a few at a time, turning them once, until they are golden brown all over. This will take about 5 minutes. Lift out with a slotted spoon and drain well on a paper towel.

Measure the sugar and cinnamon into a large plastic bag and shake to mix. Then toss the doughnuts, a few at a time, in the sugar mixture until each is well-coated. Serve freshly made.

Let the children ice the animals themselves with their favorite colors.
Animal cookie cutters are available from good kitchen stores.

ICED ANIMAL COOKIES

MAKES ABOUT 50 COOKIES

½ cup (115g) salted butter,
   softened
1¾ cups (225g) all-purpose
   flour
2½ tsps baking powder
½ tsp salt
a few drops of vanilla extract
½ cup + 1 tbsp (115g)
   granulated sugar
1 extra-large egg, beaten

For the icing
1 cup (115g) confectioners'
   sugar, sifted
about 1 tbsp fresh lemon
   juice
food coloring (red, green,
   blue, yellow)
silver balls, for eyes

Preheat the oven to 375°F. Lightly grease two baking sheets.

Rub the butter into the flour, baking powder, and salt with your fingertips until the mixture resembles fine breadcrumbs. Add the vanilla extract, sugar, and beaten egg and mix to form a fairly stiff dough. Roll out thinly onto a lightly floured work surface and cut into animal shapes using cookie cutters. Place on the prepared baking sheets.

Bake for 10–15 minutes until golden brown. Cool on a wire rack.

To make the icing, measure the confectioners' sugar into a bowl and add enough lemon juice to create a spreading consistency. Divide the icing between 2–3 small bowls (cups would do) and add a drop of different food coloring to each bowl, mixing well.

Spoon a little icing onto each of the cookies and spread out with the back of a small spoon. Finish by adding silver balls for eyes.

It is usual to shape this mixture into "S" shapes, but you can shape it into any letter or number of your choice.

JUMBLES

MAKES ABOUT 32 JUMBLES

⅔ cup (150g) salted butter, softened
¾ cup (150g) sugar
a few drops of vanilla extract
finely grated zest of 1 lemon
1 extra-large egg
2¾ cups (350g) all-purpose flour
clear honey, to glaze
demerara sugar, for dusting

Line three baking sheets with parchment paper.

Measure all the ingredients, except the honey and demerara sugar, into a bowl and work together by hand until a dough is formed. This can also be done in a food processor or with an electric mixer.

Divide the dough into 32 pieces. Roll each piece of dough into a strip about 4 inches long, then twist into an "S" shape. Place them on the prepared baking sheets and chill for about 30 minutes.

Preheat the oven to 375°F.

Bake the jumbles for 10–15 minutes until they are a pale golden color, then remove from the oven. Increase the oven temperature to 425°F and, while the jumbles are still warm, brush them well with the honey and sprinkle with the demerara sugar. Return to the oven for 2–3 minutes. Cool slightly, then lift onto a wire rack and leave to cool completely.

Children love to cut out and decorate these cookies. The dough is easy to handle and can be re-rolled successfully.

GINGERBREAD MEN

2¾ cups (350g) all-purpose
　flour
1 tsp baking soda
2 tsps ground ginger
½ cup (115g) salted butter
¾ cup + 3 tbsps (175g) light
　muscovado sugar
4 tbsps golden syrup or
　light corn syrup
1 extra-large egg, beaten
currants, to decorate

Preheat the oven to 375°F. Lightly grease three baking sheets.

Measure the flour, baking soda, and ginger into a bowl. Rub the butter in with your fingertips until the mixture resembles fine breadcrumbs, then stir in the sugar. Add the golden syrup or light corn syrup and beaten egg and mix to form a smooth dough, kneading lightly toward the end.

Divide the dough in half and lightly flour a work surface. Roll out one half to a thickness of about ¼ inch. Cut out gingerbread men using a cookie cutter and place them on the prepared baking sheets. (I used a 5½-inch cookie cutter to get 20 gingerbread men.) Place the currants for eyes and buttons. Repeat with the remaining dough. Re-roll as necessary.

Bake for 10–12 minutes until they become a slightly darker shade. Cool slightly, then lift onto a wire rack and let cool completely.

You can use small ramekins or egg cups for these easy-to-make little cakes, or you can buy pyramid molds for a more pointed shape.

COCONUT PYRAMIDS

MAKES 12 PYRAMIDS

3¼ cups (225g) shredded coconut
½ cup + 1 tbsp (115g) sugar
2 extra-large eggs, beaten
a little pink food coloring (optional)

Preheat the oven to 350°F. Line two baking sheets with parchment paper.

Measure the coconut and sugar into a bowl and mix together. Beat in enough egg to bind the mixture together and add a few drops of pink coloring, if you like.

Dip each mold, ramekin, or egg cup into cold water and drain well.

Fill the molds with the coconut mixture and press down lightly. Turn the molded coconut out onto a prepared baking sheet and continue with the remaining mixture.

Bake for about 20 minutes, or until the pyramids are tinged pale golden brown. Lift off the baking sheets and let cool on a wire rack.

These are not oversweet, so they are a slightly healthier option than other squares. Great to add to a lunch box. Try to use rolled oats for this recipe, as they give a crunchier texture than instant oats.

OAT AND SUNFLOWER SQUARES

MAKES 16 SQUARES

¼ cup (75g) salted butter
3 tbsps (75g) golden syrup
    or light corn syrup
1⅔ cups (150g) rolled oats
⅓ cup (55g) sunflower seeds

Preheat the oven to 350°F. Lightly grease a 7-inch square cake pan.

—

Heat the butter and syrup together gently until evenly blended.

—

Add the oats and sunflower seeds to the pan with the syrup mixture and stir thoroughly to mix. Spoon into the prepared pan and press the mixture down well with the back of a spoon.

—

Bake for 20–25 minutes, or until set in the middle and golden brown around the edges. Cut into 16 squares, then let cool in the pan before carefully lifting out.

This is the perfect birthday cake for any child—a chocolate castle, which you can make for a prince or a princess depending on how you decorate it.

CASTLE BIRTHDAY CAKE

SERVES 20

For the chocolate cake
¾ cup + 2 tbsps (80g) cocoa
    powder
1 cup (240ml) boiling water
3½ cups (700g) granulated
    sugar
3⅓ cups (700g) buttery
    spread, from the fridge
4 tbsps baking powder
6 cups (750g) all-purpose
    flour
1½ tsps salt
12 extra-large eggs
4 tbsps milk

For the chocolate frosting
1 cup + 2 tbsps (250g)
    salted butter, softened
2 tbsps milk
2¾ cups (350g)
    confectioners' sugar
5 tbsps cocoa powder
4 tbsps boiling water

To decorate
2 wafer cookies
1 tube edible glue
1 small packet jelly beans
8 x 4-finger KitKats or
    chocolate fingers
4 x 1.69 ounce (47.9g)
    packets M&M's
5 waffle ice cream cones

Preheat the oven to 350°F. Grease and line the bottoms of two 8-inch square cake pans with parchment paper.

Measure half of the cocoa and boiling water into a large bowl. Mix until smooth. Add half the remaining cake ingredients to the bowl and whisk with an electric mixer for 2 minutes until light and fluffy.

Divide between two pans and level the surfaces. Bake for 35–40 minutes, or until well-risen and springing back when pressed in the center with your fingertips. Remove from the pans and let cool on a wire rack.

Wash, grease, and reline the pans with parchment paper. Repeat the cake method with the remaining ingredients and divide between the pans. Bake for 35–40 minutes, as before, and let cool on a wire rack.

To make the chocolate frosting, beat the butter, milk, and half of the confectioners' sugar together until smooth, using an electric mixer. Add the remaining confectioners' sugar and beat again. Mix the cocoa and boiling water together in a small bowl to make a smooth paste. Add to the frosting and beat until well-incorporated.

Recipe continued on the next page

To assemble the cake, remove the parchment paper from all four cakes. Place one cake on a cake board, spread with frosting, and sandwich together with another cake. This will be the castle's base. Make a 4½-inch square template out of paper and place on top of the remaining two whole cakes on one corner. Slice around the template to make two 4½-inch squares. Sandwich them together with frosting and place in the center on top of the castle's base.

———

Using a 2-inch round cookie cutter, stamp 10 rounds out of the leftover cakes. Sandwich them together with frosting to make 5 rounds (these will be the turrets).

———

Place 4 of the cake turrets on top of the base cake and one on top of the center tier. Cover the whole cake with chocolate frosting.

———

Stick the wafer cookies onto the front of the cake to make the door. Glue halved jelly beans on for the doorknobs. Trim the KitKats or chocolate fingers to size and arrange in neat rows around the base and second tier of the cake to make walls. Cover the tops of the turrets with M&M's. Glue halved jelly beans onto one of the ice cream cones and place in the middle on the very top. Sit the remaining cones on the four turrets.

———

Add a flag, soldiers, princesses, and glitter, as desired!

Children love to help by putting their favorite sweets on top of these tiny cakes.

LITTLE GEMS

MAKES 40 GEMS

⅓ cup (75g) salted butter, softened
2 extra-large eggs
1 cup (115g) all-purpose flour
2½ tsps baking powder
¼ tsp salt
6 tbsps (75g) granulated sugar
1 tbsp milk

For the decoration
1 cup (115g) confectioners' sugar, sifted
about 1 tbsp fresh lemon juice
small sweets, to decorate

Preheat the oven to 350°F. Arrange about 40 petit four liners on baking sheets.

Measure all the cake ingredients into a bowl and beat well until thoroughly blended.

Spoon scant spoonfuls of the mixture into the liners, being careful not to overfill. Bake for 15–20 minutes, or until well-risen and pale golden brown. Cool on a wire rack.

To make the icing, measure the confectioners' sugar into a bowl and add enough lemon juice to create a spreading consistency. Spoon a little on top of each cooled gem and spread out with the back of a small spoon. When the icing has almost set, top with a sweet.

You can use this basic shape to make other animals, such as a cat, a teddy bear, a koala, or an owl. Chocolate sprinkles can be used in place of the coconut, if preferred.

BUNNY RABBIT BIRTHDAY CAKE

SERVES 20

For the cake
1¼ cups (275g) salted butter,
    softened
1 cup + 6 tbsps (275g)
    granulated sugar
5 extra-large eggs
2¼ cups (275g) all-purpose
    flour
4¼ tsps baking powder
½ tsp salt

For the buttercream
1 cup (225g) salted butter,
    softened
3⅔ cups (450g)
    confectioners' sugar,
    sifted
juice of ½ lemon

For the decoration
about 5 cups (about 250g)
    shredded coconut
sweets for the eyes,
    nose, and whiskers

Preheat the oven to 350°F. Grease two 7-inch and one 8-inch round cake pans and line the bottoms with parchment paper.

Measure all the cake ingredients into a large bowl and beat well for about 2 minutes until blended and smooth.

Divide the mixture between the pans and level the surfaces. Bake for 25–30 minutes (7-inch cake) and 30–35 minutes (8-inch cake), until well-risen. Let cool in the pans for a few minutes, then turn out, peel off the parchment paper, and finish cooling on a wire rack.

Meanwhile, make the buttercream by mixing the butter, confectioners' sugar, and lemon juice in a bowl until thoroughly blended.

Toast two-thirds of the coconut until golden brown.

To make the rabbit shape, cut the 7-inch cake to form the ears, paw, and tail. For the ears, cut 2 oval pieces from each side of the cake and then 1 smaller oval to form the hind paw and a circle for the tail. The 8-inch cake becomes the body and the 7-inch cake becomes the head. Assemble the rabbit on a large cake board or a foil-covered baking sheet, positioning the ears, paw, and tail.

Cover the cakes with the buttercream, then sprinkle on the toasted coconut, leaving the tail, inner ear, and tummy clear to be covered by the untoasted coconut. Finish by adding the sweets to make the eyes, nose, and whiskers. (I use thinly sliced licorice sweets to create the whiskers.)

A fun cake for a special occasion. From the outside, it looks like any other cake, but once you cut into it, it reveals itself to be as colorful as a rainbow.

RAINBOW CAKE

SERVES 20

6 eggs
1¾ cups + 2 tbsps (375g) granulated sugar
1¾ cups (375g) buttery spread, straight from the fridge
3 cups (375g) all-purpose flour
2½ tbsps baking powder
¾ tsp salt
3 tsps vanilla extract
3 tbsps milk
food coloring paste or gel (in 6 different colors)

For the cream cheese frosting
1 cup + 2 tbsps (375g) salted butter, softened
3 tbsps milk
4 cups (750g) confectioners' sugar, sifted
1½ tsps vanilla extract
¾ cup + 1 tbsp (275g) full-fat cream cheese
nonpareils or sprinkles, to decorate

Preheat the oven to 350°F. Grease and line the bottoms of two 8-inch round cake pans with parchment paper.

Measure one-third of the cake ingredients into a large bowl and whisk using an electric mixer for 2 minutes. Divide the mixture into 2 bowls and add some food coloring to each bowl (two different colors) and mix well.

Spoon into the pans and bake for 15 minutes, or until well-risen and springing back when pressed in the center with your fingertips. Remove from the pans and let cool on a wire rack.

Wash, grease, and reline the pans. Repeat the method to make four more cakes, all in different colors.

To make the cream cheese frosting, beat the butter and milk with half of the confectioners' sugar in a large bowl, using an electric mixer, until smooth. Add the remaining confectioners' sugar, the vanilla extract, and the cream cheese and beat until light and fluffy.

To assemble the cake, remove the parchment paper from all six cakes. Place the violet cake onto a cake board and spread with a little frosting. Continue to layer the cakes with frosting until you have all six cakes stacked neatly with the red cake on top. Cover the whole surface of the cake with a thin layer of frosting, then place in the fridge for 20 minutes. This will help to seal the crumbs.

Once the frosting is firm, cover with a final layer and spread to make a smooth finish. Sprinkle the top with nonpareils or sprinkles.

CHAPTER NINE

CRACKERS
AND
COOKIES

Buy a pretty tin and fill it with a variety of homemade cookies. Vary the recipe by using granulated sugar in place of the light muscovado sugar, if you would like.

SPECIAL SHORTBREAD COOKIES

MAKES ABOUT 20 COOKIES

1⅓ cups (175g) all-purpose flour

6 tbsps (75g) light muscovado sugar

½ cup + 1 tbsp (125g) salted butter

a little demerara sugar, for sprinkling

Preheat the oven to 325°F. Lightly grease two baking sheets.

—

Measure the flour and sugar into a large bowl or food processor. Add the butter and rub together with your fingertips or whiz in the processor until the mixture is just beginning to bind together. Knead gently to bring together to form a dough.

—

Roll out the dough on a lightly floured work surface to a thickness of about ¼ inch. Cut into circles using a 2-inch fluted cookie cutter and transfer the cookies to the prepared baking sheets. Prick the cookies all over with a fork and sprinkle with demerara sugar.

—

Bake for 20–25 minutes, or until pale golden. Let cool on the baking sheets for a few minutes, then lift onto a wire rack to cool completely.

To make Cherry Shortbread, follow the recipe above and then press 3 tbsps (30g) of chopped maraschino cherries into the top of each cookie before baking. Do not sprinkle with demerara sugar, as the cherries sweeten the cookies.

To make Walnut Shortbread, follow the recipe above, adding ½ cup (55g) roughly chopped walnuts after rubbing in the butter, before kneading the mixture into a dough. Dust generously with sifted confectioners' sugar once cooled.

For really good shortbread, it is essential to use butter. I like to use semolina as well as flour to give it crunch, but you can use cornstarch or rice flour instead.

THE VERY BEST SHORTBREAD

MAKES 30 FINGERS

1¾ cups (225g) all-purpose flour
⅔ cup (115g) semolina
1 cup (225g) salted butter
½ cup + 1 tbsp (115g) granulated sugar
2 tbsps demerara sugar, for dusting

Lightly grease a 9 x 13-inch baking pan.

—

Mix together the flour and semolina in a bowl or food processor. Add the butter and granulated sugar and rub together with your fingertips or whiz in the processor until the mixture is just beginning to bind together. Knead lightly until the mixture forms a smooth dough.

—

Press the dough into the prepared pan and level it with a spatula or an offset spatula, making sure the mixture is evenly spread. Prick all over with a fork and chill until firm.

—

Preheat the oven to 325°F.

—

Bake for about 50 minutes, or until a very pale golden brown. Sprinkle with the demerara sugar and let cool in the baking pan for a few minutes, then cut into 30 fingers. Carefully lift the fingers out of the pan with an offset spatula and finish cooling on a wire rack. Store in an airtight container.

To make Orange Shortbread, add the finely grated zest of one large orange to the mixture.

TIP
Maraschino cherries, dried apricots, and golden raisins make delicious additions to shortbread, but the cookies then need to be eaten on the day of making, as they soon become soggy with the moisture from the fruit.

These old-fashioned cookies are very crumbly in texture. They are best eaten within a couple days of making.

MELTING MOMENTS

MAKES ABOUT 40 COOKIES

1 cup (225g) salted butter, softened
¾ cup + 2 tbsps (75g) sugar
2 extra-large egg yolks
a few drops of vanilla extract
2¼ cups (275g) all-purpose flour
3¼ tsps baking powder
½ tsp salt
½ cup (55g) old-fashioned rolled oats
20 maraschino cherries, halved (optional)

Preheat the oven to 350°F and line two baking sheets with parchment paper.

——

Measure the butter, sugar, egg yolks, vanilla extract, flour, baking powder, and salt into a mixing bowl and beat together to form a soft dough.

——

Divide the mixture into about 40 pieces. Form each one into a ball and roll in the oats to cover. Place on the prepared baking sheets, leaving space between them. Flatten each ball slightly and top each one with a halved maraschino cherry, if using.

——

Bake for about 20 minutes or until golden. Leave cool on the baking sheets for a few minutes, then lift onto a wire rack to finish cooling.

These are neither fork cookies nor shortbread, but a combination of the two! You could use any flavored chocolate and omit the orange zest, if you would like. Be creative!

ORANGE AND CHOCOLATE FORK SHORTBREAD COOKIES

MAKES 25 COOKIES

¾ cup (175g) salted butter, softened
6 tbsps (75g) sugar
1⅓ cups (175g) all-purpose flour
⅔ cup (75g) cornstarch
finely grated zest of 1 small orange
4 ounces (115g) orange chocolate, chopped into pieces

Preheat the oven to 350°F. Line two baking sheets with parchment paper.

—

Measure the butter and sugar into a food processor and whiz until soft. Add the flour, cornstarch, and orange zest and whiz again until the mixture comes together. Stir in the chocolate pieces.

—

Knead lightly until the mixture forms a smooth dough. Divide into 25 balls and place well apart on the prepared baking sheets. Dip a fork in a little water and use this to flatten the cookies.

—

Bake for 25 minutes until pale golden. Let cool on the baking sheets for a few minutes, then lift onto a wire rack to cool completely.

Don't expect these cookies to be as crisp as shortbread—they should be slightly chewy. They will keep in an airtight container for a week.

CHOCOLATE CHIP COOKIES

MAKES 20 COOKIES

½ cup (115g) salted butter, softened
6 tbsps (75g) granulated sugar
¼ cup (55g) light muscovado sugar
½ tsp vanilla extract
1 extra-large egg, beaten
1¼ cups (150g) all-purpose flour
1¾ tsps baking powder
½ tsp salt
⅔ cup (115g) plain chocolate chips

Preheat the oven to 375°F and line two large baking sheets with parchment paper.

—

Measure the butter and sugars into a large bowl and beat thoroughly until evenly blended.

—

Add the vanilla extract to the beaten egg, then add this a little at a time to the butter and sugar mixture in the bowl, beating well between each addition.

—

Mix in the flour, baking powder, and salt, and lastly stir in the chocolate chips. Spoon tablespoons of the mixture onto the prepared baking sheets, leaving room for the cookies to spread.

—

Bake on the top shelf of the oven for 10–12 minutes, or until the cookies are golden. Watch them like a hawk, as they will turn dark brown very quickly. Let the cookies rest on the baking sheets for a few minutes, then lift off with an offset spatula and place on a wire rack to cool completely. Store in an airtight container.

To make Chocolate and Orange Cookies, follow the recipe above, but chop a bar of plain orange chocolate into small pieces and use instead of the chocolate chips.

Dead easy to make, these are wonderful cookies. Expect an irregular shape. They are very soft when they come out of the oven but will harden up considerably on cooling.

DOUBLE CHOCOLATE COOKIES

MAKES ABOUT 36 COOKIES

6¼ ounces (180g) dark chocolate, broken into pieces

¼ cup (55g) salted butter

1 × 14-ounce (397g) can full-fat condensed milk

1¾ cups (225g) all-purpose flour

2½ tsps baking powder

½ tsp salt

⅔ cup (115g) white chocolate chips

Melt the chocolate with the butter in a heatproof bowl set over a saucepan of simmering water, stirring occasionally.

—

Remove from the heat, stir in the condensed milk, and cool.

—

Mix in the flour, baking powder, salt, and chocolate chips and chill the mixture in the fridge for about 30 minutes, until firm enough to handle.

—

Preheat the oven to 350°F and line two baking sheets with parchment paper.

—

Roll the mixture into 36 balls and place well apart on the prepared baking sheets. Press down to flatten.

—

Bake for about 15 minutes. The cookies should still look soft and will glisten. Don't overcook them as they soon become very hard. Leave to cool on the baking sheets for a few minutes, then remove the cookies carefully with an offset spatula and place on a wire rack to cool completely.

Both the flowers and the leaves of lavender can be used, although it is best to use only young leaves. If you are using fresh lavender, make sure it is unsprayed. Dried lavender is stronger in flavor, so use half the quantity.

LAVENDER COOKIES

MAKES ABOUT 36 COOKIES

¾ cup (175g) salted butter, softened

2 tbsps fresh, finely chopped lavender flowers and leaves (pick the flowerlets and the leaves off the stems to measure), or 1 tbsp dried lavender

½ cup + 1 tbsp (115g) sugar

1¾ cups (225g) all-purpose flour

2 tbsps (30g) demerara sugar

Place the softened butter and lavender in a mixing bowl and beat together (this will bring out the maximum flavor from the lavender).

—

Beat the sugar into the butter and lavender, then stir in the flour, bringing the mixture together with your hands and kneading lightly until smooth.

—

Divide the mixture in half and roll out to form 2 sausage shapes 6 inches long. Roll the cookie "sausages" in the demerara sugar until evenly coated. Wrap in parchment paper or foil and chill until firm.

—

Preheat the oven to 350°F and line two large baking sheets with parchment paper.

—

Cut each "sausage" into about 18 slices and place on the prepared baking sheets, allowing a little room for them to spread.

—

Bake for 15–20 minutes, until the cookies are pale golden brown at the edges. Leave to cool on the baking sheets for a few minutes, then lift them off with a fish spatula or an offset spatula and let sit on a wire rack to cool completely.

These cookies first made their appearance in an old red Cordon Bleu cookbook, and I've been making them for years.

FORK COOKIES

MAKES ABOUT 16 COOKIES

½ cup (115g) salted butter, softened
¼ cup (55g) sugar
finely grated zest of 1 lemon
1¼ cups (150g) all-purpose flour
1¾ tsps baking powder
½ tsp salt

Preheat the oven to 375°F and line two baking sheets with parchment paper.

———

Measure the butter into a bowl and beat to soften further. Gradually beat in the sugar and lemon zest, then the flour, baking powder, and salt. Bring the mixture together with your hands to form a dough.

———

Form the dough into 16 balls about the size of a walnut and place well apart on the prepared baking sheets. Dip a fork in a little water and use this to flatten the cookies.

———

Bake for 15 minutes until a very pale golden. Let cool on the baking sheets for a few minutes, then lift onto a wire rack to cool completely.

To make Chocolate Fork Cookies, follow the recipe above, but omit the lemon zest and use only 1 cup (120g) all-purpose flour, ½ tsp baking powder, and ¼ tsp salt along with 3 tbsps (15g) cocoa powder. Bake until browned.

These cookies have a delicate lemony flavor.

SHREWSBURY COOKIES

MAKES ABOUT 24 COOKIES

½ cup (115g) salted butter, softened

6 tbsps (75g) sugar, plus extra for sprinkling

1 extra-large egg, separated

1⅔ cups (200g) all-purpose flour

finely grated zest of 1 lemon

⅓ cup (55g) currants

1–2 tbsps milk

Preheat the oven to 400°F and line two large baking sheets with parchment paper.

—

Measure the butter and sugar into a bowl and cream together until light and fluffy. Beat in the egg yolk.

—

Sift in the flour and add the grated lemon zest. Mix well. Add the currants and enough milk to form a fairly soft dough.

—

Knead the mixture gently on a lightly floured surface and roll out to a thickness of ¼ inch. Cut into about 24 rounds, using a 2½-inch fluted cookie cutter. Place on the prepared baking sheets.

—

Bake for 10 minutes.

—

Meanwhile, lightly beat the egg whites. Remove the cookies from the oven, brush with the beaten egg white, sprinkle with a little sugar, and return the cookies to the oven for an additional 4–5 minutes, or until pale golden brown. Leave to cool on the baking sheets for a few minutes, then lift onto a wire rack to cool completely.

Take care not to bake these cookies too long, as they become hard and crisp.

CORNISH FAIRINGS

MAKES ABOUT 24 COOKIES

1 cup (115g) all-purpose flour
¼ tsp ground ginger
¼ tsp pumpkin pie spice
¼ tsp ground cinnamon
½ tsp baking soda
¼ cup (55g) salted butter, softened
¼ cup (55g) sugar
¼ cup (75g) golden syrup or light corn syrup

Preheat the oven to 350°F and line a large baking sheet with parchment paper.

—

Measure the flour, spices, and baking soda into a bowl. Rub the butter into the flour with your fingertips until the mixture resembles fine breadcrumbs, then mix in the sugar.

—

Gently heat the golden syrup or light corn syrup, then stir into the mixture to make a soft dough.

—

Roll the dough into 24 balls roughly the size of a cherry and place on the prepared baking sheet, allowing room for them to spread.

—

Bake for about 10 minutes, then take the baking sheet out of the oven and carefully hit it on a solid surface to make the cookies crack and spread. Bake for an additional 5 minutes, until they are a good even brown. Let cool on the baking sheet for a few minutes, then lift onto a wire rack to cool completely.

TIP
Banging the baking sheet partway through cooking makes the mixture crack and flatten.

These oat squares are crunchy and traditional. Take care not to overbake them, as they can become hard and dark.

FAST OAT SQUARES

MAKES 24 OAT SQUARES

1 cup (225g) salted butter
1 cup (225g) demerara sugar
¼ cup (75g) golden syrup or light corn syrup
2¾ cups (275g) old-fashioned rolled oats

Preheat the oven to 325°F. Line a 9 x 13-inch baking pan with parchment paper.

—

Measure the butter, demerara sugar, and golden syrup or light corn syrup into a saucepan. Slowly melt over a low heat until the sugar has dissolved. Remove from the heat and stir in the oats. Mix well, then turn into the prepared pan and press flat, using the back of a spoon.

—

Bake for 30–35 minutes until evenly pale golden brown. Make sure you don't overcook them or they will become hard. If you don't cook them for long enough, the middle will be soft. Remove from the oven and let cool in the pan for 10 minutes. Cut into 24 squares, using a small sharp knife, and allow to finish cooling in the pan.

—

Once completely cool, transfer the squares onto a paper towel to absorb any excess oil. Store in an airtight container with parchment paper in between the oat squares so they don't stick together.

To make Chocolate Chip Oat Squares, allow the mixture to cool after stirring in the oats. Stir in ⅔ cup (115g) dark chocolate chips, then turn into the prepared pan and cook as above.

To make Muesli Oat Squares, replace 1¾ cups (175g) of the rolled oats with your favorite muesli, then turn into the prepared pan and cook as above. If you like a lot of raisins, add an extra ¼–⅓ cup (30–55g) to the oat squares mixture.

A variation of an oat square jammed full of dried fruits and seeds. You could use chia and sunflower seeds instead of pumpkin and sesame, and swap the cranberries and golden raisins for apricots and raisins. A flexible recipe that is great for a picnic or a packed lunch.

FRUITY GRANOLA BARS

MAKES 12 BARS

1⅔ cups (150g) old-fashioned rolled oats
¼ cup (30g) pumpkin seeds
¼ cup (30g) sesame seeds
½ cup (115g) salted butter
2 tbsps honey
½ cup + 2 tbsps (115g) light muscovado sugar
½ cup (55g) cranberries, chopped
⅓ cup (55g) golden raisins
a pinch of sea salt (optional)

Preheat the oven to 350°F. Grease an 8-inch square cake pan and line the bottom and sides with a piece of parchment paper.

—

Place the oats and seeds on a baking sheet and toast in the oven for 10–15 minutes until the oats are lightly golden. Let cool.

—

Melt the butter, honey, and sugar together in a large saucepan. Add the toasted oats, seeds, and dried fruits and mix well. Add a pinch of sea salt, if using. Spoon into the prepared pan and smooth the surface with the back of a spoon.

—

Bake for 25 minutes until pale golden and the mixture is firm to the touch in the center. Let cool in the pan for 15 minutes, then turn out carefully and slice into 12 bars. Let cool completely on a wire rack.

The flavor and consistency will depend on the muesli used. These are good for a lunch box, for a snack at school or work, or to take on a picnic.

MUESLI COOKIES

MAKES ABOUT 24 COOKIES

¾ cup (175g) salted butter, softened
½ cup + 1 tbsp (115g) granulated sugar
1 extra-large egg
1⅓ cups (175g) all-purpose flour
2 tsps baking powder
½ tsp salt
1¾ cups (200g) muesli
demerara sugar, for sprinkling

Preheat the oven to 350°F and line two large baking sheets with parchment paper.

—

Measure all the ingredients, except the muesli and demerara sugar, into a large bowl and beat together until well-blended and smooth. Stir in 1½ cups (175g) of the muesli.

—

Spoon 24 small spoonfuls of the mixture onto the prepared baking sheets, leaving room for the cookies to spread. Sprinkle the top of each one with a little extra muesli and demerara sugar.

—

Bake for 15–20 minutes, or until golden brown at the edges. Leave to cool on the baking sheets for a few minutes, then lift onto a wire rack to cool completely.

Cheesy crackers always go well with drinks. If you make these ahead of time, they are best heated again in the oven before serving.

RICH CHEESY CRACKERS

MAKES ABOUT 60 CRACKERS

1⅓ cups (175g) all-purpose flour
½ tsp fine sea salt
1 tsp mustard powder
⅓ cup (75g) salted butter
1½ cups (175g) sharp Cheddar, grated
2 extra-large eggs
sesame or poppy seeds, for sprinkling

Sift the flour, salt, and mustard powder into a bowl and rub the butter in with your fingertips until the mixture resembles fine breadcrumbs. Stir in the grated cheese.

—

Beat the eggs, then stir just enough egg into the flour mixture to form a soft dough (there will be some egg left over for glazing). Wrap the dough in plastic wrap and chill for about 15 minutes.

—

Preheat the oven to 400°F and line two baking sheets with parchment paper.

—

Roll the dough out on a lightly floured work surface to a thickness of about ¼ inch and cut into 2-inch rounds or triangles. Place on the prepared baking sheets and brush with the remaining beaten egg. Sprinkle lightly with sesame or poppy seeds. Re-roll the trimmings once only.

—

Bake for 15–18 minutes, or until crisp and golden. Let cool on the baking sheets for a few minutes, then lift onto a wire rack to cool completely.

Savory crackers are great with drinks, and these cheesy, nutty ones are delicious. Children like to roll these little balls, and they could give them as a present to a relative.

DORCHESTER CRACKERS

MAKES ABOUT 20 CRACKERS

1 cup (115g) sharp
　　Cheddar, grated
1 cup (115g) all-purpose flour
a little salt
½ cup (115g) salted butter,
　　softened
½ tsp mustard powder
20 pistachios, shelled

Preheat the oven to 375°F and line two large baking sheets with parchment paper.

—

Measure all the ingredients, except the nuts, into a large bowl and work together to form a dough.

—

Roll into 20 balls about the size of a walnut and place well apart on the prepared baking sheets. Top each cracker with a pistachio, then just slightly flatten each one with your hand.

—

Bake for 15 minutes, or until golden brown. Leave to cool on the baking sheets for a few minutes, then lift onto a wire rack to cool completely.

—

Serve warm or cold.

TIP
Try whole or halved cashew nuts, instead of pistachios.

With flecks of rosemary and a slight chewiness from the sun-dried tomatoes, these are delicious savory crackers that capture the best Mediterranean flavors and look as lovely as they taste.

SUN-DRIED TOMATO AND ROSEMARY CRACKERS

MAKES 48 CRACKERS

1 cup (115g) Parmesan, grated
½ cup (55g) sun-dried tomatoes, chopped
2 tbsps chopped fresh rosemary, plus extra for rolling
1 cup (125g) all-purpose flour
½ cup (115g) salted butter, cubed

Measure the Parmesan, tomatoes, and rosemary into a food processor. Whiz until finely chopped. Add the flour and butter and whiz again until the mixture comes together and forms a dough.

———

Divide the dough in half and roll each half into a tube measuring about 6 inches long and 1¼ inch diameter. Roll the tube in the extra rosemary, then wrap in plastic wrap and chill in the fridge for 30 minutes.

———

Preheat the oven to 400°F. Line two large baking sheets with parchment paper.

———

Slice each tube into 24 thin rounds and arrange on the baking sheets. Bake for 10–15 minutes until lightly golden. Let cool on the baking sheets for a few minutes, then lift onto a wire rack to cool completely.

These make a lovely gift when beautifully presented in a box. They can be made in advance, but do not keep them in the cupboard, as they can quickly go stale. Freeze them once cooled.

PUFF PASTRY CHEESE STRAWS

MAKES 32 STRAWS

11.3 ounces (320g) of
    pre-rolled puff pastry
all-purpose flour, for dusting
3 tbsps black olive tapenade
1 extra-large egg, beaten
½ cup (55g) Parmesan,
    grated
½ cup (55g) sharp
    Cheddar, grated
2 tbsps poppy seeds

Preheat the oven to 425°F and line two large baking sheets with parchment paper.

—

Unroll the pastry sheet on a floured work surface with the long side nearest to you. Spread the tapenade over the bottom half of the pastry. Brush the top half with the beaten egg. Sprinkle both cheeses on top of the tapenade in an even layer. Fold the top half of the pastry over the cheese-covered section. Using a rolling pin, carefully re-roll the pastry back to its original rectangle size (about 15 x 9 inches).

—

Slice the pastry in half horizontally, then slice each half into 16 strips, ¾ inch wide. Twist the strips and place on the prepared baking sheets, leaving space between them. Brush with the remaining beaten egg and sprinkle with the poppy seeds.

—

Bake for 15–18 minutes, then turn the straws over and continue to bake for an additional 5 minutes, until golden brown and crisp. Let cool on the baking sheets for a few minutes, then lift onto a wire rack to cool completely.

CHAPTER TEN

FANCY COOKIES

These cookies must be made with butter. The mixture holds its shape beautifully for piping, so use it for all shapes of piped cookies.

VIENNESE FINGERS

MAKES ABOUT 20 COOKIES

½ cup (150g) salted butter, softened
¼ cup (30g) confectioners' sugar
1 cup (150g) all-purpose flour
2½ ounces (75g) dark chocolate, broken into pieces

Preheat the oven to 375°F. Lightly grease two baking sheets. Fit a piping bag with a medium star nozzle.

Measure the butter and confectioners' sugar into a bowl and beat well until pale and fluffy. Sift the flour into the bowl and beat well until thoroughly mixed.

Spoon mixture into the piping bag and pipe out finger shapes about 3 inches long, spacing them well apart.

Bake for 10–15 minutes, or until a pale golden brown. Leave to cool on the baking sheets for a few minutes, then lift onto a wire rack to cool completely.

Melt the chocolate gently in a heatproof bowl set over a saucepan of hot water, making sure the bottom of the bowl doesn't touch the water, stirring occasionally. Dip both ends of the cookies into the chocolate and let set on the wire rack.

Using parchment paper makes it so much simpler to get these cookies off the baking sheets. You can simply use a well-greased baking sheet, but be careful not to leave them for too long or they will harden before you have a chance to lift them off.

FLORENTINES

MAKES ABOUT 20 FLORENTINES

¼ cup (55g) salted butter

¼ cup (55g) demerara sugar

3 tbsps (55g) golden syrup or light corn syrup

½ cup (55g) all-purpose flour

4 maraschino cherries, finely chopped

⅔ cup (55g) candied orange or lemon peel, finely chopped

½ cup (55g) mixed almonds and walnuts, finely chopped

6 ounces (175g) dark chocolate, broken into pieces

Preheat the oven to 350°F. Line three baking sheets with parchment paper.

Measure the butter, sugar, and syrup into a small saucepan and heat gently until the butter has melted. Remove from the heat and add the flour, chopped cherries, candied orange or lemon peel, and nuts to the saucepan and stir well to mix.

Spoon small spoonfuls of the mixture onto the prepared baking sheets, leaving plenty of room for them to spread. Bake for 8–10 minutes, or until golden brown. Allow the Florentines to cool before lifting onto a wire rack with an offset spatula. (If they have been baked on greased baking sheets, allow them to harden for a few moments only before lifting onto wire racks to cool completely.) If the Florentines become too hard to remove, pop them back into the oven for a few moments to allow them to soften.

Melt the chocolate in a heatproof bowl set over a saucepan of hot water, making sure the bottom of the bowl doesn't touch the water, stirring occasionally. Spread a little melted chocolate over the flat base of each Florentine, mark a zigzag in the chocolate with a fork, and let set, chocolate side up, on the wire rack. Store in an airtight container.

TIP

These are luxurious cookies, but you do need patience and an accurate scale to make them.

These make a very special present! Look out for a pretty or unusual plate in an antique shop or garage sale, and arrange the petits fours on this. Cover with clear cellophane and decorate with a ribbon. The milk and sugar glaze is optional for these petits fours, but it does create a nice shine.

PETITS FOURS AUX AMANDES

MAKES 24 PETITS FOURS

2 extra-large egg whites
1 cup + 3 tbsps (115g)
    almond flour
6 tbsps (75g) sugar
a little almond extract

To decorate
maraschino cherries,
    chopped

To finish (optional)
1 tbsp sugar
2 tbsps milk

Preheat the oven to 350°F. Line two baking sheets with parchment paper. Fit a piping bag with a large star nozzle.

Whisk the egg whites until stiff. Fold in the almond flour, sugar, and almond extract. Spoon the mixture into the prepared piping bag and pipe the mixture into small rosettes. Decorate each rosette with a small piece of maraschino cherry.

Bake for about 15 minutes, or until golden. Leave to cool on the baking sheets for a few minutes, then lift onto a wire rack to cool completely.

To finish, mix the sugar and milk together and lightly brush over the petits fours.

These are irresistible, but keep them in a cool place or they'll become very soft.

CHOCOLATE GANACHE PETITS FOURS

MAKES 24 PETITS FOURS

For the chocolate liners
6 ounces (175g) dark
chocolate, broken into
pieces
1 tsp sunflower oil

For the chocolate ganache
⅔ cup (150ml) heavy cream
4 ounces (100g) dark
chocolate, broken into
pieces
a little rum or brandy,
to flavor

To decorate
pistachios, chopped
edible gold leaf (optional)

First make the chocolate liners. Melt the chocolate gently with the oil in a heatproof bowl set over a saucepan of hot water, making sure the bottom of the bowl doesn't touch the water, stirring occasionally. Allow to cool slightly, then brush the inside of about 24 petit four paper liners with a thin layer of chocolate (you can use a fine brush to do this, or even just a fingertip). Let set in a cool place. Give the liners three or four coats of chocolate, leaving them to set each time.

To make the ganache, pour the cream into a small saucepan and bring to a boil. Remove from the heat and add the chocolate pieces and a little rum or brandy. Stir until the chocolate has melted.

Return the saucepan to the heat, bring to a boil, then take off the heat and let cool. When firm, spoon the chocolate ganache into a piping bag fitted with a medium star nozzle and pipe rosettes of the ganache into the chocolate casings.

Carefully peel off the paper liners. Decorate the top of each petit four with a small piece of pistachio or a touch of gold leaf (optional), and chill until required.

Traditionally, macaroons were always made on rice paper, but as this is not always easy to get hold of, I've used parchment paper.

MACAROONS

MAKES 16 MACAROONS

2 extra-large egg whites
8 blanched almonds, halved
1 cup (100g) almond flour
¾ cup + 2 tbsps (175g) sugar
3 tbsps (30g) semolina
a few drops of almond
extract

Preheat the oven to 300°F. Line two baking sheets with parchment paper.

Put the egg whites into a bowl, dip in the halved almonds, and set them aside. Whisk the egg whites until they form soft peaks. Gently fold in the almond flour, sugar, semolina, and almond extract.

Spoon the mixture in small spoonfuls onto the prepared baking sheets and smooth out with the back of a spoon to form circles. Place an almond half in the center of each.

Bake for 20–25 minutes, or until a pale golden brown. Let cool on the baking sheets for a few minutes, then lift onto a wire rack to cool completely.

I use a quick method for making the pastry here rather than the classic way.

SUGARED PRETZELS

MAKES 10 PRETZELS

1 cup + 3 tbsps (150g)
   all-purpose flour, plus
   extra for dusting
5 tbsps (65g) salted butter
3 tbsps (35g) granulated
   sugar
1 extra-large egg, beaten
a few drops of vanilla extract

To finish
1 extra-large egg, beaten
1 tbsp nibbed or pearled
   sugar
a little confectioners' sugar,
   for dusting

Measure the flour into a large bowl, add the butter, and rub in with your fingertips until the mixture resembles fine breadcrumbs. Stir in the sugar, then the egg and vanilla extract, and mix until the pastry comes together. Knead very gently on a lightly floured work surface until smooth, then wrap in plastic wrap and chill for about 30 minutes, or until firm enough to roll.

Preheat the oven to 400°F. Lightly grease two baking sheets.

Divide the dough equally into 10 pieces and roll each into a ball. Roll each ball into a thin sausage measuring approximately 12 inches, then twist into the traditional pretzel shape, like a loose knot. Place on the prepared baking sheets and brush gently with the beaten egg.

Scatter the nibbed or pearled sugar over the top of the pretzels and bake for 15 minutes, or until barely changing color. Lift onto a wire rack and dust thickly with confectioners' sugar while still hot.

Also known as "Diggers," these traditional Australian cookies are really easy to make and taste delicious.

ANZAC COOKIES
MAKES ABOUT 45 COOKIES

⅔ cup (150g) salted butter, softened

1 tbsp golden syrup or light corn syrup

¾ cup + 2 tbsps (175g) granulated sugar

⅔ cup (75g) all-purpose flour

1 tsp baking powder

¼ tsp salt

1 cup (75g) shredded coconut

1¼ cups (115g) rolled oats

Preheat the oven to 350°F. Lightly grease two baking sheets.

Measure the butter, golden syrup or light corn syrup, and sugar into a medium saucepan and heat gently until the butter has melted and the sugar has dissolved. Stir in the flour, baking powder, salt, coconut, and oats and mix well until evenly blended.

Place spoonfuls of the mixture well apart on the prepared baking sheets and flatten slightly with the back of the spoon. You should have enough mixture for about 45 mounds, and you will need to bake them in batches.

Bake for 8–10 minutes, or until they have spread out flat and are lightly browned at the edges. Let cool on the baking sheets for a few minutes, then carefully lift off with an offset spatula and place on a wire rack to cool completely. If the cookies harden too much to lift off the baking sheets, pop them back in the oven for a few minutes to soften.

Store in an airtight container.

These slim, crisp, curled cookies are wonderful with light mousses, ice cream, and fruit salads.

ALMOND TUILES

MAKES ABOUT 20 COOKIES

⅓ cup (75g) salted butter, softened
6 tbsps (75g) granulated sugar
1 extra-large egg white
⅓ cup + 1 tbsp (55g) all-purpose flour
½ cup (75g) blanched almonds, finely chopped

To finish
a little confectioners' sugar, for dusting

Preheat the oven to 400°F. Lightly grease two baking sheets.

Measure the butter and sugar into a bowl and beat well until pale and fluffy.

Place the egg white in a separate bowl and sift the flour over the top. Mix well, then stir into the butter mixture, along with the finely chopped almonds.

Place small spoonfuls of the mixture onto the prepared baking sheets, leaving ample room for the cookies to spread (bake about 4 at a time).

Bake for 6–8 minutes, or until they are browned around the edge but not in the middle. Remove from the oven and let rest for a second or two, then remove from the baking sheets with an offset spatula and curl over a rolling pin until set.

When cool, store in an airtight container. Serve with a dusting of confectioners' sugar.

TIP
These keep well in an airtight container or, if made a long time in advance, in the freezer. Store them in a rigid box or container so they cannot be broken.

Bought Easter cookies are usually larger than these. If you like them that way, simply use a larger cookie cutter.

EASTER COOKIES

MAKES ABOUT 24 COOKIES

½ cup (115g) salted butter, softened
6 tbsps (75g) sugar
1 extra-large egg, separated
1⅔ cups (200g) all-purpose flour, plus extra for dusting
½ tsp pumpkin pie spice
½ tsp ground cinnamon
⅓ cup (55g) currants
¼ cup (30g) candied orange or lemon peel, chopped
1-2 tbsps milk
a little sugar, for sprinkling

Preheat the oven to 400°F. Lightly grease three baking sheets.

Measure the butter and sugar into a bowl and beat together until light and fluffy. Beat in the egg yolk. Sift in the flour and spices and mix well. Add the currants and chopped candied orange or lemon peel and enough milk to give a fairly soft dough.

Knead the mixture lightly on a lightly floured work surface and roll out to a thickness of ¼ inch. Cut into rounds using a 2½-inch fluted cookie cutter.

Place on the prepared baking sheets and bake for 8-10 minutes.

Meanwhile, lightly beat the egg white. Remove the cookies from the oven, brush them with the beaten egg white, sprinkle with a little sugar, and return to the oven for an additional 4-5 minutes, or until pale golden brown. Lift onto a wire rack to cool.

Store in an airtight container.

TIP
If bought or homemade cookies have gone a little soft, place them on a baking sheet and crisp them in a 350°F oven for a few minutes.

I must confess that I rarely make these, as it is so easy to buy good ones! Serve plain with ice cream or mousses, or fill with whipped cream and serve with fruit.

BRANDY SNAPS

MAKES ABOUT 24 SNAPS

¼ cup (55g) salted butter
¼ cup (55g) demerara sugar
3 tbsps (55g) golden syrup or light corn syrup
½ cup (55g) all-purpose flour
½ tsp ground ginger
½ tsp fresh lemon juice

Preheat the oven to 350°F. Line two baking sheets with parchment paper and oil the handles of four wooden spoons.

Measure the butter, sugar, and syrup into a small saucepan and heat gently until the butter has melted and the sugar has dissolved. Allow the mixture to cool slightly, then sift in the flour and the ginger. Add the lemon juice and stir well to mix thoroughly.

Place small spoonfuls of the mixture on the prepared baking sheets, at least 4 inches apart and only 4 snaps at a time. Bake for about 8 minutes, or until the mixture is well spread out and a dark golden color.

Remove from the oven and let sit for a few minutes to firm, then lift from the parchment paper using a fish spatula. Turn over and roll each around the handle of a wooden spoon. Let set on a wire rack, then slip out the spoon. Repeat until all the mixture has been used.

When cold, store in an airtight container.

TIP

To make Brandy Snap Baskets, mold the cooked mixture around the bottom of a greased cup or an orange and use your fingers to flute the top. You don't need to grease the orange, as its natural oils will prevent the brandy snap mixture from sticking.

*If you notice that the underside of the shortbread is not pale gold,
return the pan to the oven for an additional 5–10 minutes.*

BISHOP'S FINGERS

MAKES 12 FINGERS

1 cup (115g) all-purpose flour
⅓ cup (30g) almond flour
3 tbsps (30g) semolina
½ cup (115g) salted butter
¼ cup (55g) sugar
a few drops of almond
    extract
⅓ cup (30g) sliced almonds
a little sugar, for dusting

Preheat the oven to 325°F. Lightly grease a 7-inch square pan.

Mix together the flour, almond flour, and semolina in a bowl
or food processor. Add the butter, sugar, and almond extract
and rub together with your fingertips until the mixture is just
beginning to bind together. Knead lightly until smooth.

Press the dough into the prepared pan and level the surface
with the back of a metal spoon or an offset spatula. Sprinkle over
the sliced almonds.

Bake for 30–35 minutes, or until a very pale golden brown.
Score the shortbread into 12 fingers with a knife, sprinkle with
sugar, and let cool in the pan.

When completely cold, cut into fingers, lift out carefully,
and store in an airtight container.

This shortbread is always popular. The different textures are the principal appeal—the crunch of the shortbread base, the caramel in the middle, and the chunky chocolate on top.

MILLIONAIRES' SHORTBREAD

MAKES 24 SQUARES

For the shortbread
2 cups (250g) all-purpose flour
6 tbsps (75g) granulated sugar
¾ cup (175g) salted butter, softened

For the caramel
½ cup (115g) salted butter
½ cup + 2 tbsps (115g) light muscovado sugar
2 × 14-ounce (397g) cans full-fat condensed milk

For the topping
7 ounces (200g) dark or milk chocolate, broken into pieces

TIP
A marbled chocolate top looks stunning. Simply melt just over 2 ounces (55g) each of dark, milk, and white chocolate in separate bowls. Place the chocolate in spoonfuls over the set caramel, alternating the 3 types. Use a skewer to marble the edges of the chocolates together, then let set.

Preheat the oven to 350°F. Lightly grease a 9 x 13-inch baking pan.

To make the shortbread, mix the flour and granulated sugar in a bowl. Rub the butter in with your fingertips until the mixture resembles fine breadcrumbs. Knead until it forms a dough, then press into the bottom of the prepared pan. Prick the shortbread lightly with a fork and bake for about 20 minutes or until firm to the touch and very lightly browned. Cool in the pan.

To make the caramel, measure the butter and muscovado sugar into a large nonstick pan. Heat gently until the butter has melted and the sugar has dissolved. Add the condensed milk and stir continuously and evenly with a flat-ended wooden spoon for about 5 minutes, or until the mixture is thick and has turned a golden toffee color—take care, as it burns easily.

Pour the caramel over the shortbread and let cool.

To make the topping, melt the chocolate gently in a bowl set over a saucepan of hot water, making sure the bottom of the bowl doesn't touch the water, stirring occasionally. Pour over the cold caramel and let set.

Cut into squares or bars.

Be generous with the raspberry jam, it makes all the difference. As the shortcrust pastry contains a lot of fat and no sugar, there is no need to line the pan with parchment paper.

BAKEWELL SLICES

MAKES 24 SLICES

For the shortcrust pastry
1⅓ cups (175g) all-purpose flour, plus extra for dusting
⅓ cup (75g) salted butter

For the sponge
7 tbsps (100g) salted butter, softened
½ cup (100g) sugar
1⅓ cups (175g) all-purpose flour
3 tsps baking powder
½ tsp salt
2 extra-large eggs
2 tbsps milk
½ tsp almond extract

To finish
about 4 tbsps raspberry jam
sliced almonds, for sprinkling

To make the pastry, measure the flour into a bowl and rub the butter in with your fingertips until the mixture resembles fine breadcrumbs. Add 2–3 tablespoons cold water gradually, mixing to form a soft dough.

Roll out the dough onto a lightly floured work surface and use to line a 9 x 13-inch baking pan.

Preheat the oven to 350°F.

Measure all the sponge ingredients into a bowl and beat until well-blended.

Spread the pastry with raspberry jam, then top with the sponge mixture.

Sprinkle with the sliced almonds and bake for about 25 minutes, or until the sponge has shrunk from the sides of the pan and springs back when pressed in the center with your fingertips. Let cool in the pan, then cut into slices.

CHAPTER ELEVEN

TARTS
AND
PASTRIES

This classic "upside-down" French tart is usually served warm rather than as a cold cake.

TARTE TATIN
SERVES 6

8 tbsps (120ml) water
1 cup (200g) sugar
Salted butter, for greasing
7 ounces (200g) tart apples
    (such as Granny Smith),
    peeled, cored, and cut into
    ¾-inch (2cm) pieces
4 large sweet-tart apples
    (such as Honeycrisp)
All-purpose flour, for dusting
13¼ ounces (375g) block of
    all-butter puff pastry
Whipped cream or crème
    fraîche, for serving

You will need a 9-inch (23cm) round cake pan with tall sides.

First make the caramel. Measure 6 tablespoons (90ml) of the water and ¾ cup plus 2 tablespoons (175g) of the sugar into a stainless-steel saucepan. Stir gently over low heat until the sugar is fully dissolved, then remove the spoon and increase the heat. Boil until the caramel is a golden straw color, then immediately pour into the cake pan, letting it spread evenly over the bottom. Set aside to cool for about 30 minutes, then butter the sides of the pan above the caramel line.

Meanwhile, place the tart apples, the remaining 2 tablespoons sugar, and the remaining 2 tablespoons water in a medium saucepan. Stir over medium heat, then cover with a lid and simmer until the apples are soft, 5 to 10 minutes. Remove from the heat, then use a fork to mash the apples to a purée. Let cool.

Preheat the oven to 425°F.

Peel and core the sweet-tart apples, then thinly slice so they are about ¼ inch (5mm) thick. Arrange a layer over the caramel in the pan in a circular pattern. Start from the outside of the pan and work inward, using larger pieces for the outer edge of the circle and smaller slices for the inner ring. Scatter the remaining apples on top and press down. Add the cooled apple purée in spoonfuls over the sliced apples and carefully spread out in an even layer.

Lightly dust a work surface with flour, then roll out the puff pastry to a circle 1 inch (2.5cm) bigger than the pan. Cover the apples with the pastry and tuck in the edges. Make a small cross in the top of the pastry with a sharp knife, to let the steam out. Bake until the pastry is crisp and golden and the apples are soft, 35 to 40 minutes.

Carefully turn the tarte tatin out onto a plate and spoon the syrup over the apples. Serve with whipped cream or crème fraîche.

Another lovely tart with a crisp sweet pastry crust and a sharp lemon filling.

LEMON TART WITH LEMON
SERVES 8 PASSION FRUIT CURD

For the pâté sucrée
1⅓ cups (175g) all-purpose
    flour, plus extra for dusting
⅓ cup (75g) salted butter,
    softened
6 tbsps (75g) sugar
3 extra-large egg yolks

For the filling
5 extra-large eggs
1 cup + 2 tbsps (225g) sugar
½ cup (125ml) heavy cream
3 large lemons

To finish
6 tbsps lemon curd
2 passion fruits

First make the pâté sucrée (sweet pastry). Measure the flour and butter into a bowl. Rub the butter in with your fingertips until the mixture resembles fine breadcrumbs. Stir in the sugar, then add the egg yolks. Mix until the ingredients come together to form a firm dough. Roll out the pastry onto a lightly floured work surface and use to line a 9-inch pie pan. Prick the pastry all over with a fork. Chill in the fridge for 30 minutes.

Preheat the oven to 400°F.

Line the pan with parchment paper and pie weights. Blind-bake for 15 minutes, then remove the paper and weights and bake for an additional 5 minutes until golden and crisp.

Lower the oven temperature to 325°F.

To make the filling, mix the eggs, sugar, and cream together in a large bowl. Zest the lemons and add to the mixture. Squeeze the juice from the lemons and add ⅔ cup (150ml) to the bowl.

Pour the mixture into the pan and carefully slide back into the oven. Bake for about 30–35 minutes until the filling is set, but with a slight wobble. Let cool.

Meanwhile, mix the lemon curd and passion fruit pulp together in a bowl. Serve alongside the tart , or drizzle over the top.

These little tarts look best if each one is filled with a single type of fruit. Use red currant glaze for red fruits, and apricot glaze for orange or green fruits, such as green grapes and kiwifruit. Fill the pastry crusts at the last moment, as they soften quickly.

GLAZED FRUIT TARTLETS

MAKES 12 TARTLETS

For the pâté sucrée
1 cup (115g) all-purpose
    flour, plus extra for dusting
¼ cup (55g) salted butter,
    softened
¼ cup (55g) sugar
2 extra-large egg yolks

For the filling and glaze
⅔ cup (150ml) heavy cream
1½–1¾ cups (225g) fresh
    fruits (such as raspberries
    and blueberries)
about 4 tbsps red currant
    jelly (or apricot jam)

You will need twelve 3½-inch tartlet pans.

First make the pâté sucrée (sweet pastry). Measure the flour into a bowl. Rub the butter in with your fingertips until the mixture resembles fine breadcrumbs. Stir in the sugar, then add the egg yolks and mix until the ingredients come together to form a dough. Knead the mixture gently until smooth. Wrap the dough in plastic wrap and let rest in the fridge for about 30 minutes.

Preheat the oven to 400°F.

Roll out the pastry on a lightly floured work surface and cut out about 12 rounds using a 3½-inch fluted cookie cutter. Re-roll the trimmings once only. Ease the pastry rounds into tartlet pans and prick lightly with a fork. Place a small piece of parchment paper or foil in each pastry crust and fill with pie weights.

Bake the pastry crusts for about 15 minutes or until golden brown. Turn out onto a wire rack, remove the paper and pie weights, and let cool.

To make the filling, whip the cream until it forms soft peaks and spoon a little into each tartlet crust. Arrange the fruits on top.

Warm the red currant jelly or apricot jam in a small saucepan and brush liberally over the fruits to glaze.

These lovely little shortbread crusts can actually be filled with anything you like—they are a good way of stretching a small amount of fruit.

LEMON AND STRAWBERRY CREAM TARTLETS

MAKES 10 TARTLETS

For the shortbread
½ cup (115g) salted butter, softened
¼ cup (55g) sugar
⅓ cup (55g) semolina
1 cup (115g) all-purpose flour

For the filling
about 3 tbsps good lemon curd
⅔ cup (150ml) heavy cream, whipped
a few sliced strawberries

You will need a 12-cup cupcake pan.

First make the shortbread. Measure the butter, sugar, semolina, and flour into a bowl and work together to form a smooth dough. Wrap in plastic wrap and chill in the fridge for about 15 minutes.

Preheat the oven to 300°F.

On a lightly floured work surface, roll out the shortbread to just under ¼ inch in thickness. Cut out 10 circles using a 3-inch fluted cookie cutter, then press the circles gently into the pan. Prick the bottoms well.

Bake for 20–25 minutes or until firm and golden. Leave the shortbread in the pans to harden slightly, then ease out of the pans and let cool completely on a wire rack.

To make the filling, mix together the lemon curd and whipped cream.

Just before serving, spoon a little of the filling into each shortbread crust and top with sliced strawberries.

TIP

The shortbread crusts can be made ahead, and they can be frozen for up to 2 months. Once filled, however, they go soft very quickly, so serve and eat straightaway.

I've used premade filo pastry in this recipe, for ease. Try to find the shorter packets of filo pastry, as then you won't need to trim the pastry to size.

FILO APPLE STRUDELS

MAKES 8 STRUDELS

For the filling
2 medium (350g) tart
   cooking apples, peeled,
   cored, and roughly
   chopped
juice of ½ lemon
⅓ cup (75g) demerara sugar
½ cup (30g) fresh
   breadcrumbs
6 tbsps (55g) golden raisins
1 tsp ground cinnamon
8 sheets filo pastry,
   7 x 13 inches
½ cup (115g) salted butter,
   melted

For the topping
2 tbsps granulated sugar
2 tbsps water
confectioners' sugar, for
   dusting

Preheat the oven to 400°F. Lightly grease two baking sheets.

First prepare the filling. Mix the apples, lemon juice, sugar, breadcrumbs, golden raisins, and cinnamon together in a bowl.

Unfold 1 sheet of filo pastry and brush liberally with melted butter. Spoon one-eighth of the apple mixture to cover the middle third of the longest edge of the pastry, leaving a small border. Fold this border in, then bring the two short sides over the apple to cover it. Roll the filled pastry over and over to form a neat strudel. Put it on one of the prepared baking sheets, then repeat the process with the remaining 7 pastry sheets and apple mixture.

Brush the strudels with melted butter and bake for 15–20 minutes, or until golden brown and crisp.

Meanwhile, mix the granulated sugar and water together in a small saucepan and heat gently until all the sugar has dissolved. Spoon the syrup over the warm strudels and dust with confectioners' sugar to serve.

TIP
Any leftover filo will keep in the fridge for 2 days. Alternatively, you can wrap it carefully, put it into the freezer straightaway, and use within 1 month.

This delicious tart is an economical choice in the fall, when you can use your own free apples or get them cheaply from elsewhere. You will need an 8-inch fluted pie pan.

FRENCH APPLE TART

SERVES 6 TO 8

For the pastry
1⅓ cups (175g) all-purpose flour, plus extra for dusting
⅓ cup (75g) salted butter, cubed
1 extra-large egg yolk

For the filling
2 pounds, about 4 large (900g) cooking apples
¼ cup (55g) salted butter
4 tbsps apricot jam
¼ cup (55g) sugar, plus extra for sprinkling
finely grated zest of ½ lemon
½ pound, about 2 small (225g) dessert apples
1–2 tbsps fresh lemon juice

For the glaze
4 tbsps apricot jam

To make the pastry, measure the flour into a large bowl, add the butter, and rub in with your fingertips until the mixture resembles fine breadcrumbs. Add the egg yolk, mix into the flour mixture, and bring the mixture to a dough, adding a little water if necessary. Knead the pastry very lightly, then wrap in plastic wrap and chill in the fridge for about 30 minutes.

Preheat the oven to 400°F.

To make the apple filling, cut the cooking apples into quarters, remove the core, and chop the apples into chunks (no need to peel).

Melt the butter in a large saucepan and then add the prepared apples and 2 tablespoons water. Cover and cook very gently for 10–15 minutes until the apples have become soft and mushy.

Rub the apples through a sieve into a clean saucepan, add the apricot jam, sugar, and lemon zest. Cook over high heat for 10–15 minutes, stirring continuously, until all the excess liquid has evaporated and the apple mixture is thick. Set aside to cool.

Roll out the pastry thinly on a lightly floured work surface and use to line an 8-inch fluted tart pan with a removable bottom. Cover with parchment paper and fill with pie weights. Blind-bake for 10–15 minutes.

Recipe continued on the next page

Remove the paper and weights and bake for an additional 5 minutes until the pastry at the bottom has dried out. Remove from the oven but do not turn off the oven.

Spoon the cooled apple purée into the tart crust and level the surface. Peel, quarter, and core the dessert apples, then slice them very thinly. Arrange in neat overlapping circles over the apple purée, brush with the lemon juice, and sprinkle with 1 teaspoon sugar. Return the tart to the oven and bake for 25 minutes or until the pastry and the edges of the apples are lightly browned.

To make the glaze, sieve the apricot jam into a small saucepan and heat gently until runny. Brush all over the top of the apples and pastry.

Serve warm or cold.

This tart looks wonderful cooked because the top layer of pastry molds itself around the apricot halves. I use canned apricots, as I find them to be more reliable and a readily obtainable alternative to fresh. You will need a 10-inch fluted pie pan.

AUSTRIAN APRICOT
SERVES 8 TO 10 AND ALMOND TART

For the pastry
2¼ cups (275g) all-purpose flour, plus extra for dusting
1 cup + 3 tbsps (150g) confectioners' sugar, sifted
⅔ cup (150g) chilled salted butter, cubed
1 extra-large egg, beaten

For the filling
¾ cup (175g) almond paste or marzipan, grated (see page 398 for almond paste recipe)
28 ounces (800g) canned apricot halves in natural juice, drained and dried on paper towel

TIP
You can prepare the tart ahead of time. Cover the uncooked tart in plastic wrap and keep in the fridge for up to 24 hours before baking. Remove the tart from the fridge and let sit at room temperature for about 20 minutes before baking.

First make the pastry. Measure the flour and confectioners' sugar into a large bowl and rub the butter in with your fingertips until the mixture resembles breadcrumbs. Stir in the beaten egg and bring together to form a dough. Form into a smooth ball, wrap in plastic wrap, and chill in the fridge for 30 minutes.

—

Preheat the oven to 350°F and put a heavy sheet pan in the oven to heat.

—

Cut off a little less than half the pastry, wrap it in plastic wrap, and return it to the fridge. Take the larger piece and roll out onto a lightly floured work surface to a circle of about 11½ inches. Line the bottom and sides of a 10-inch deep fluted tart pan with a removable bottom with the pastry, then trim the excess from the top edge with a knife. Use the trimmings to patch the pastry if necessary.

—

Spread the grated almond paste or marzipan evenly over the bottom. Place the apricots on top of the almond paste, evenly spaced, rounded side up.

—

Roll out any trimmings along with the remaining pastry to a circle large enough to fit the top of the tart pan. Use a little water to dampen the rim of the pastry in the pan, then, with the aid of the rolling pin, lift the top circle of pastry into position. Trim off any excess pastry, then press the edges together so no juices can escape. Again, use the pastry trimmings to patch if necessary.

—

Transfer to the oven to bake on the hot sheet pan for 30–35 minutes, or until pale golden. Watch the pastry carefully: if it is browning too quickly, protect the edge with strips of foil.

A familiar option on pub dessert menus, and a popular choice with adults and children alike. Delicious served with cream, ice cream, or custard.

DEEP TREACLE TART

SERVES 6

For the pastry
1¼ cups (150g) all-purpose
    flour, plus extra for dusting
1 tbsp confectioners' sugar
⅓ cup (75g) salted butter
1 extra-large egg

For the filling
1⅓ cups (450g) golden
    syrup or light corn syrup
about 2 cups (150g) fresh
    white or brown
    breadcrumbs
finely grated zest and juice
    of ½ large lemon

First make the pastry. Measure the flour and confectioners' sugar into a large bowl and rub the butter in with your fingertips until the mixture resembles fine breadcrumbs. Add the egg and mix to a firm dough.

—

Roll the pastry out thinly onto a lightly floured work surface and use to line an 9-inch round cake pan. Chill in the fridge for 30 minutes.

—

Preheat the oven to 400°F and put a heavy baking sheet in the oven to heat.

—

To make the filling, heat the syrup in a large saucepan and stir in the breadcrumbs and lemon zest and juice. If the mixture looks runny, add a few more breadcrumbs (it depends whether you use white or brown bread). Pour the syrup mixture into the pastry crust and level the surface.

—

Bake on the hot baking sheet for 15 minutes, then lower the oven temperature to 350°F and bake for an additional 25–30 minutes until the pastry is golden and the filling set. Let cool in the pan.

—

Serve warm or cold.

It's fiddly and time-consuming to make these pastries in their various traditional shapes, but they'll be better than any you can buy! They are best eaten on the day they are made. The basic recipe filling is almond paste, but do try the alternative fillings, too.

DANISH PASTRIES

MAKES 16 PASTRIES

For the pastry dough
3½ cups (450g) bread flour
½ tsp salt
1½ cups (350g) salted
    butter, softened
1 x ¼-ounce (7g) packet
    fast-acting dried yeast
¼ cup (55g) granulated
    sugar
⅔ cup (150ml) warm milk
3 extra-large eggs, beaten

For the filling and topping
1 cup (225g) almond paste
    or marzipan (see page
    398 for almond paste
    recipe)
1–2 tbsps warm water
1 cup (115g) confectioners'
    sugar
⅔ cup (55g) sliced almonds,
    toasted
11 total (55g) maraschino
    cherries, chopped

Lightly grease three baking sheets.

Measure the flour and salt into a bowl and rub in ¼ cup (55g) of the butter with your fingertips. Add the yeast and sugar and stir to mix. Make a well in the center, add the warm milk and 2 of the beaten eggs, and mix to a soft dough. Knead the dough until smooth. Place it in a clean bowl, cover with plastic wrap, and let rise in a warm place for about 1 hour or until the dough has doubled in bulk.

Punch down the dough, knead until smooth, then roll out to an oblong about 14 x 8 inches. Cover the top two-thirds of the oblong with half the remaining butter, dotting pieces of butter over the dough. Fold the bottom third of dough up and the top third down to form a parcel. Seal the edges, then give the dough a quarter turn so that the folded side is to the left. Roll out to the same-size oblong as before. Dot over the remaining butter in the same way and fold the dough as before. Wrap the dough in plastic wrap and let rest in the fridge for about 15 minutes.

Set the dough so that the fold is on the left again and roll and fold the dough, with no butter, twice more. Wrap the dough in plastic wrap and return to the fridge for 15 minutes.

To make crescents, divide the dough into quarters and roll out one section to a 9-inch circle. Divide the circle into four equal wedges. Place a small sausage of almond paste at the wide end of each wedge and roll up loosely toward the point. Bend them around to form a crescent. Repeat with the remaining dough or try a different shape.

Recipe continued on the next page

To make pinwheels, roll out a quarter of dough to form an 8-inch square. Cut into four squares. Place a small piece of almond paste in the center of each square. Make cuts from each corner almost to the center and fold four alternate points to the center, pressing them down firmly.

To make kite shapes, roll out a quarter of dough to form an 8-inch square. Cut into four squares. Place a small amount of flattened almond paste in the center of each square. Make an "L-shape" cut ½ inch from the edge. Lift the "L-shape" piece and fold it over the almond paste disc.

To make envelopes, roll out a quarter of dough to form a 16-inch square. Cut this into four squares. In the center of each square, place a piece of flattened almond paste or some other filling (vanilla cream or apple mixture is especially good here). Fold two opposite corners or all four corners into the middle over the almond paste disc. Press the edges down lightly.

Arrange the pastries on the prepared baking sheets, cover with oiled plastic wrap or put the sheets inside oiled plastic bags, and leave to proof for about 20 minutes in a warm place, until they are beginning to look puffy.

Preheat the oven to 425°F.

Brush each pastry with beaten egg and bake for about 15 minutes until golden brown. Lift onto a wire rack to cool.

Make up some glacé icing by gradually mixing the warm water into the confectioners' sugar. Spoon a little icing over the pastries while they are still warm. Sprinkle with toasted sliced almonds and small pieces of maraschino cherry.

ALTERNATIVE DANISH PASTRY FILLINGS

ALMOND FILLING

This is softer and moister than almond paste. Use it in any of the pastry shapes.

1¼ cups (115g) almond flour
½ cup + 1 tbsp (115g) sugar
a little beaten egg

Mix the almond flour and sugar together and bind with enough egg to form a soft paste.

VANILLA CREAM

This is particularly good in the "envelopes."

1 tbsp all-purpose flour
1 tsp cornstarch
1 extra-large egg yolk
1 tbsp sugar
⅔ cup (150ml) milk
2–3 drops of vanilla extract

Mix together the flours, egg yolk, and sugar, and blend with a little of the milk. Bring the remaining milk to a boil, pour onto the flour mixture, blend, and then return to the saucepan. Heat gently, stirring, until the mixture comes to a boil. Allow to cool then flavor with a few drops of vanilla extract.

APPLE FILLING

Use this filling in any of the pastry shapes.

1 pound, about 2 medium (450g) cooking apples, quartered and cored (no need to peel)
1 tbsp (15g) salted butter
finely grated zest and juice of ½ lemon
4 tbsps light muscovado sugar
½ cup (75g) golden raisins (optional)

Place the apples in a saucepan with the butter and the lemon zest and juice. Cover and cook until soft. Rub the apples through a sieve, return to the rinsed-out saucepan, and add the sugar. Cook until the sugar has dissolved and the apple mixture is thick. Add the golden raisins, if using, and let cool before using.

Pâté sucrée is the classic French sweet pastry. I make mine in a food processor, which is easier than the traditional way, on a work surface.

FRANGIPANE TARTLETS

MAKES 12 TARTLETS

For the pâté sucrée
1 cup (115g) all-purpose flour
¼ cup (55g) salted butter, softened
¼ cup (55g) sugar
2 extra-large egg yolks

For the frangipane
¼ cup (55g) salted butter, softened
¼ cup (55g) sugar
1 extra-large egg, beaten
⅔ cup (65g) almond flour
a few drops of almond extract
⅔ cup (55g) sliced almonds

To finish
3 tbsps apricot jam
2 tbsps almond flour

You will need twelve 4-inch tartlet pans.

First make the pâté sucrée (sweet pastry). Measure the flour into a bowl. Rub the butter in with your fingertips until the mixture resembles fine breadcrumbs. Stir in the sugar, then add the egg yolks and mix until the ingredients come together to form a dough. Knead the mixture gently until smooth. Wrap the dough in plastic wrap and let rest in the fridge for about 30 minutes.

Roll out the pastry on a lightly floured work surface and cut out about 12 rounds using a 4-inch plain cookie cutter. Re-roll the trimmings once only. Ease the pastry rounds into the tartlet pans and prick lightly with a fork. Chill while you are making the frangipane.

Preheat the oven to 375°F.

To make the frangipane, measure the butter and sugar into a bowl and beat well together until light and fluffy. Gradually beat in the egg, then stir in the almond flour and almond extract. Divide the frangipane between the chilled tartlet crusts and scatter the sliced almonds on top.

Bake for about 15 minutes, until the frangipane is golden and firm to the touch. Ease the tartlets out their pans and onto a wire rack to cool.

Sieve the apricot jam into a small saucepan and warm gently. Brush the tartlets with the apricot jam to glaze, and decorate the outside edge with a thin line of almond flour. Allow the tartlets to cool completely before serving.

Choux pastry must be well cooked until it is really firm and has turned a good straw color. The profiteroles look wonderful piled up in a pyramid.

PROFITEROLES

MAKES 12 PROFITEROLES

For the choux pastry
¼ cup (55g) salted butter
½ cup + 2 tbsps (150ml) water
⅔ cup (75g) all-purpose flour, sifted
2 extra-large eggs, beaten, plus 1 extra egg, beaten, to glaze

For the chocolate sauce
⅓ cup (75ml) heavy cream
3 ounces (75g) dark chocolate, broken into pieces

For the filling
¾ cup + 1 tbsp (200ml) heavy cream

TIP
These can be made and assembled up to 4 hours ahead. Unfilled buns can be made up to a day ahead. Not for freezing.

Preheat the oven to 425°F and line a baking sheet with parchment paper.

To make the pastry, place the butter and water in a small saucepan until the water is boiling and the butter has melted. Remove from the heat and immediately add the flour, all at once. Quickly beat with a wooden spoon until the mixture comes together and makes a smooth, thick dough. Add the beaten egg, a little at a time, beating after each addition, until the egg is incorporated and the dough is thick and smooth.

Spoon 12 domes of pastry onto the prepared baking sheet. Brush with the extra beaten egg and bake for 10 minutes. Lower the oven temperature to 375°F and bake for an additional 20 minutes.

Remove the buns from the oven and turn the oven off. Slice each bun in half and put the buns cut side up back onto the baking sheet. Return to the cooling oven for 15–20 minutes to dry out.

Meanwhile, to make the chocolate sauce, pour the cream into a saucepan and heat until hot. Add the chocolate and stir until melted. Remove from the heat and set aside in a cool place to thicken up.

Once the buns have dried out and are crisp, dip one half into the chocolate sauce and place on a wire rack to set. Repeat with the remaining 11 bun tops.

Pour the cream into a large bowl and whisk until it forms soft peaks. Place a generous dollop of cream onto the remaining bun bases, then sandwich a chocolate half on top. Repeat to make 12.

These are sheer luxury and well worth making. Serve for tea or as a dessert.

CHOCOLATE ÉCLAIRS
MAKES ABOUT 12 ÉCLAIRS

For the choux pastry
¼ cup (55g) salted butter, cubed
½ cup + 2 tbsps (150ml) water
½ cup (65g) all-purpose flour, sifted
2 extra-large eggs, beaten

For the filling
¼ cup (300ml) heavy cream

For the icing
2 ounces (55g) dark chocolate, broken into pieces
1 tbsp (15g) salted butter
2 tbsps water
⅔ cup (75g) confectioners' sugar, sifted

TIP
Do not fill choux pastry items too long before serving, as the pastry tends to go soggy.

Preheat the oven to 425°F. Lightly grease two baking sheets.

To make the choux pastry, put the butter and water into a small saucepan and place over a low heat. Allow the butter to melt, then bring slowly to a boil. Remove the saucepan from the heat, add the flour all at once, and beat until the mixture forms a soft ball and leaves the sides of the saucepan. Allow to cool slightly.

Add the eggs to the mixture a little at a time, beating really well between each addition to give a smooth, shiny paste. It is easiest to use a handheld electric mixer for this.

Spoon the mixture into a large piping bag fitted with a ½-inch plain nozzle. Pipe onto the prepared baking sheets into shapes about 5–6 inches long, leaving room to spread. Bake for 10 minutes, then lower the temperature to 375°F and bake for an additional 20 minutes. (It is important that the éclairs are golden brown all over. Any pale, undercooked parts will become soggy once they have cooled.) Remove them from the oven and split down the side to allow the steam to escape. Let cool completely on a wire rack.

Whip the cream until it is just firm enough to pipe. Fill the éclairs with whipped cream, using a piping bag fitted with a plain nozzle.

To make the icing, place the chocolate in a bowl set over a saucepan of hot water, making sure the bottom of the bowl doesn't touch the water. Add the butter and water to the chocolate and place the saucepan over a low heat until the chocolate and butter have melted, stirring occasionally. Remove from the heat and add the sifted confectioners' sugar, beating well until smooth.

Spoon the icing over the top of each éclair, then let set.

CHAPTER TWELVE

BREADS

These old-fashioned English muffins are traditionally pulled apart through the middle, not cut, and eaten warm and slathered with butter. Any left over will store for 2–3 days in an airtight container and are then best split in half and eaten toasted.

ENGLISH MUFFINS

MAKES ABOUT 14 MUFFINS

5⅓ cups (675g) bread flour,
   plus extra for dusting
2 tsps sugar
1 × ¼ ounce (7g) packet
   fast-acting dried yeast
1½ tsps salt
1¾ cups + 3 tbsps (450ml)
   tepid milk
1 tsp fine semolina,
   for dusting

Measure the dry ingredients into a bowl or stand mixer, then pour in the milk in a continuous stream while mixing the ingredients, to form a dough. Knead the dough with your hands or with a mixer fitted with a dough hook until smooth and elastic.

—

Turn the dough out onto a lightly floured work surface and roll to a thickness of about ½ inch with a floured rolling pin.

—

Cut the dough into rounds using a 3-inch round cookie cutter and place on a well-floured baking sheet. Dust the tops with the semolina, cover loosely, and leave in a warm place until doubled in size (approximately 1 hour).

—

Lightly oil a griddle or heavy-bottomed frying pan and place on the stovetop over medium heat. Cook the muffins, in 2–3 batches, for about 7 minutes on each side, turning the heat down once the muffins go into the pan. When cooked, they should be well-risen and brown on both sides.

—

Cool slightly on a wire rack before splitting and buttering to serve.

*This is a good everyday loaf. You can make it in other shapes if you prefer.
Individual rolls will take less time to proof and bake.*

WHITE COTTAGE LOAF

MAKES 1 STANDARD ROUND LOAF

3½ cups (450g) bread flour
1 × ¼-ounce (7g) packet
  fast-acting dried yeast
3 tbsps (40g) salted butter,
  melted
1 tsp salt
1 cup + 3 tbsps (300ml)
  warm water

To glaze
1 extra-large egg, beaten
1 tbsp milk

Measure all the ingredients into a bowl and mix together by hand or with a stand mixer fitted with a dough hook until combined to make a fairly sticky, soft dough. Knead on a floured work surface, adding a little extra flour if needed, for about 4–5 minutes.

Transfer to a large oiled bowl, cover tightly with plastic wrap (make sure no air can escape), and let rise in a warm place for 1–1½ hours, or until the dough has doubled in size.

Line a baking sheet with parchment paper. Tip the dough out onto a floured work surface and punch down by hand until smooth. Cut off a quarter of the dough and shape into a round ball. Shape the remaining dough into a large ball and place on the prepared sheet. Sit the small ball on top of the large ball.

Flour the handle of a wooden spoon and push the handle vertically through the center of the two balls until you hit the baking sheet, then remove the handle carefully. Slide the baking sheet into a large plastic bag so the dough and baking sheet are completely covered. Seal the end of the bag completely. Let proof in a warm place for 35–45 minutes, or until doubled in size.

Preheat the oven to 425°F.

Brush the loaf with the milk and egg mixture and bake for 20–25 minutes, or until golden and the bread sounds hollow when tapped on the bottom. Let cool on a wire rack.

To make a dense, more substantial roll, you could use all barley flour instead of the mix given here.

QUICK MALT ROLLS

MAKES 12 ROLLS

2¾ cups (350g) bread flour, plus extra for dusting
3¼ cups (350g) barley flour
1½ tsps salt
1½ tsps sugar
1 × ¼-ounce (7g) packet fast-acting dried yeast
3 tbsps (40g) salted butter
1¾ cups + 2 tbsps (about 450ml) tepid milk and water, mixed

Lightly grease two baking sheets.

—

Measure the dry ingredients and the butter into a bowl or stand mixer. If mixing by hand, rub the butter in with your fingertips. If using a mixer, briefly mix in the butter.

—

Add the milk and water mixture in a continuous stream while mixing the ingredients to a dough. Knead thoroughly until smooth and elastic. Alternatively, use a mixer fitted with a dough hook to knead the dough for an additional 2 minutes.

—

Turn the dough out onto a floured work surface and divide into 12 even pieces. Shape the pieces into rounds and place on the prepared baking sheets, allowing room for expansion. Cover the rolls with oiled plastic wrap and let rest in a warm place to proof until doubled in size.

—

Preheat the oven to 425°F.

—

Uncover the rolls and bake for 10–15 minutes, or until they have browned on top and sound hollow when the bottom is tapped. Lift onto a wire rack to cool.

TIP
To glaze the rolls, brush the dough with a little milk and sprinkle with malted wheat flakes just before baking them.

*This loaf is made in an 8-inch round cake pan and breaks off into
12 individual rolls—perfect for a picnic or special meal.*

CROWN LOAF

MAKES 1 CROWN

2¾ cups (350g) bread flour,
   plus extra for dusting
2 tsps fast-acting dried yeast
1 tsp salt
1 tbsp (20g) salted butter,
   melted
¾ cup + 3 tbsps (225ml)
   warm water and a little
   milk, to glaze

Lightly grease an 8-inch round cake pan.

———

Measure all the ingredients, except the milk, into a bowl and mix
together by hand or with an electric mixer fitted with a dough
hook until combined to make a fairly sticky dough.

———

Remove from the bowl and tip onto a floured work surface.
Knead by hand for about 4–5 minutes, adding a little extra flour
if needed.

———

Transfer to a large oiled bowl, cover tightly with plastic wrap
(make sure no air can escape), and let rise in a warm place
for 1–1½ hours, or until the dough has doubled in size.

———

Tip onto a lightly floured work surface and punch down by hand
for about 5 minutes. Divide the dough into 12 evenly sized balls.
Arrange the balls in the pan so they are snug and touching. Cover
the pan with plastic wrap and let proof in a warm place for
about 30 minutes, or until doubled in size.

———

Preheat the oven to 425°F.

———

Glaze the loaf with a little milk, then bake for 20–25 minutes,
until lightly golden on top and well-risen. Let cool in the pan
for a few minutes, then remove from the pan and let cool on a
wire rack.

This is good with soup or a cheeseboard and best eaten on the day of making.

CHEESE AND OLIVE CROWN LOAF

MAKES 1 CROWN

2 cups (250g) bread flour
1½ tsps fast-acting dried
    yeast
½ tsp salt
1½ tbsps olive oil
⅔ cup (175ml) slightly
    warm water
⅓ cup + 1 tbsp (55g) black
    olives, pitted and chopped
½ cup (55g) finely grated
    Parmesan
1 egg, beaten
¼ cup (30g) sharp, grated
    Cheddar

Measure the flour, yeast, salt, olive oil, and water into a bowl. Mix using a wooden spoon until you have a wettish dough.

—

Tip the dough onto a lightly floured work surface. Knead by hand for 5–8 minutes until the dough is smooth and shiny. Place in an oiled bowl, cover with plastic wrap, and let rise for about 1½ hours, or until doubled in size.

—

Lightly grease an 8-inch round cake pan.

—

Punch down the dough by hand for a few minutes, then scatter over the olives and Parmesan and knead again. Divide the dough into 12 balls and arrange them in a circle in the prepared pan, starting from the outside. Cover with plastic wrap and let proof for 30 minutes, or until doubled in size.

—

Preheat the oven to 425°F.

—

Brush the tops with beaten egg and sprinkle with the Cheddar. Bake for 25–30 minutes, or until well-risen and golden brown on the top and underneath. Cool on a wire rack.

This recipe makes very good bread, very quickly! It needs mixing, shaping, and rising only once before baking, which takes about 1¼ hours altogether. Use walnut oil instead of olive oil, if you wish. This bread makes the best toast ever!

HONEY-GLAZED WALNUT BREAD

MAKES 2 × 8-INCH STANDARD ROUND LOAVES

1 cup (115g) walnut pieces
3¼ cups (350g) barley flour
2¾ cups (350g) bread flour, plus extra for dusting
1 × ¼-ounce (7g) packet fast-acting dried yeast
2 tsps salt
1 tbsp molasses
2 cups + 2 tbsps (500ml) warm milk (1 part boiling to 2 parts cold)
2 tbsps olive oil
¾ cup (115g) sunflower seeds

To glaze
1 tbsp beaten egg
1 tbsp clear honey

TIPS
You could make 16 rolls with the dough instead. Just remember, they will need less time in the oven.

To freeze the bread, seal in freezer-proof bags, label, and freeze for up to 6 months. To defrost, thaw in the plastic bag for 5–6 hours at room temperature. The bread is best served warm, so refresh in a preheated oven at 325°F for about 15 minutes or until warmed through.

Grease two baking sheets. Briefly process the walnuts, or coarsely chop by hand, taking care to keep the pieces quite large. Set aside until ready to use.

—

Combine the flours, yeast, and salt together in a large bowl. Add the molasses, milk, and olive oil and mix to form a dough, either with your hands or an electric mixer. Add a little more milk, if necessary, to make the dough slightly sticky.

—

Turn the dough out onto a lightly floured work surface and knead for about 10 minutes. Alternatively, use a stand mixer fitted with a dough hook and leave running for about 5 minutes. When ready, the dough should be smooth and elastic and leave the bowl and your hands clean.

—

Reserve about 2 tablespoons of sunflower seeds, then work the rest of the seeds and the chopped walnuts into the dough. Divide the dough in half, then shape each piece into a smooth round and set in the center of the prepared baking sheets. Enclose each baking sheet inside a large plastic bag, sealing a little air inside so that the plastic is not in contact with the bread. Let rise in a warm place for 30–45 minutes, or until doubled in size. If your kitchen is cool, this may take as long as 1–1½ hours.

—

Preheat the oven to 400°F.

—

To glaze the loaves, mix together the egg and honey and brush gently over the surface of the dough. Sprinkle the loaves with the reserved seeds and bake for 20–25 minutes, or until the loaves are a good chestnut brown and sound hollow when tapped on the bottom. Cool on a wire rack.

This textured loaf is packed with flavor and keeps well.

FARMHOUSE BROWN SEEDED LOAVES

MAKES 2 × 8-INCH STANDARD ROUND LOAVES

⅓ cup (40g) flaxseed
1⅔ cups (150g) rolled oats
1 cup + 3 tbsps (300ml)
   boiling water
3½ cups (450g) bread flour,
   plus extra for dusting
¾ cup + 2 tbsps (115g)
   whole wheat bread flour
⅓ cup (55g) sunflower seeds
1 tsp salt
1 × ¼-ounce (7g) fast-acting
   dried yeast
1⅓–1½ cups (about 350ml)
   warm water

To finish
a little milk, to glaze
a few rolled oats,
   to decorate

Measure the flaxseed and rolled oats into a bowl, pour over the boiling water, and mix. This can be done by hand or with an electric mixer. Allow to absorb for about 10 minutes and cool slightly.

———

Add all the remaining ingredients and mix to form a soft dough. Tip out onto a floured work surface and knead by hand for about 5 minutes, or in a stand mixer fitted with a dough hook. Put into an oiled bowl, cover with plastic wrap, and let rise in a warm place for about 1–1½ hours.

———

Punch down by hand for a few minutes, then divide and shape into 2 rounds.

———

Line a baking sheet with parchment paper. Place the rounds on the prepared sheet. Slip the sheet into a large plastic bag and let proof in a warm place for about 30 minutes or until doubled in size.

———

Preheat the oven to 425°F.

———

Brush the rounds with milk and scatter with oats. Bake for 20–25 minutes, or until golden brown and the loaves sound hollow when tapped on the bottom. Cool on a wire rack.

TIP
This can be made into one large loaf, but it will take a little longer to bake.

This generously fruited savory loaf with added walnuts is delicious with cheese.

WALNUT AND RAISIN LOAF

MAKES 1 LARGE OR 2 SMALLER LOAVES

1¾ cups (225g) bread flour, plus extra for dusting
1⅔ cups (225g) whole wheat bread flour
1 tsp salt
1 tbsp light muscovado sugar
1 tsp ground cinnamon
3 tbsps (40g) salted butter, melted
1¼ cups (300ml) warm water
1 × ¼-ounce (7g) packet fast-acting dried yeast
1 cup (115g) walnuts, finely chopped
¾ cup (115g) raisins

To glaze
1 extra-large egg, beaten

Measure the flours, salt, sugar, cinnamon, butter, water, and yeast into a bowl and mix together by hand or with an electric mixer fitted with a dough hook, until combined to make a fairly sticky dough.

———

Knead for 4–5 minutes on a lightly floured work surface or in the mixer, adding a little extra flour, if needed.

———

Transfer to a large oiled bowl, cover tightly with plastic wrap (make sure no air can escape), and let rise in a warm place for 1–1½ hours, or until the dough has doubled in size.

———

Tip the dough onto a lightly floured work surface and flatten the ball slightly. Add the chopped walnuts and raisins and knead into the dough. Shape into a long thick sausage shape about 4 x 16 inches or two smaller sausage shapes.

———

Line a baking sheet with parchment paper. Place the dough on the prepared sheet and slide into a large plastic bag, so the dough and baking sheet are completely covered. Seal the end of the bag. Let proof in a warm place for 35–45 minutes, or until doubled in size.

———

Preheat the oven to 425°F.

———

Brush the dough with the beaten egg and bake for 20–25 minutes (a little less for two smaller loaves), or until golden brown and the bread sounds hollow when tapped on the bottom. Cool on a wire rack.

Perfect with cheese or smoked salmon. Use a selection of different seeds,
such as pumpkin, sunflower, flax, and chia.

SEEDED NUT LOAF

MAKES 1 × 2-LB LOAF

4 extra-large eggs
3 tbsps olive oil
1 cup (115g) dried cranberries,
   finely chopped
1 tsp salt
¾ cup (115g) mixed seeds
1½ cups (150g) pistachios,
   chopped
⅔ cup (75g) walnuts,
   chopped
½ cup (75g) skin-on whole
   almonds, chopped

Preheat the oven to 350°F. Grease and line the bottom and sides of a 9 × 5-inch loaf pan with parchment paper.

—

Break the eggs into a large bowl and beat with a fork until combined. Add all the remaining ingredients and mix well.

—

Pour into the prepared pan and bake for 45–50 minutes until golden brown and firm in the center. Cool on a wire rack.

*Sourdough is a delicious crisp loaf and makes wonderful toast, too.
A starter dough is needed, and there are various ways to make a starter.
We have used a quick starter dough for home baking.*

QUICK SOURDOUGH LOAF

MAKES 1 STANDARD LOAF

For the starter
1¼ cups (125g) dark rye flour
1 cup (125g) bread flour
1 tsp fast-acting dried yeast
1¼ cups (300ml) slightly
   warm water

For the loaf
2¾ cups (350g) bread flour,
   plus extra for dusting
1 tsp fast-acting dried yeast
2 tsps salt
⅔ cup (150ml) slightly warm
   water

Mix all the starter ingredients together in a large bowl. Cover with plastic wrap and let rest at room temperature for 24 hours.

—

The next day, add the loaf ingredients to the starter and mix well to form a dough.

—

Tip the dough out onto a lightly floured work surface and knead for 10 minutes, adding a little more flour if it is very sticky.

—

Transfer to a large oiled bowl, cover tightly with plastic wrap, and let rise until doubled in size—this will take about an hour.

—

Tip the dough out onto a lightly floured work surface and gently shape into a round or oblong, whichever you prefer. Line a large baking sheet with parchment paper and dust with flour. Carefully transfer the dough onto the prepared baking sheet, cover with a tea towel, and let rise for another hour, or until doubled in size.

—

Preheat the oven to 425°F.

—

Dust the bread with a little flour and, using a sharp knife, slash a cross in the center (this will stop the loaf from bursting). Place the sheet in the oven along with a second lipped baking sheet on the shelf below. Drop 4–5 ice cubes into the lipped baking sheet (this will create steam and give the loaf a lovely crust), and bake for 30–35 minutes, or until the loaf sounds hollow when the underside is tapped. Cool on a wire rack.

Soda bread is quick and easy to make, as it uses no yeast, so it does not have to rise.

IRISH SODA BREAD

MAKES 1 STANDARD ROUND LOAF

3½ cups (450g) bread flour,
  plus extra for dusting
1 tsp baking soda
1 tsp salt
1 cup + 3 tbsps (300ml)
  buttermilk or ⅔ cup
  (150ml) milk and ½ cup
  (150ml) Greek yogurt,
  mixed
about 6 tbsps warm water

Preheat the oven to 400°F. Lightly grease a baking sheet.

—

Mix together the dry ingredients in a large bowl. Add the buttermilk (or milk and yogurt mixture) and enough warm water to form a very soft dough.

—

Turn the dough out onto a lightly floured work surface and shape into a neat round about 7 inches in diameter.

—

Place on the baking sheet and make a shallow cross in the top with a sharp knife. Bake for 30 minutes, then turn the bread upside-down and continue baking for 10–15 minutes, or until the bread sounds hollow when tapped on the bottom. Cool on a wire rack.

TIP
Rolled oats can be added to give the bread more texture. Simply replace ½ cup (55g) of the flour with the same quantity of oats. Soda bread is best eaten on the day of making.

This is a flat Italian bread with an exciting topping, perfect with soups and pâté.

FOCACCIA WITH ONION AND BALSAMIC TOPPING

MAKES 1 RECTANGULAR LOAF

3 cups + 3 tbsps (400g) bread flour
⅔ cup (115g) semolina
4 tbsps olive oil
1 tsp salt
1 × ¼-ounce (7g) fast-acting dried yeast
1¼ cups (300ml) warm water

For the onion and balsamic topping
1 tbsp olive oil
2 large onions, sliced
1½ tsps balsamic vinegar
1 tsp sugar
1 tsp fresh thyme leaves
salt and freshly ground black pepper

To finish
sea salt, for sprinkling

Measure all the ingredients for the bread into a bowl and mix by hand or with a stand mixer fitted with a dough hook until you have a fairly sticky, soft dough. Tip out onto a floured work surface and knead by hand for 4–5 minutes, adding a little extra flour if needed. Transfer to a large oiled bowl, cover tightly with plastic wrap (make sure no air can escape), and let rise in a warm place for 1–1½ hours, or until doubled in size.

While the dough is rising, make the topping. Heat the oil in a frying pan over high heat. Add the onions and fry for a few minutes. Cover with a lid, turn the heat down to low, and cook for about 20 minutes until the onions are soft.

Remove the lid and turn the heat up to drive off any excess water. Add the vinegar and sugar and fry until golden brown. Add the thyme and season with salt and freshly ground black pepper. Remove from the heat and set aside to cool.

Once the dough has risen, tip onto a lightly floured work surface and punch down, using your hands, for about 5 minutes. Roll out into a rectangle about 16 x 11 inches. Line a baking sheet with parchment paper and transfer the dough to the sheet. Spread the cold onion mixture over the dough and slide the baking sheet and dough into a large plastic bag. Seal the bag so no air can escape and let proof for about 30 minutes, or until doubled in size.

Preheat the oven to 425°F.

Remove the dough from the bag and bake for 20–25 minutes, or until golden on top and underneath. Cool on a wire rack. Sprinkle with sea salt to serve.

Naan breads are rustic, fluffy breads baked in the oven. They are easy to shape into different sizes and are good vehicles for different flavors.

GARLIC AND CILANTRO NAAN BREADS

MAKES 6 NAAN BREADS

2⅓ cups (300g) bread flour, plus extra for dusting

1 × ¼-ounce (7g) packet fast-acting dried yeast

2 tbsps (30g) salted butter, melted

1 tsp salt

2 garlic cloves, crushed

¾ cup + 3 tbsps (225ml) warm milk

1 small bunch of cilantro, finely chopped

olive oil, for brushing

Measure the flour, yeast, melted butter, and salt into a large bowl. Mix the garlic into the milk, then pour into the dry ingredients and mix well into a dough.

—

Tip out onto a lightly floured work surface and knead for 10 minutes until smooth.

—

Place in a large oiled bowl, cover, and let rise for 1½ hours, or until doubled in size.

—

Preheat the boiler to high and lightly grease a baking sheet.

—

Tip the dough out onto a lightly floured work surface. Add the cilantro and knead until smooth. Divide into 6 equal pieces. Using a rolling pin, roll each piece into a tear shape about the size of your hand.

—

Place three naans on the prepared sheet and brush the tops with oil. Broil for 2–4 minutes on each side until cooked and golden brown. Repeat with the remaining three naans.

The quickest of flatbreads, this is like a pizza base with herbs and garlic. The very best garlic bread for sharing!

HERB AND GARLIC FLATBREAD

MAKES 1 LARGE ROUND FLATBREAD

For the flatbread
1⅓ cups (175g) all-purpose
   flour, plus extra for dusting
2 tsps baking powder
½ tsp salt
1 extra-large egg
⅓ cup (70ml) milk

For the topping
½ cup (115g) salted butter,
   softened
1 large garlic clove, crushed
   to a paste (as with a
   microplane)
1 tbsp chopped parsley
1 tbsp snipped chives
1 tsp chopped thyme leaves
a pinch of sea salt

Preheat the oven to 400°F. Slide a baking sheet into the oven to get hot.

—

To make the flatbread, measure the flour and baking powder into a bowl. Add the salt. Combine the egg and milk in a small bowl and beat to mix. Pour into the flour and mix to form a soft dough.

—

Tip out onto a floured work surface and knead gently. Shape into a ball and place on a large piece of parchment paper. Using a rolling pin, roll out the dough to a large round measuring about 12 inches in diameter.

—

To make the topping, mix the butter, garlic, parsley, chives, thyme, and sea salt together in a bowl. Spread the herb butter over the dough base. Carefully transfer the flatbread, on the parchment paper, to the hot baking sheet and bake for about 12 minutes, until golden and crisp underneath.

—

Slice into wedges and serve at once.

CHAPTER THIRTEEN

FRUIT LOAVES

These can be made in advance as they keep very well and can also be frozen. Barley malt syrup is a thick consistency and can be bought in a jar.

GOLDEN RAISIN MALT LOAVES

MAKES 2 × 1-LB LOAVES

1¾ cups (225g) all-purpose flour
½ tsp baking soda
1 tsp baking powder
1½ cups (225g) golden raisins
¼ cup (55g) demerara sugar
½ cup (175g) barley malt syrup
1 tbsp molasses
2 extra-large eggs, beaten
½ cup + 2 tbsps (150ml) cold black tea

Preheat the oven to 300°F. Grease two 8½ x 4½-inch loaf pans, then line the bottom of each pan with parchment paper.

—

Measure the flour, baking soda, and baking powder into a bowl and stir in the golden raisins.

—

Gently heat the sugar, barley malt syrup, and molasses together. Pour onto the dry ingredients, along with the beaten eggs and the tea. Beat well until smooth.

—

Pour into the prepared pans and level the surfaces. Bake for about 1 hour or until well-risen and firm to the touch. Let cool in the pans for 10 minutes, then turn out, peel off the parchment paper, and finish cooling on a wire rack.

—

These loaves are best kept for 2 days before eating.

TIP
Freeze the loaves as soon as they are cold.

This tea cake has quite a pale color even when cooked, because of the thick pale honey used. It is a very good way of using up overripe bananas.

BANANA AND HONEY TEA CAKE

MAKES 1 × 2-LB LOAF

1¾ cups (225g) all-purpose
   flour
2½ tsps baking powder
½ tsp salt
¼ tsp freshly grated nutmeg
½ cup (115g) salted butter
2 medium (225g) bananas
½ cup + 1 tbsp (115g)
   granulated sugar
finely grated zest of 1 lemon
2 extra-large eggs
6 tbsps thick pale honey

For the topping
2 tbsps honey
nibbed sugar or crushed
   sugar cubes, for sprinkling

Preheat the oven to 325°F. Lightly grease a 9 x 5-inch loaf pan, then line the bottom with parchment paper.

Measure the flour, baking powder, salt, and nutmeg into a large bowl and rub the butter in using your fingertips until the mixture resembles fine breadcrumbs.

Peel and mash the bananas and stir into the flour mixture, along with the sugar, lemon zest, eggs, and honey. Beat well until evenly mixed.

Turn into the prepared pan and level the surface. Bake for about 1¼ hours or until a fine skewer inserted into the center comes out clean. Cover the tea cake loosely with foil during the end of the cooking time if it is browning too much. Let cool in the pan for a few minutes, then turn out, peel off the parchment paper, and finish cooling on a wire rack.

To make the topping, gently warm the honey in a small saucepan, then brush over the top of the cold tea cake. Sprinkle with the nibbed sugar.

Like any fruit loaf, this is easy to make. I've found this to be a popular choice at festivals and charity events, sold in slices or whole.

ICED APRICOT FRUIT LOAF

MAKES 1 × 2-LB LOAF

7 tbsps (75g) maraschino
  cherries, quartered
3 extra-large eggs
1⅓ cups (175g) all-purpose
  flour
2 tsps baking powder
½ tsp salt
½ cup (115g) salted butter,
  softened
½ cup + 2 tbsps (115g) light
  muscovado sugar
¾ cup + 3 tbsps (115g) dried
  apricots, chopped
1 cup (150g) golden raisins

For the icing
1 cup (115g) confectioners'
  sugar, sifted
1 tbsp apricot jam
1 tbsp water
2 dried apricots, chopped

Preheat the oven to 325°F. Lightly grease a 9 x 5-inch loaf pan, then line the bottom with parchment paper.

—

Place the cherries in a sieve and rinse under running water. Drain well, then dry thoroughly on a paper towel.

—

Break the eggs into a large bowl, then measure in the remaining loaf ingredients including the cherries. Beat well until the mixture is smooth.

—

Turn into the prepared pan and level the surface. Bake for about 1 hour 10 minutes or until the loaf is golden brown, firm to the touch, and shrinking away from the sides of the pan. A fine skewer inserted into the center of the loaf should come out clean. Let cool in the pan for 10 minutes, then turn out, peel off the parchment paper, and finish cooling on a wire rack.

—

To make the icing, measure the confectioners' sugar into a bowl. Heat the apricot jam and water together until the jam melts, then pour onto the confectioners' sugar. Mix to a smooth spreading consistency, then spoon over the top of the cold loaf. Decorate the loaf by sprinkling the chopped apricots down the center.

There are many versions of this traditional tea cake. In Welsh, "bara brith" means "speckled bread." Similar breads are made in different parts of Britain, such as Barm Brack in Ireland and Selkirk Bannock in Scotland.

BARA BRITH

MAKES 1 × 2-LB LOAF

1¼ cups (175g) currants
1¼ cups (175g) golden raisins
1 cup + 3 tbsps (225g) light
   muscovado sugar
1¼ cups (300ml) strong
   hot black tea
2¼ cups (275g) all-purpose
   flour
1 tbsp baking powder
½ tsp salt
1 extra-large egg, beaten

Measure the fruit and sugar into a bowl, pour over the hot tea, cover, and leave overnight.

—

Preheat the oven to 300°F. Lightly grease a 9 x 5-inch loaf pan, then line the bottom with parchment paper.

—

Stir the flour, baking powder, salt, and egg into the fruit mixture and mix thoroughly.

—

Turn into the prepared pan and level the surface. Bake for about 1½ hours or until well-risen and firm to the touch. A skewer inserted into the center should come out clean. Let cool in the pan for 10 minutes, then turn out, peel off the parchment paper, and finish cooling on a wire rack.

—

Serve sliced and buttered.

This is a lovely, moist loaf that really doesn't need to be buttered. It freezes very well. Any bananas left in the fruit bowl are ideal for this cake—the riper they are, the better.

BANANA LOAF

MAKES 1 × 2-LB LOAF

½ cup (115g) salted butter, softened
¾ cup + 2 tbsps (175g) sugar
2 extra-large eggs
2 ripe bananas, mashed
1¾ cups (225g) all-purpose flour
1 tbsp baking powder
½ tsp salt
2 tbsps milk

Preheat the oven to 350°F. Lightly grease a 9 x 5-inch loaf pan, then line the bottom and sides with parchment paper.

—

Measure all the ingredients into a mixing bowl and beat for about 2 minutes, until well-blended.

—

Spoon the mixture into the prepared pan and level the surface. Bake for about 1 hour, until well-risen and golden brown. A fine skewer inserted in the center should come out clean. Let cool in the pan for a few minutes, then turn out, peel off the parchment paper, and finish cooling on a wire rack.

—

Slice thickly to serve.

I've seen loaves similar to these for sale in Wycombe market. They may not look madly exciting, but they are very popular, and delicious.

CRUNCHY ORANGE SYRUP LOAVES

MAKES 2 × 1-LB LOAVES

½ cup (115g) salted butter, softened
1⅓ cups (175g) all-purpose flour
1 tbsp baking powder
½ tsp salt
¾ cup + 2 tbsps (175g) granulated sugar
2 extra-large eggs
4 tbsps milk
finely grated zest of 1 orange

For the topping
juice of 1 orange
1⅔ cups (115g) sanding sugar

Preheat the oven to 350°F. Lightly grease two 8½ x 4½-inch loaf pans, then line the bottom of each pan with parchment paper.

—

Measure all the loaf ingredients into a large bowl and beat well for about 2 minutes.

—

Divide the mixture evenly between the pans and level the surface of each. Bake for about 30 minutes or until the loaves spring back when the surface is lightly pressed.

—

While the loaves are baking, make the crunchy topping. Measure the orange juice and sugar into a small bowl and stir to mix. Spread the mixture over the baked loaves while they are still hot, then let cool completely in the pans. Turn out and remove the parchment paper once cold.

This tea cake freezes well. It's delicious spread with good butter, and I like coming across the walnuts in the cake—they create an interesting texture.

WALNUT AND CRANBERRY TEA CAKE

MAKES 1 × 2-LB LOAF

½ cup + 1 tbsp (115g) sugar
½ cup (175g) golden syrup or light corn syrup
¾ cup + 2 tbsps (200ml) milk
⅓ cup (55g) golden raisins
½ cup (55g) dried cranberries
1¾ cups (225g) all-purpose flour
1 tbsp baking powder
½ tsp salt
½ cup (55g) walnuts, roughly chopped
1 extra-large egg, beaten

Preheat the oven to 350°F. Lightly grease a 9 x 5-inch loaf pan, then line the bottom with parchment paper.

—

Measure the sugar, syrup, milk, golden raisins, and cranberries into a saucepan and heat gently until the sugar has dissolved. Set aside to cool.

—

Measure the flour, baking powder, and salt into a bowl and add the roughly chopped walnuts. Add the cooled syrup mixture to the dry ingredients along with the beaten egg and stir well until the mixture is smooth.

—

Pour into the prepared pan and level the surface. Bake for 1 hour, until firm to the touch and a skewer inserted into the center comes out clean. Cover the top of the tea cake loosely with foil toward the end of the cooking time if it is becoming too brown. Let cool in the pan for 10 minutes, then turn out, peel off the parchment paper, and finish cooling on a wire rack.

—

Serve buttered.

TIP
To break up walnuts, or pulverize cookies or cornflakes, put them in a strong plastic bag and crush with a rolling pin.

Expect this cake to have a sugary top, which is quite normal. Freeze one of the loaves and store the second one in the fridge. Serve sliced and buttered, or spread with low-fat cream cheese. Use small zucchinis, as they will not produce as much liquid as the large ones.

ZUCCHINI LOAVES

MAKES 2 × 2-LB LOAVES

3 extra-large eggs
1 cup (250ml) sunflower oil
1¾ cups (350g) sugar
2¾ cups (350g) small and thin zucchinis, grated
1⅓ cups (165g) all-purpose flour
1⅓ cups (165g) buckwheat flour
1 tsp baking powder
2 tsps baking soda
1 tbsp ground cinnamon
1 cup + 3 tbsps (175g) raisins
1¼ cups (150g) walnuts, chopped

Preheat the oven to 350°F. Grease two 9 x 5-inch loaf pans, then line the bottom of each pan with parchment paper.

—

Measure all the ingredients into a large bowl and mix well to make a thick batter.

—

Pour into the prepared pans. Bake for about 1 hour or until the loaves are firm and a skewer inserted into the center comes out clean. Let cool in the pan for 10 minutes, then turn out, peel off the parchment paper, and finish cooling on a wire rack.

—

Store in the fridge and use within 3 weeks.

A wonderful moist tea cake to serve buttered. The fruit is soaked in tea overnight. You can make two 1-lb loaves from this recipe instead of one large loaf, but shorten the cooking time to 30–40 minutes.

BORROWDALE TEA CAKE

MAKES 1 × 2-LB LOAF

¾ cup (115g) golden raisins
¾ cup (115g) currants
¾ cup (115g) raisins
2 cups (475ml) strong
    black tea
1 cup + 3 tbsps (225g) light
    muscovado sugar
2 extra-large eggs
4 cups (450g) whole wheat
    flour
2 tbsps baking powder
1 tsp salt

Put the golden raisins, currants, and raisins in a bowl along with the tea. Cover and let soak overnight.

—

Preheat the oven to 350°F. Grease a 9 x 5-inch loaf pan, then line the bottom with parchment paper.

—

Mix the sugar and eggs together until light and fluffy. Add the flour, baking powder, and salt along with the soaked fruits and any remaining liquid, and mix thoroughly together.

—

Spoon the mixture into the prepared loaf pan and level the surface. Bake for about 1 hour or until a skewer inserted into the center comes out clean. Let cool in the pan, then turn out and peel off the parchment paper.

—

Serve sliced and spread with butter.

*Don't overdo the marmalade or the fruit will sink to the bottom of the loaf.
Too much marmalade alters the sugar proportion of the recipe, loosening
the mixture, which causes the fruit to drop.*

MARMALADE LOAF

MAKES 1 LOAF

¼ cup (40g) maraschino
   cherries, quartered
½ cup (115g) salted butter,
   softened
½ cup + 1 tbsp (115g) sugar
¾ cup (115g) golden raisins
¾ cup (115g) currants
2 extra-large eggs
1⅓ cups (175g) all-purpose
   flour
2 tsps baking powder
½ tsp salt
1 rounded tbsp chunky
   marmalade

To finish
1 tbsp chunky marmalade, or
   a little sugar for sprinkling

Preheat the oven to 325°F. Grease a 9 x 5-inch loaf pan and line
the bottom with parchment paper.

—

Place the cherries in a sieve and rinse under running water.
Drain well, then dry thoroughly on a paper towel.

—

Measure all the remaining ingredients into a large bowl,
add the cherries, and mix well until blended.

—

Turn into the prepared pan and level the top. Bake for about
1½ hours or until a skewer inserted into the center of the loaf
comes out clean. Let cool in the pan for 10 minutes, then turn
out, peel off the parchment paper, and finish cooling on a wire
rack.

—

To finish, warm the marmalade in a small saucepan and then
spoon over the top of the loaf and let set. Or simply sprinkle
the top of the loaf with sugar before serving.

TIP
Store dried fruits in the freezer, well-wrapped, and use within 2 years.

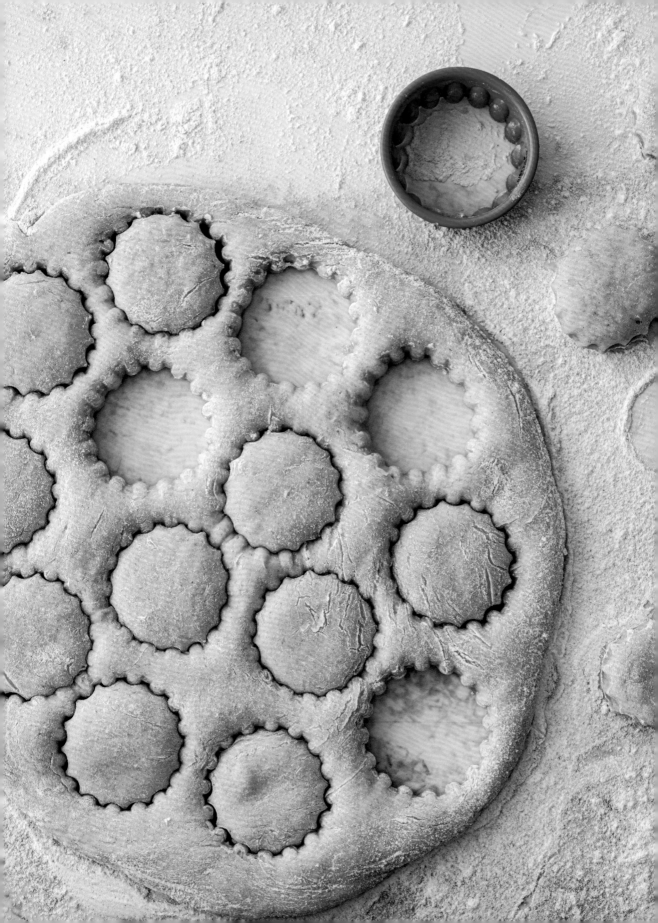

CHAPTER FOURTEEN

BUNS
AND
SCONES

The secret to making good scones is not to handle them too much before baking, and to make the mixture on the sticky side. Either eat the scones fresh or let them cool completely, then freeze them. Thaw them at room temperature and then refresh in a 350°F oven for about 10 minutes.

VERY BEST SCONES

MAKES 20 SCONES

3⅔ cups (450g) all-purpose flour, plus extra for dusting
2½ tbsps baking powder
1 tsp salt
⅓ cup (75g) salted butter, softened
¼ cup (55g) sugar
2 extra-large eggs
about 1 cup (225ml) milk

TIP

Make Whole Wheat Scones by using 4 cups (450g) whole wheat flour instead of all-purpose. You may need to add a little more liquid to make the dough.

You could make 8–10 large scones using a 3½-inch cookie cutter.

Preheat the oven to 425°F. Lightly grease two baking sheets.

Measure the flour, baking powder, and salt into a large bowl. Add the butter and rub it in with your fingertips until the mixture resembles fine breadcrumbs. Stir in the sugar.

Beat the eggs together in a liquid measuring cup and add milk until the mixture totals a generous 1¼ cups (300ml). Place about 2 tablespoons of the mixture aside in a cup for glazing the scones later. Gradually add the egg mixture to the dry ingredients, stirring until you have a soft dough. The scone mixture should be on the wet side, sticking to your fingers, as the scones will rise better this way.

Turn the dough onto a lightly floured surface and flatten it out with your hand or a rolling pin to a thickness of ½–¾ inch. Use a 2-inch fluted cookie cutter to stamp out the scones by pushing the cookie cutter straight down into the dough (as opposed to twisting it), then lifting it straight out. This will ensure that the scones rise evenly and keep their shape. Gently push the remaining dough together, knead lightly, then re-roll and cut more scones.

Arrange the scones on the prepared baking sheets and brush the tops with the reserved beaten egg mixture to glaze. Bake for 10–15 minutes, until well-risen and golden. Transfer to a wire rack and let cool, covered with a clean tea towel to keep them moist.

Serve cut in half and spread generously with strawberry jam. Top with a good spoonful of whipped cream, if you like.

Making good scones is so easy if the mixture is not too dry and the dough is not overhandled. Wrap them in a clean tea towel after baking to keep them moist.

SPECIAL FRUIT SCONES

MAKES 14 SCONES

1¾ cups (225g) all-purpose flour, plus extra for dusting
1 tbsp baking powder
½ tsp salt
¼ cup (55g) salted butter, softened
3 tbsps (30g) sugar
2 tbsps (20g) golden raisins
3 tbsps (20g) dried apricots, snipped into pieces
2 tbsps (15g) dried cranberries, roughly chopped
1 extra-large egg
a little milk

Preheat the oven to 425°F. Lightly grease two baking sheets.

Measure the flour, baking powder, and salt into a large bowl, add the butter, and rub it in with your fingertips until the mixture resembles fine breadcrumbs. Stir in the sugar and dried fruit.

Break the egg into a liquid measuring cup, then add milk until the mixture totals about ⅔ cup (150ml). Stir the egg and milk into the flour and mix to form a soft but not sticky dough.

Turn out onto a lightly floured work surface, knead lightly, and roll out to a ½-inch thickness. Cut into rounds with a fluted 2-inch cookie cutter and place them on the prepared baking sheets. Brush the tops with a little milk.

Bake for about 10 minutes or until pale golden brown. Lift the scones onto a wire rack to cool.

Eat as fresh as possible.

Serve these warm with cold meats, soup, or a cheeseboard—and with butter, of course!

CHEESE SCONE ROUND

SERVES 6

1¾ cup (225g) all-purpose flour, plus extra for dusting
1 tsp salt
½ tsp mustard powder
¼ tsp cayenne pepper
3½ tsps baking powder
2 tbsps (30g) salted butter, softened
1⅓ cups (150g) sharp Cheddar, grated
1 extra-large egg
a little milk

Preheat the oven to 425°F. Lightly grease a baking sheet.

—

Measure the flour, salt, mustard powder, cayenne pepper, and baking powder into a large bowl. Add the butter and rub it in with your fingertips until the mixture resembles fine breadcrumbs. Stir in 1 cup (115g) of the grated cheese.

—

Break the egg into a liquid measuring cup, then add milk until the mixture totals about ⅔ cup (150 ml). Stir the egg and milk into the dry ingredients and mix to form a soft but not sticky dough.

—

Turn out onto a lightly floured work surface and knead lightly. Roll out to a 6-inch circle and place on the prepared baking sheet.

—

Score into 6 wedges, then brush with a little milk. Sprinkle with the remaining grated cheese and bake for about 15 minutes, or until golden brown and firm to the touch. Slide onto a wire rack to cool.

—

Eat as fresh as possible.

Making one large scone is fastest of all, as you don't have to roll and cut out the mixture. If you don't have a baking pan, shape the dough into an oblong on a baking sheet.

GRUYÈRE AND OLIVE SCONE BAKE

MAKES 12 SQUARES

3⅔ cups (450g) all-purpose flour, plus extra for dusting
2½ tsps baking powder
2 tsps salt
½ cup (115g) salted butter, softened
1¾ cups (225g) plus ¼ cup (30g) grated Gruyère
¾ cup + 2 tbsps (115g) pitted black olives, roughly chopped
2 extra-large eggs
a little milk

Preheat the oven to 450°F. Lightly grease a 9 × 13-inch baking pan.

—

Measure the flour, baking powder, and salt into a large bowl. Add the butter and rub it in with your fingertips until the mixture resembles fine breadcrumbs. Stir in 200g (7oz) of the grated Gruyère and the roughly chopped olives.

—

Break the eggs into a liquid measuring cup and add milk until the mixture totals about 1¼ cups (300ml). Add to the flour mixture, mixing to form a soft dough.

—

Knead the dough quickly and lightly until smooth, then roll out on a lightly floured work surface to an oblong to fit the pan. Transfer to the prepared pan and score into 12 squares, then brush the top with a little milk.

—

Bake for about 15 minutes. Sprinkle the top with the remaining ¼ cup grated Gruyère and bake for an additional 5 minutes or until the scone is well-risen and golden. Turn out onto a wire rack to cool.

These scones are particularly moist, excellent if you want to keep them a day or two. They can be made sweet or savory: for savory potato scones, omit the sugar and add an additional ½ teaspoon of salt to the flour.

POTATO SCONES

MAKES 6 SCONES

1⅓ cups (175g) all-purpose flour, plus extra for dusting
4 tsps baking powder
½ tsp salt
¼ cup (55g) salted butter, softened
3 tbsps (40g) sugar
½ cup (115g) fresh mashed potato
1 egg, beaten

Preheat the oven to 425°F. Lightly grease two baking sheets.

Measure the flour, baking powder, and salt into a large bowl, add the butter, and rub it in with your fingertips until the mixture resembles fine breadcrumbs.

Stir in the sugar and mashed potato, mixing with a fork to prevent the potato from forming lumps. Add enough egg to form a soft but not sticky dough.

Turn the mixture out onto a lightly floured work surface and knead very lightly. Roll out to a thickness of about ¾ inch and cut into rounds using a 2¾-inch fluted cookie cutter (use a plain cookie cutter for savory scones).

Transfer to the prepared baking sheet and bake for 12–15 minutes, or until well-risen and golden brown.

Serve warm and buttered.

These are also known as drop scones. In the old days, they were made on a solid metal griddle over an open fire. Now it is more practical to use a large nonstick frying pan.

PANCAKES

MAKES ABOUT 24 PANCAKES

1⅓ cups (175g) all-purpose flour
1 tbsp baking powder
½ tsp salt
¼ cup (40g) sugar
1 extra-large egg
about ¾ cup + 2 tbsps (200ml) milk

Prepare a griddle or heavy-bottomed frying pan (preferably nonstick) by heating and greasing with oil or vegetable shortening.

—

Measure the flour, baking powder, salt, and sugar into a large bowl. Make a well in the center and add the egg and ½ cup (100ml) milk. Beat to form a smooth, thick batter, then beat in enough of the remaining milk to make the batter the consistency of thick cream.

—

Drop the mixture in spoonfuls onto the hot griddle or pan, spacing them well apart. When bubbles rise to the surface, turn the pancakes over with an offset spatula and cook on the other side for an additional 30 seconds–1 minute, until golden brown. Lift off onto a wire rack and cover them with a clean tea towel to keep them soft.

—

Cook the remaining mixture in the same way.

—

Serve warm with butter and golden syrup or maple syrup.

Serve as soon as they are made, with butter and syrup. If you do make them in advance and need to reheat them, arrange them in a single layer on an ovenproof plate, cover tightly with foil, and reheat in a 350°F oven for about 10 minutes.

ORANGE PANCAKES

MAKES ABOUT 24 PANCAKES

2 oranges
a little milk
1⅓ cups (175g) all-purpose
    flour
1 tbsp baking powder
½ tsp salt
¼ cup (40g) sugar
1 extra-large egg

Finely grate the zest from the oranges and set aside, and then squeeze the juice. Pour the juice into a liquid measuring cup and add milk until the mixture totals just over ¾ cup (200ml).

Measure the flour, baking powder, salt, sugar, and orange zest into a mixing bowl. Make a well in the center and add the egg and half the orange juice and milk mixture. Beat well to make a smooth, thick batter, then beat in enough of the remaining orange juice and milk to make the batter the consistency of thick cream.

Heat a large nonstick frying pan over a medium heat and grease with a little oil or vegetable shortening.

Drop the mixture in large spoonfuls onto the hot pan, spacing them well apart to allow the mixture to spread. When bubbles appear on the surface, turn the pancakes over with an offset spatula and cook on the other side for 30 seconds–1 minute, until golden brown. Transfer to a wire rack and cover with a clean tea towel.

Cook the remaining mixture in the same way.

Serve warm with butter and honey or maple syrup, and a little extra grated orange zest, if desired.

This Northumberland griddle cake "sings" or sizzles as it cooks on the griddle, hence its name. "Hinny" is northern slang for "honey," a term of endearment applied especially to children and young women. Traditionally the Singin' Hinny is made in one large round, but you can make two or three smaller ones in the same way.

SINGIN' HINNY

SERVES 4-6

2¾ cups (350g) all-purpose flour, plus extra for dusting
½ tsp baking soda
1 tsp cream of tartar
⅓ cup (75g) lard or vegetable shortening (not butter)
¾ cup (115g) currants
about ¾ cup + 2 tbsps (200ml) milk
butter, to serve

Prepare a griddle or large heavy-bottomed frying pan (preferably nonstick) by heating and lightly greasing it with oil or vegetable shortening.

—

Measure the flour, baking soda, and cream of tartar into a large bowl, add the lard or vegetable shortening, and rub it in with your fingertips until the mixture resembles fine breadcrumbs. Stir in the currants.

—

Gradually add the milk, mixing to form a soft but not sticky dough. Turn out onto a lightly floured work surface. Knead lightly, then roll out to a large round about ¼ inch thick.

—

Lift the scone round onto the prepared hot griddle and cook on a gentle heat for about 5 minutes on one side, then carefully turn over and cook on the other side for an additional 5 minutes or until both sides are a good brown.

—

Slide the Singin' Hinny onto a wire rack to cool slightly.

—

Split in half and butter, then sandwich back together and serve hot.

Make these with all-purpose or whole wheat flour and eat them really fresh spread with butter. If you use whole wheat flour, the mixture will need a little more milk. It is traditional to use baking soda and cream of tartar, but you can use 4½ teaspoons of baking powder and ½ teaspoon of salt instead.

GRIDDLE SCONES

MAKES 12 SCONES

1¾ cups (225g) all-purpose
   flour, plus extra for dusting
1 tsp baking soda
2 tsps cream of tartar
2 tbsps (30g) salted butter
3 tbsps (30g) sugar
about ⅔ cup (150ml) milk

Prepare a griddle or heavy-bottomed frying pan (preferably nonstick) by heating and lightly greasing with oil or vegetable shortening.

—

Measure the flour, baking soda, and cream of tartar into a large bowl. Add the butter and rub it in with your fingertips until the mixture resembles fine breadcrumbs. Stir in the sugar.

—

Gradually add the milk, mixing to form a soft but not sticky dough.

—

Divide the dough in half and knead each piece very lightly on a lightly floured work surface. Roll out each piece into a round about ½ inch thick, then cut each round into 6 equal wedges. Cook the wedges in batches on the prepared hot griddle for about 5 minutes on each side until evenly brown. Lift onto a wire rack to cool.

—

Eat as fresh as possible.

The spa town of Bath is famous for its buns, distinguished by the coarse sugar topping. They are said to have been created in the eighteenth century.

BATH BUNS
MAKES 12 BUNS

3½ cups (450g) bread flour,
    plus extra for dusting
1 × ¼-ounce (7g) packet
    fast-acting dried yeast
1 tsp salt
¼ cup (55g) sugar
¼ cup (55g) salted butter,
    melted and cooled
2 extra-large eggs, beaten
⅔ cup (150ml) tepid milk
1 cup + 3 tbsps (175g)
    golden raisins
¾ cup (55g) candied orange
    or lemon peel, chopped

To finish
1 extra-large egg, beaten, to
    glaze
nibbed sugar or coarsely
    crushed sugar cubes

Measure the flour, yeast, salt, and sugar into a large bowl and mix well.

———

Make a well in the center and pour in the melted and cooled butter, the eggs, and the milk. Add the golden raisins and chopped orange or lemon peel and mix to form a smooth, soft dough.

———

Turn the dough out onto a lightly floured work surface and knead for about 5 minutes or until smooth and elastic. Place in an oiled bowl and cover with oiled plastic wrap, or put the bowl inside a large plastic bag. Let rise until doubled in size, about 1 hour in a warm room.

———

Lightly grease two baking sheets.

———

Turn the risen dough out of the bowl and knead well until the dough is again smooth and elastic. Divide into 12 equal pieces. Shape each piece of dough into a bun and place on the prepared baking sheets. Cover again with oiled plastic wrap and let rest in a warm place until doubled in size, about 30 minutes.

———

Preheat the oven to 400°F.

———

Brush the buns with the beaten egg and sprinkle with nibbed sugar. Bake for about 15 minutes, or until golden brown and they sound hollow when the bottom is tapped. Lift onto a wire rack to cool.

———

Serve buttered.

For sweet cakes it is traditional to use a fluted cookie cutter, but you may find a plain cookie cutter easier for these, as it will cut through the fruit in the dough more easily.

WELSH CAKES

MAKES 10 CAKES

2¾ cups (350g) all-purpose flour, plus extra for dusting
2 tbsps baking powder
¾ tsp salt
¾ cup (175g) salted butter
½ cup + 1 tbsp (115g) sugar
¾ cup (115g) currants
¾ tsp pumpkin pie spice
1 extra-large egg
about 2 tbsps milk

To finish
sugar, for sprinkling

Prepare a griddle or heavy-bottomed frying pan by heating and lightly greasing with oil.

—

Measure the flour, baking powder, and salt into a large bowl and rub the butter in with your fingertips until the mixture resembles fine breadcrumbs. Add the sugar, currants, and spice.

—

Beat the egg with the milk, then pour into the flour mixture. Mix to form a firm dough, adding a little more milk if necessary.

—

Roll out the dough on a lightly floured work surface to a thickness of ¼ inch, then cut into rounds with a 3-inch plain round cookie cutter.

—

Cook the Welsh Cakes on the hot griddle over a low heat for about 3 minutes on each side, or until golden brown (be careful not to cook them too fast, otherwise the centers will not be fully cooked).

—

Cool on a wire rack, then sprinkle with sugar.

—

Eat on the day of making, and spread with butter, if desired.

These are very traditional English cakes, probably the first things most of us made at school. They're inexpensive, can be large or tiny, and need no special equipment. They are best eaten on the day of making.

ROCK CAKES

MAKES 12 CAKES

1¾ cups (225g) all-purpose
  flour
1½ tbsps baking powder
½ tsp salt
½ cup (115g) salted butter,
  softened
¼ cup (55g) granulated
  sugar
⅓ cup (55g) currants
½ cup (75g) golden raisins
⅓ cup (52g) dried apricots,
  chopped
1 extra-large egg
3 tbsps milk
a little demerara sugar,
  for sprinkling

Preheat the oven to 400°F. Lightly grease two baking sheets.

—

Measure the flour, baking powder, and salt into a large bowl. Add the butter and rub it in with your fingertips until the mixture resembles fine breadcrumbs. Stir in the sugar and dried fruit.

—

Beat the egg and milk together and add to the fruity mixture. If the mixture is too dry, add a little more milk.

—

Using 2 small spoons, shape the mixture into about 12 rough mounds on the prepared baking sheets. Sprinkle generously with demerara sugar. Bake for about 15 minutes, or until a pale golden brown at the edges. Cool on a wire rack.

TIP
Use whole wheat flour, if you like, although you may need a little more milk to mix.

These "upside-down" buns should be eaten very fresh, on the day of making. You need 12 mini brioche pans to give the buns their pretty shape, but you can make them plain using a 12-cup muffin pan, if you like.

COBURG BUNS

MAKES 12 BUNS

about ⅔ cup (55g) sliced almonds
1¼ cups (150g) all-purpose flour
2¾ tsps baking powder
½ tsp salt
½ tsp pumpkin pie spice
½ tsp ground ginger
½ tsp ground cinnamon
¼ cup (55g) salted butter, softened
¼ cup (55g) sugar
1 extra-large egg
1 tbsp golden syrup or light corn syrup
4 tbsps milk

Preheat the oven to 350°F. Lightly grease 12 mini brioche pans or use a 12-cup muffin pan.

—

Place a few almond slices in the bottom of each pan.

—

Measure all the ingredients into a large bowl and beat for about 2 minutes until the mixture is well-blended and smooth.

—

Divide the mixture between the pans and bake for about 15 minutes, until well-risen, golden, and firm to the touch. Let cool for a few minutes, then turn out so that the almond slices are on top, and finish cooling on a wire rack.

These used to be baked as one large bun, but now it is standard to have individual buns. For a more definite cross on the top of the buns, make shortcrust pastry (using ½ cup all-purpose flour and 2 tablespoons salted butter and a little water), cut it into thin strips, and lay it over the top of the buns before baking.

HOT CROSS BUNS

MAKES 12 BUNS

3½ cups (450g) bread flour, plus extra for dusting
1 tsp salt
1 tsp pumpkin pie spice
1 tsp ground cinnamon
½ tsp freshly grated nutmeg
1 × ¼-ounce (7g) packet fast-acting dried yeast
¼ cup (55g) granulated sugar
¼ cup (55g) salted butter, melted and cooled
⅔ cup (150ml) tepid milk
5 tbsps tepid water
1 extra-large egg, beaten
½ cup (75g) currants
¾ cup (55g) candied orange or lemon peel, chopped

To finish
55g (2oz) plain flour
2 tbsps granulated sugar

Lightly grease two baking sheets.

—

Measure the flour, salt, spices, yeast, and sugar into a large bowl and stir to mix.

—

Make a well in the center and pour in the melted and cooled butter, the milk, water, and egg. Add the currants and chopped orange or lemon peel and mix to form a soft dough.

—

Turn out onto a lightly floured work surface and knead for about 10 minutes until smooth and elastic. Transfer to an oiled bowl, cover with oiled plastic wrap, and let rise until the dough has doubled in size, about 1½ hours in a warm room. (Because this is an enriched dough, it will take longer to rise than a plain dough.)

—

Turn the risen dough out onto a lightly floured work surface again and knead for 2–3 minutes. Divide the dough into 12 equal pieces and shape each one into a round bun. Place onto the prepared baking sheets and cover with oiled plastic wrap. Let rise again in a warm place until doubled in size, about 30 minutes.

—

Preheat the oven to 425°F.

—

Mix the plain flour with 4 tablespoons of water to make a paste and pipe or drizzle over the buns to make the crosses. Bake for about 15 minutes, until brown and hollow-sounding when the bottom is tapped.

—

While the buns are baking, dissolve the granulated sugar in 2 tablespoons of water over a gentle heat. As soon as the buns come out of the oven, brush them with the syrup to create a sticky glaze.

CHAPTER FIFTEEN

HOT PUDDINGS
AND
PIES

One of my favorite desserts. I always decorate my sweet pies with lots of pastry leaves, so that they look more inviting.

CLASSIC APPLE PIE

SERVES 6

1½ pounds, about 2 large (675g) cooking apples, peeled, cored, and cut into thick slices
6 tbsps (75g) sugar
4 whole cloves
3 tbsps cold water

For the pastry
1⅓ cups (175g) all-purpose flour, plus extra for dusting
¼ cup (55g) salted butter, cubed
¼ cup (55g) vegetable shortening, cubed
milk, to glaze
granulated sugar, for sprinkling

TIP

You can freeze the pie after cooking and when completely cool. Allow to defrost almost completely before reheating and serving. Uncooked homemade pastry is an excellent standby for the freezer. Pack it in separate quantities of 8 ounces (225g) and 1 pound (450g), labeling it clearly. Defrost in the fridge or kitchen until pliable enough to roll and use.

Use a 9-inch pie dish.

Arrange half the apple slices in the bottom of the dish. Sprinkle with the sugar and arrange the cloves evenly among the apples. Cover with the remaining apple slices and add the cold water.

To make the pastry, measure the flour, butter, and vegetable shortening into a food processor. Whiz until breadcrumb stage. Add about 2 tablespoons cold water and whiz again until it comes together to form a stiff dough. Tip out onto a floured work surface and gently knead into a ball.

Roll out the dough on a lightly floured work surface to a size that will cover the top of the pie dish. Lift the dough onto the dish and trim the edges. If you like, cut the trimmings into decorative shapes and lightly press onto the dough. Chill in the fridge for 30 minutes.

Preheat the oven to 400°F.

Brush the pie with a little milk, then sprinkle the top with granulated sugar. Make a small slit in the center of the pie for the steam to escape. Bake for 40–45 minutes, until the apples are tender and the pastry is crisp and pale golden. Cover the pie loosely with foil toward the end of the cooking time if the pastry starts to brown before the apples are cooked.

Serve warm with whipped cream or ice cream.

A great family favorite as a pudding to follow a weekend lunch. You can use reduced-fat milk for a healthier pudding, or slices of brioche instead of sliced white bread to make it even richer! Use a rectangular dish, as the bread will fit better.

MY MOTHER'S BREAD
SERVES 6-8 **AND BUTTER PUDDING**

½ cup (115g) salted butter, melted

1¾ cups (250g) currants and golden raisins

6 tbsps (75g) granulated sugar

finely grated zest of 1 lemon

½ tsp pumpkin pie spice

about 8–12 thin slices white bread, crusts removed, and each cut into 3 strips

3 extra-large eggs

1¼ cups (300ml) milk

⅔ cup (150ml) heavy cream

2 tbsps demerara sugar, for sprinkling

Grease a 10 × 7-inch ovenproof baking dish with a little of the melted butter. Measure the dried fruit, granulated sugar, lemon zest, and spice into a bowl and toss to mix well.

Take enough bread strips to cover the bottom of the dish and dip one side of each strip in melted butter. Lay them in the prepared dish, buttered side down. Sprinkle with half the dried fruit mixture. Repeat the bread layer, placing the bread buttered side up, and sprinkle with the remaining dried fruit mixture. Place a third and final layer of bread strips on top, buttered side up.

Beat together the eggs, milk, and cream until combined. Pour over the pudding. Sprinkle with demerara sugar, then let rest for about 1 hour if time allows.

Preheat the oven to 350°F.

Bake for about 40 minutes, or until the top is golden brown and crisp and the pudding is slightly puffed up.

Serve hot with whipped cream, though there are some who insist that it is just as delicious cold!

TIP

You can prepare the pudding ahead of time and keep it covered in the fridge for up to 6 hours before baking. Don't sprinkle over the demerara sugar topping until 1 hour before you are ready to bake.

Something like the old-fashioned Eve's pudding, but this one includes its own creamy lemon sauce. If buying lemon curd, check that it contains butter, sugar, and lemons. It may be labeled lemon cheese or luxury lemon curd.

BAKED APPLE LEMON SPONGE
SERVES 6-8

For the base
1¼ cups (300ml) half-and-half
6 tbsps lemon curd
2 tbsps granulated sugar
1 heaped tsp all-purpose flour
1¾ pounds, about 3–4 medium (750g) cooking apples, peeled, cored, and very thinly sliced

For the topping
2 extra-large eggs
1⅓ cups (175g) all-purpose flour
½ cup + 1 tbsp (115g) granulated sugar
½ cup (115g) salted butter, softened
1 tbsp baking powder
½ tsp salt
2 tbsps milk
1–1½ tbsps demerara sugar

Preheat the oven to 325°F. Place a heavy baking sheet to heat in the oven. You will need a 10 × 7-inch ovenproof baking dish.

To prepare the base, measure the half-and-half, lemon curd, sugar, and flour into a bowl and beat until smooth. Mix the sliced apples into the cream mixture, then spoon into the baking dish and level with the back of a spoon.

To make the topping, measure all the ingredients except the demerara sugar into a mixing bowl. Beat until smooth, then spread gently over the fruit in the baking dish.

Sprinkle with demerara sugar. Bake on the hot baking sheet for about 30 minutes, or until perfect golden brown.

Cover the pudding with foil, then continue to bake for an additional 45 minutes or until the sponge springs back when lightly pressed in the center with a fingertip.

Serve warm with whipped cream or crème fraîche.

TIPS
The unbaked pudding can be kept covered in the fridge for up to 6 hours. Bring it up to room temperature before baking in the oven on the hot baking sheet.

I find it easiest to use a mandoline slicer for the apples, or the thin slicing disc in the food processor.

A great family favorite for a cold winter's day.

TREACLE SPONGES

MAKES 4 INDIVIDUAL SPONGES

8 tbsps golden syrup or light corn syrup, plus extra to serve
1 tbsp fresh lemon juice
finely grated zest of 1 lemon
½ cup (115g) salted butter, softened
½ cup + 1 tbsp (115g) sugar
2 extra-large eggs
1 cup (115g) all-purpose flour
2½ tsps baking powder
¼ tsp salt

Grease four 6-ounce heatproof pudding bowls and line the bottom of each one with a square of nonstick parchment paper.

Mix the syrup with the lemon juice and divide between the pudding bowls.

Measure all the remaining ingredients into a mixing bowl and beat well for 2 minutes or until well-blended.

Divide the mixture between the bowls and smooth the tops. Cover each basin with a pleated lid of parchment paper and then foil, to allow for the steam and expanding pudding.

Steam in a steamer, or place in a large saucepan with enough boiling water to come halfway up each bowl, for about 45 minutes (see Tip).

Turn out and serve with warm golden syrup or honey.

TIP

Keep the water boiling in the saucepan, topping up when needed with more boiling water. Stand the pudding bowls on an old, heatproof upturned teacup saucer to keep them off the saucepan's bottom.

This is a very adaptable recipe and one of my family's favorites. You can use a variety of different fruits, either fresh or canned. It's a good dessert to serve for Sunday lunch. Just place the pudding on the top oven shelf, above the roast, and let it cook there. It couldn't be easier.

STICKY APRICOT PUDDING

SERVES 6-8

1⅓ cups (175g) all-purpose flour
1 tbsp baking powder
½ tsp salt
¼ cup (55g) granulated sugar
¼ cup (55g) salted butter, softened
1 extra-large egg
finely grated zest of 1 lemon
⅔ cup (150ml) milk
1 × 15-ounce (410g) can apricot halves (or other canned fruit), drained

For the topping
¼ cup (55g) salted butter, melted
¼ cup (55g) demerara sugar

Preheat the oven to 450°F. Grease an 11 x 8-inch ovenproof baking dish.

—

Measure the flour, baking powder, salt, sugar, butter, egg, lemon zest, and milk in a large bowl. Beat together until the mixture forms a soft, cake batter consistency.

—

Spread the mixture into the prepared baking dish and arrange the apricots, cut side down, over the top.

—

Brush or drizzle the melted butter for the topping over the apricots, then sprinkle with the demerara sugar.

—

Bake for about 35 minutes, or until the top has caramelized to a deep golden brown.

—

Serve warm, with crème fraîche, whipped cream, or ice cream.

TIP
You can replace the apricots with whatever fruit you have on hand. Both sliced dessert and cooking apples work well. Arrange the apple slices evenly over the top of the sponge mixture. Other good alternatives are rhubarb and plums. Cut the plums in half and remove the stones, then arrange them cut side down.

This baked creamy "custard" tastes like sheer luxury but is not difficult to make. Choose a shallow dish or individual dishes that will withstand being put under the broiler, and be careful not to overcook the mixture, or it will form bubbles. Use the leftover egg whites to make a meringue dessert (see pages 362–74).

CRÈME BRÛLÉE
SERVES 6–8

4 extra-large egg yolks
3 tbsps (30g) granulated
    sugar
a few drops of vanilla extract
1¼ cups (300ml) half-and-half
1¼ cups (300ml) heavy cream
about ¼ cup (55g)
    demerara sugar

TIP
You could replace the granulated sugar and vanilla extract with vanilla sugar. Simply store two or three vanilla pods in a jar of granulated sugar. After about two weeks, the sugar is imbued with the fragrance of the vanilla.

Preheat the oven to 325°F. Grease an 18-ounce (1½ pint) shallow ovenproof dish or 6–8 small ramekins.

—

Beat the egg yolks with the granulated sugar and vanilla extract.

—

Heat the creams to scalding (just too hot to put your finger in!), let cool slightly, then pour into the egg yolks in a steady stream, beating all the time.

—

Pour into the dish or ramekins. Stand the dish or ramekins in a roasting pan half-filled with hot water. Bake for 45 minutes (for the single dish) or about 25–30 minutes (for the ramekins), or until set.

—

Remove from the oven and let cool. Cover, then chill in the fridge overnight. These can be made 2 days ahead.

—

Preheat the broiler to hot.

—

Sprinkle the top of the custard with the demerara sugar to about a ¼-inch thickness and place under the broiler, on a high shelf, until the sugar melts then caramelizes to a golden brown. This takes 3–4 minutes. Keep a careful watch to make sure the sugar does not burn. Alternatively, use a cook's blowtorch to caramelize the sugar.

—

Let cool, then chill for 2–3 hours before serving. Chilling again after caramelizing the sugar gives time for the hard topping to become slightly less hard, easier to crack and serve. If you let it chill considerably longer, the caramel will melt and soften, which is not nearly so attractive and does not taste as good.

The combination of toffee, bananas, and cream makes this one of the most popular desserts around. Make sure you use a nonstick pan for the toffee and watch it very closely as you are making it, as it can burn easily.

BANOFFEE PIE

SERVES 6

For the crust
1¼ cups (175g) graham crackers
¼ cup (65g) salted butter

For the toffee filling
½ cup (115g) salted butter
½ cup + 2 tbsps (115g) light muscovado sugar
2 × 14-ounce (397g) cans full-fat condensed milk

For the topping
3 bananas, sliced
a little fresh lemon juice
1¼ cups (300ml) heavy cream
a little grated Belgian milk or dark chocolate, for sprinkling

You will need a 9-inch springform pan.

To make the crust, put the graham crackers into a plastic bag and crush them to crumbs with a rolling pin. Melt the butter in a small saucepan, remove from the heat, and stir in the crushed graham crackers. Mix well.

Spread the mixture over the bottom and sides of the pan. Press the mixture with the back of a metal spoon.

To make the toffee filling, measure the butter and sugar into a large nonstick pan. Heat gently until the butter has melted and the sugar has dissolved. Add the condensed milk and stir continuously and evenly with a flat-ended wooden spoon for about 5 minutes, or until the mixture is thick and has turned a golden toffee color—take care, as it burns easily. Turn it into the prepared graham cracker crust and let cool and set.

To make the topping, toss the bananas in lemon juice and arrange the slices over the toffee in a neat layer. Lightly whip the heavy cream until it has soft peaks and spread evenly over the bananas. Sprinkle the whole pie with grated chocolate.

Remove the sides of the springform pan and transfer to a flat plate.

Serve well-chilled.

TIP
Most condensed milk cans now have ring pulls, so the old method of simmering the can in a pan of water for 4 hours to caramelize the condensed milk is not advised.

This is an all-American creation that is delicious served with coffee, or as a dessert served with whipped cream or ice cream.

PECAN PIE

SERVES 6

For the rich shortcrust pastry
1⅓ cups (175g) all-purpose flour, plus extra for dusting
2 tbsps (15g) confectioners' sugar
⅓ cup (75g) salted butter, cubed
1 extra-large egg yolk
about 1 tbsp cold water

For the filling
2 tbsps (30g) salted butter, softened
¾ cup + 3 tbsps (175g) light muscovado sugar
3 extra-large eggs
⅔ cup (200ml) maple syrup
1 tsp vanilla extract
1½ cups (150g) pecan halves

You will need a 9-inch fluted tart pan with a removable bottom.

To make the pastry, measure the flour, confectioners' sugar, and butter into a food processor and whiz until the mixture resembles fine breadcrumbs. Add the egg yolk and water and whiz again until it comes together to form a firm dough. Wrap in plastic wrap and let rest in the fridge for about 30 minutes.

Preheat the oven to 400°F.

Roll out the dough onto a lightly floured work surface and use to line the tart pan. Prick the pastry all over with a fork, line parchment paper or foil, and fill with pie weights. Blind-bake for about 15 minutes.

Remove the pie weights and parchment paper and return the crust to the oven for 5 minutes or until it is pale golden and dried out.

Remove from the oven and lower the temperature to 350°F.

To make the filling, beat the butter with the sugar. Add the eggs, maple syrup, and vanilla extract and beat well.

Place the pie pan on a baking sheet and layer the pecan halves flat side down over the pastry base. Pour in the filling. Bake at the lowered temperature for 30–35 minutes until set. The filling will rise up in the oven but will fall back once it's cooling. Let cool slightly.

Serve warm with whipped cream or ice cream.

CHAPTER SIXTEEN

SOUFFLÉS
AND
MERINGUES

Meringues are easily broken, so store them in a rigid airtight container or plastic container, with a paper towel in between them. If you use turbinado sugar, expect darker meringues, but they will taste just as good!

BASIC WHITE MERINGUES

MAKES 18 MERINGUES

3 extra-large egg whites
¾ cup + 2 tbsps (175g)
    granulated sugar

For the filling
1¼ cups (300ml) heavy
    cream, whipped
confectioners' sugar, for
    dusting (optional)

Preheat the oven to 250°F. Line two baking sheets with parchment paper.

Place the egg whites in a large bowl and whisk until stiff but not dry. Add the sugar, a small spoonful at a time, whisking well after each addition, until all the sugar has been added. The meringue should be stiff and glossy.

Fit a ½-inch plain nozzle into a large nylon piping bag and stand, nozzle down, in a large liquid measuring cup. Spoon the meringue into the bag. Squeeze the meringue mixture toward the nozzle and twist the top of the piping bag to seal. Pipe the meringue into 18 "shells" 2 inches in diameter on the prepared baking sheets. Alternatively, use 2 large spoons to shape the mixture into 18 mini meringues.

Bake for about 1–1½ hours, or until they are a creamy color and can be lifted easily from the parchment paper without sticking. Turn off the oven, leave the door ajar, and let the meringues rest until cold.

Serve them sandwiched with whipped cream and dusted with confectioners' sugar, if desired.

To make Brown Sugar Meringues, follow the recipe above but instead of ¾ cup + 2 tbsps (175g) granulated sugar use half light muscovado sugar and half granulated sugar.

A favorite for all ages. Traditionally the inside of the meringue is soft and marshmallow-like and the outside is crisp. Don't worry if the pavlova cracks on the top—this is all part of its charm.

MANGO AND PASSION FRUIT PAVLOVA

SERVES 8

4 extra-large egg whites
1 cup + 2 tbsps (225g) sugar
2 tsps cornstarch
2 tsps white wine vinegar

For the filling
4 tbsps lemon curd
2 mangoes, sliced into
 thin strips
4 passion fruit, halved
 and pulp and seeds
 scooped out
1¼ cups (300ml) heavy
 cream, whipped

Preheat the oven to 325°F. Place a sheet of parchment paper on a baking sheet and mark a 9-inch circle on it.

Place the egg whites in a large bowl and whisk until stiff and cloud-like. Add the sugar one small spoonful at a time, whisking well after each addition, until all the sugar has been added.

Blend the cornstarch and vinegar together and whisk into the meringue mixture.

Spread the meringue out to cover the circle on the parchment paper, building up the sides so they are higher than the middle. Place in the oven but immediately lower the temperature to 300°F. Bake for about 1 hour until firm to the touch and a pale beige color.

Turn the oven off and allow the pavlova to cool while still in the oven. If you keep the oven door closed you will encourage a more marshmallowy meringue.

Remove the cool pavlova from the baking sheet and parchment paper and slide onto a serving plate.

Stir the lemon curd and half the fruit in with the whipped cream and spread into the center of the meringue. Top with the remaining mango slices and passion fruit, then chill in the fridge for 1 hour before serving.

This is rather an unusual idea, and it makes a generous roulade, an excellent size for a party. It also freezes extremely well. Simply wrap it in foil to freeze, then allow about 8 hours to thaw before serving.

RASPBERRY MERINGUE ROULADE

SERVES 8-10

5 extra-large egg whites
1 cup + 6 tbsps (275g) sugar
⅔ cup (55g) sliced almonds

For the filling
1¼ cups (300ml) heavy
    cream
3 cups (350g) raspberries

Preheat the oven to 425°F. Line a 9 × 13-inch baking pan with parchment paper.

Place the egg whites in a large bowl and whisk until very stiff. Gradually add the sugar, one small spoonful at a time, whisking well between each addition. Whisk until very, very stiff and all the sugar has been added.

Spread the meringue mixture into the prepared pan and sprinkle with the almonds. Place the pan fairly near the top of the oven and bake for about 8 minutes until pale golden. Lower the oven temperature to 325°F and bake for an additional 15 minutes until firm to the touch.

Remove the meringue from the oven and turn it almond side down onto a sheet of parchment paper. Remove the paper from the bottom of the cooked meringue and allow to cool for about 10 minutes.

Meanwhile, whisk the cream until it stands in stiff peaks, and gently mix in the raspberries. Spread the cream and raspberries evenly over the meringue.

Start to roll the meringue from a long end fairly tightly until rolled up like a roulade. Wrap in parchment paper and chill before serving.

TIP
Leftover egg yolks should be stored in the fridge in a small container. Pour a tablespoon of cold water over the top, and then cover with plastic wrap. Use within a week.

This has become a classic, the raspberries and hazelnuts being a particularly good combination. Fill the meringue about 3 hours before serving; it will then cut into portions without splintering.

HAZELNUT MERINGUE CAKE

SERVES 6-8

1 cup (140g) hazelnuts
4 extra-large egg whites
1¼ cups (250g) granulated
   sugar
a few drops of vanilla extract
½ tsp white wine vinegar

For the filling
1¼ cups (300ml) heavy
   cream
1¾ cups + 2 tbsps (225g)
   raspberries
confectioners' sugar, for
   dusting

TIPS

If you don't have round cake pans, you can cook the mixture on two flat baking sheets, spread out into two circles. It won't look quite so neat, but it tastes the same! Walnuts can be used in place of the hazelnuts in the meringue. Choose a fruit to complement the walnuts, such as strawberries or ripe peaches in season.

Preheat the oven to 375°F. Lightly brush two 8-inch round cake pans with oil, then line the bottom of each pan with parchment paper.

Place the hazelnuts on a baking sheet and roast in the oven for about 10 minutes, then tip onto a clean tea towel and rub well together to remove the skins. (Some stubborn ones may need to go back into the oven but don't worry about getting every last bit of skin off, it's not necessary.) Grind the nuts in a food processor.

Place the egg whites in a large bowl and whisk until stiff. Add the sugar, one small spoonful at a time, whisking well between each addition. Whisk until the mixture is very stiff, stands in peaks, and all the sugar has been added.

Whisk in the vanilla extract and wine vinegar, then fold in the prepared nuts. Divide the mixture between the prepared pans and smooth the top with an offset spatula.

Bake for 30–40 minutes, but no longer. The top of the meringue will be crisp and the inside soft and marshmallow-like. Turn out of the pans and let cool on a wire rack.

Whip the cream until thick and use about two-thirds to sandwich the meringues together along with two-thirds of the raspberries. Spread the remaining cream over the top, scatter on the remaining raspberries, and dust with confectioners' sugar.

Ordinary meringue could be used for these nests, but they won't be quite so firm, nor will they store so well. Meringue cuite is traditional because it holds its shape so well and is drier. Vary the fruit in these nests depending on the season.

SUMMER FRUIT MERINGUE NESTS

MAKES 6 NESTS

For the meringue cuite
4 extra-large egg whites
1¾ cups (225g) confectioners' sugar
a few drops of vanilla extract (optional)

For the filling
¾ cup (115g) strawberries, halved if large
1 cup (115g) raspberries
⅔ cup (115g) blueberries
about 2 tbsps red currant jelly

TIP
To fill a piping bag, stand the bag and nozzle point down in a liquid measuring cup and then fold the top edges of the bag over the top of the liquid measuring cup. That way it is much easier to spoon the meringue (or cream or frosting) into the bag without getting it all over yourself!

Preheat the oven to 275°F. Line a baking sheet with parchment paper.

Place the egg whites in a large bowl and whisk until foaming. Sift the confectioners' sugar through a fine sieve into the egg whites. Set the bowl over a saucepan of gently simmering water and whisk the whites and sugar together until very thick and holding its shape. Add the vanilla extract, if using, and whisk again to mix. Be careful not to let the bowl get too hot or the meringue mixture will crust around the edges.

Spoon the mixture into a piping bag fitted with a large star nozzle. Pipe into 6 basket shapes on the prepared baking sheet, starting at the center of each nest and lastly building up the sides.

Bake for about 45 minutes until crisp and dry. Carefully lift off the baking sheet and allow to cool on a wire rack.

Use the summer fruits to fill the cold "nests."

Warm the red currant jelly in a small saucepan and gently spoon over the fruit to glaze.

To make Baby Meringues, follow the ingredients and recipe above, then pipe the mixture into 30 tiny shapes such as baskets, shells, spiral oblongs, and fingers. Bake until crisp and dry, then carefully lift off the baking sheets onto a wire rack to cool.

To make different fillings, whip 1¼ cups (300ml) heavy cream with 1 tbsp brandy or liqueur of your choice until it holds its shape. Divide between 2 bowls. Stir ¼ cup (30g) chopped nuts into one bowl, and leave the other cream plain. Sandwich the spiral oblongs and tiny shells together with the nutty cream mixture, pipe a little plain cream into the baskets, and use it to sandwich the fingers together. Top the baskets and the sandwiched fingers with a small single piece of fruit, if you like. These are perfect for a party; the different shapes and fillings make a wonderful centerpiece for the dessert table.

Lemon meringue pie is a classic popular dessert, with a crisp pastry crust and sharp lemon filling. The meringue topping adds sweetness and crunch.

LEMON MERINGUE PIE

SERVES 6-8

For the pastry
1⅓ cups (175g) all-purpose
   flour, plus extra for dusting
2 tbsps confectioners' sugar
⅓ cup (75g) salted butter,
   cubed
1 extra-large egg, beaten

For the filling
¼ cup (30g) cornstarch
¾ cup (200ml) water
finely grated zest and juice
   of 2 lemons
¼ cup (55g) granulated
   sugar
3 extra-large egg yolks

For the topping
3 extra-large egg whites
¾ cup + 2 tbsps (175g)
   granulated sugar

TIP
You can make a cheat's version of the lemon filling by pouring one 14-ounce (397g) can of condensed milk into a bowl, then beating in 3 extra-large egg yolks and the finely grated zest and strained juice of 3 lemons. The mixture will seem to thicken on standing, then loosen again as soon as it is stirred. This is caused by the combination of condensed milk and lemon juice and is nothing to worry about. Pour the mixture into the pastry-lined dish.

You will need a 9-inch round cake pan.

To make the pastry, measure the flour and confectioners' sugar into a food processor. Add the butter and whiz until the mixture resembles fine breadcrumbs. Add the egg and mix to a firm dough.

Roll out the dough on a lightly floured work surface and use parchment paper to line the bottom and sides of the dish. Prick the pastry all over with a fork and chill in the fridge for 30 minutes.

Preheat the oven to 400°F. Line the pastry crust with parchment paper, add pie weights, and blind-bake for about 15 minutes. Remove the weights and paper and return to the oven for an additional 5 minutes until the pastry is lightly golden. Let cool.

Reduce the oven temperature to 300°F.

Measure the cornstarch and ¾ cup (200ml) water into a saucepan and whisk to combine. Add the lemon zest and juice and place the saucepan over a medium heat. Whisk continuously until the mixture has boiled and thickened. Remove from the heat, add the granulated sugar and yolks, and whisk again. Pour into the pastry crust.

To make the topping, place the egg whites in a large bowl and whisk until stiff. Gradually add the sugar, one small spoonful at a time, whisking well between each addition, until shiny and glossy. Spoon into a piping bag and pipe blobs over the surface in a neat pattern or use two large spoons. Bake for 35–40 minutes until pale golden on top and firm to the touch. Let cool for about 15 minutes before removing from the pan.

Serve slightly warm with whipped cream.

A vacherin meringue, which is rather grand, is piped in a spiral pattern.

GINGER AND PEAR VACHERIN

SERVES 6-8

4 extra-large egg whites
1 cup + 2 tbsps (225g)
    granulated sugar

For the filling
1¾ cups + 2 tbsps (450ml)
    heavy cream
1 x 15-ounce (410g) can
    pears in natural juice,
    drained and cut
    into long thin strips
¾ cup finely chopped
    crystallized ginger
2 ounces (55g) dark
    chocolate, melted
confectioners' sugar, for
    dusting

Preheat the oven to 300°F. Line three baking sheets with parchment paper and mark each with an 8-inch circle.

Place the egg whites in a large bowl and whisk until stiff. Add the sugar, one small spoonful at a time, whisking well between each addition, until the mixture is very stiff, stands in peaks, and all the sugar has been added.

Spoon the meringue mixture into a large piping bag fitted with a ½-inch plain nozzle, and pipe the meringue to fill the circles on the parchment paper; pipe in circles in a spiral pattern, starting at the center.

Bake for 1–1¼ hours, or until the meringues are crisp and dry and lightly colored. Allow to cool in the oven and then peel off the parchment paper.

Place the cream in a large bowl and lightly whip. Spoon a third into a small bowl (this is for the top layer). Spread half of the remaining cream over one round. Top with half of the pears and ginger. Place the second round on top and spread with the remaining cream. Top with the remaining pears and ginger. Place the final round on top and gently press down. Spread the reserved cream on top and swirl.

Drizzle with the melted chocolate and sprinkle with confectioners' sugar to serve.

TIP
You can make the meringue circles the day before, but don't keep the filled cake for too long.

This is impressive to serve but surprisingly easy to make.

BAKED ALASKA WITH
SERVES 6-8 **ITALIAN MERINGUE**

For the sponge base
2 extra-large eggs
6 tbsps (75g) granulated
    sugar
½ cup (55g) all-purpose
    flour
¾ tsp baking powder
¼ tsp salt

For the filling
1 tbsp sherry (optional)
1½ cups (225g) strawberries
1¾ pints (1 liter) strawberry
    ice cream

For the Italian meringue
1 cup + 2 tbsps (225g)
    granulated sugar
4 extra-large egg whites
⅔ cup (55g) sliced almonds,
    for sprinkling
confectioners' sugar, to
    serve (optional)

Preheat the oven to 375°F. Lightly grease a 9-inch round cake pan and line the bottom with parchment paper.

To make the sponge, measure the eggs and sugar into a large bowl and beat with an electric mixer until the mixture is pale and thick enough to just leave a trail when the whisk is lifted. Sift the flour, baking powder, and salt over the surface and gently fold in with a metal spoon. Turn into the prepared pan and tilt the pan to allow the mixture to spread evenly to the sides. Bake for 20–25 minutes, until springy to the touch and beginning to shrink from the sides of the pan. Turn out and let cool on a wire rack.

Place the cold sponge on an ovenproof serving dish, sprinkle with the sherry, if using, then scatter with the strawberries, leaving a small gap around the edge. Slice the ice cream and arrange it in a dome shape over the strawberries. Place in the freezer.

Preheat the oven to 450°F.

To make the Italian meringue, measure the sugar into a stainless steel saucepan. Add 6 tablespoons of water and stir over a low heat until the granules have dissolved. Increase the heat and boil until the syrup reaches 248°F on a sugar thermometer. Remove from the heat and set aside. Place the egg whites in a stand mixer and whisk at full speed until stiff. Slowly pour in the syrup, whisking all the time, until thick and glossy.

Take the cake from the freezer and pile the meringue over the top and sides, making sure that it is all covered. Sprinkle over the almonds and bake for 3–4 minutes, or until well-browned. Dust with confectioners' sugar, if using, and serve immediately.

Soufflés like this are not difficult to make, but need a bit of care with the timing.

HOT CHOCOLATE SOUFFLÉS

SERVES 4

4 ounces (115g) dark
 chocolate, broken into
 pieces
1¼ cups (300ml) milk
3 tbsps (40g) salted butter
⅓ cup (40g) all-purpose
 flour
¼ tsp vanilla extract
4 extra-large eggs, separated
¼ cup (55g) granulated
 sugar
sifted confectioners' sugar,
 for dusting

TIP

If you are serving a soufflé
for a dinner party, make
the sauce base ahead of
time, including the addition
of the yolks and flavoring.
Fold in the whisked egg
whites 40 minutes
before baking.

To make Orange Soufflés,
omit the chocolate and
water and add the finely
grated zest of 2 small
oranges and the juice of
½ orange to the mixture.
Also omit the vanilla extract
and increase the granulated
sugar to 6 tbsps (75g).

To make Coffee Soufflés,
omit the chocolate and
water and add 2 tbsps strong
coffee to the milk; omit the
vanilla extract.

Preheat the oven to 375°F and place a baking sheet inside to heat. Grease four 8-ounce individual soufflé dishes or a 2-quart soufflé dish.

Place the chocolate in a saucepan with 2 tablespoons water and 2 tablespoons of the milk. Stir over a low heat until the chocolate has melted.

Add the remaining milk and bring to a boil. Remove the saucepan from the heat.

Melt the butter in a small saucepan, stir in the flour, and cook over a low heat for 2 minutes without browning, stirring continuously. Remove from the heat and stir in the hot chocolate milk. Return to the heat and bring to a boil, stirring until thickened. Add the vanilla extract and let cool.

Beat the egg yolks, one at a time, into the cooled chocolate sauce, then sprinkle in the sugar.

Place the egg whites in a large bowl and whisk until they are stiff but not dry. Stir 1 tablespoon into the mixture, then carefully fold in the remainder.

Pour into the individual soufflé dishes or large soufflé dish and run a small spoon or your finger around the edge to help it rise and prevent it catching on the edge. Bake on the hot baking sheet for 10 minutes for the individual soufflés or about 40 minutes for the large soufflé.

Dust with confectioners' sugar and serve at once with whipped cream.

This is one of my favorite lemon puddings. I have even baked it ahead of time and reheated it very satisfactorily, set inside of a roasting pan of water for 30 minutes in a 350°F oven. The top of the pudding is a spongy mousse while underneath is a sharp lemon sauce.

HOT LEMON SOUFFLÉ PUDDING

SERVES 4-6

⅓ cup (75g) salted butter, softened
1¼ cups (250g) sugar
3 extra-large eggs, separated
⅔ cup (75g) all-purpose flour
1 tsp baking powder
¼ tsp salt
finely grated zest and juice of 2 lemons
1¾ cups + 2 tbsps (450ml) milk

Preheat the oven to 375°F. Grease a shallow 2-quart ovenproof baking dish.

Measure the butter and sugar into a bowl. Add the egg yolks, flour, baking powder, and salt, then beat until smooth. Slowly add the lemon zest, juice, and milk. Do not worry if the mixture looks curdled at this stage—this is quite normal.

Place the egg whites in a large bowl and whisk until they form soft peaks. Carefully fold the whites into the lemon mixture using a large metal spoon.

Pour the mixture into the prepared ovenproof dish and place in a baking pan or roasting pan. Pour in enough boiling water to come halfway up the dish and bake for about 30 minutes, or until pale golden brown on top.

TIP
Buy thin-skinned lemons that feel heavy for their size. To get maximum juice from them, it helps if the fruit is warm, or at least at room temperature. Before grating the zest, wash and dry the fruit well. Grate the zest on the small-holed side of the grater, and remember to scrape everything off the back of the grater after grating. A pastry brush is a useful tool to do this.

CHAPTER SEVENTEEN

CHEESECAKES

This cheesecake easily serves 8-10, as it is quite sweet and rich, so it should be served in small portions. Expect the cheesecake to crack on cooling.

AMERICAN CHOCOLATE
SERVES 8-10 RIPPLE CHEESECAKE

For the crust
¾ cup/1 sleeve (150g)
    chocolate graham
    crackers
¼ cup (55g) salted butter

For the cheesecake
5 ounces (150g) dark
    chocolate, broken into
    pieces
3 cups + 2 tbsps (700g)
    full-fat cream cheese
½ cup + 1 tbsp (115g) sugar
½ tsp vanilla extract
1 extra-large egg

Preheat the oven to 325°F. Lightly grease a 9-inch springform pan.

To make the crust, place the graham crackers in a plastic bag and crush with a rolling pin. Melt the butter in a medium saucepan. Remove the saucepan from the heat and stir in the graham cracker crumbs. Press into the prepared pan and let set.

To make the cheesecake filling, melt the chocolate gently in a bowl set over a saucepan of hot water, making sure the bottom of the bowl doesn't touch the water, stirring occasionally. Cool slightly.

Measure the cream cheese into a large bowl and beat until soft. Add the sugar and beat again until well-mixed. Beat in the vanilla extract, then the egg.

Spoon half the cheese mixture onto the graham cracker crust, separating the spoonfuls. Add the melted chocolate to the remaining cheese mixture and stir well to mix. Spoon this chocolate mixture in between the plain mixture. Swirl the top with a knife to give a marbled effect.

Bake for about 1 hour or until the cheesecake becomes puffy around the edges but is still very soft in the center. Turn off the oven but leave the cheesecake in the oven to cool. Chill well and then loosen the cheesecake from the sides of the pan using a small offset spatula.

Serve well-chilled.

A sophisticated cheesecake. If you like, you can add a little more brandy to the filling. If ginger is a favorite flavor, the quantity used can be increased as well.

CHOCOLATE, BRANDY, AND GINGER CHEESECAKE

SERVES 8

For the crust
4 ounces (115g) ginger cookies
¼ cup (55g) salted butter
2 tbsps (30g) demerara sugar

For the cheesecake
4 ounces (115g) dark chocolate, broken into pieces
2 tsps powdered gelatin
3 tbsps warm water
2 extra-large eggs, separated
¼ cup (55g) granulated sugar
½ cup (115g) full-fat cream cheese
⅔ cup (150ml) sour cream
4 tbsps brandy

To decorate
⅔ cup (150ml) heavy cream, whipped (optional)
chocolate curls (page 402)
¼ cup finely sliced crystallized ginger

Lightly grease a 9-inch springform pan.

—

To make the crust, place the cookies in a plastic bag and crush with a rolling pin. Melt the butter in a medium saucepan. Remove the saucepan from the heat and stir in the cookie crumbs and sugar. Press into the prepared pan and let set.

—

Melt the chocolate gently in a bowl set over a saucepan of hot water, making sure the bottom of the bowl doesn't touch the water, stirring occasionally. Allow to cool slightly.

—

Place the gelatin powder in a small bowl and add the warm water. Stir for a few minutes until dissolved. Be sure never to boil any gelatin mixture or it will lose its thickening quality.

—

Beat together the egg yolks, sugar, and cream cheese in a large bowl. Add the sour cream and cooled chocolate.

—

Place the egg whites in a large bowl and whisk until frothy. Fold into the cheese mixture.

—

Warm the brandy gently in a small saucepan. Add the dissolved gelatin to the brandy and stir to combine. Fold into the cheese mixture.

—

Pour onto the cookie crust base and chill in the fridge to set.

—

When set, carefully remove the cheesecake from the pan before decorating with whipped cream, if you like, and chocolate curls and slices of crystallized ginger.

An excellent, quick cheesecake that's always popular with my family.
You can vary the fruit topping, depending on what is in season.

EASY LEMON CHEESECAKE

SERVES 8

For the crust
1 × 9-cracker sleeve graham
    crackers
⅓ cup (75g) salted butter
2 tbsps (30g) demerara
    sugar

For the cheesecake
1 × 14-ounce (397g) can
    full-fat condensed milk
1 cup + 2 tbsps (250g)
    full-fat mascarpone
    cheese
finely grated zest and juice
    of 3 large lemons

For the topping
⅔ cup (150ml) heavy cream,
    whipped
strawberries

You will need a 9-inch springform pan.

Put the graham crackers into a plastic bag and crush with a rolling pin. Melt the butter in a medium saucepan. Remove the saucepan from the heat and stir in the graham cracker crumbs and sugar. Press evenly over the bottom and sides of the pan, then let set.

To make the cheesecake filling, mix together the condensed milk, mascarpone, and lemon zest. Add the lemon juice a little at a time, whisking until the mixture thickens.

Pour the mixture onto the graham cracker crust and let chill in the fridge for 3–4 hours or overnight.

Carefully remove the cheesecake from the pan before decorating with swirls of whipped cream and fresh strawberries.

This is a very quick and easy cheesecake to make. It's delicious to eat, too, as the yogurt gives the filling a wonderfully fresh flavor.

QUICK CHILLED CHEESECAKE

SERVES 6-8

For the crust
1¼ cups (175g) graham
  crackers
⅓ cup (75g) salted butter
3 tbsps (40g) demerara
  sugar

For the cheesecake
1 cup (225g) full-fat
  cream cheese
3 tbsps (30g) granulated
  sugar
⅔ cup (150ml) heavy cream
½ cup (150g) full-fat
  Greek yogurt
juice of 1½ lemons

For the topping
1½ cups (175g) raspberries
  or other soft fruits
1–2 tbsps red currant jelly

You will need a 9-inch springform pan.

Put the graham crackers into a plastic bag and crush with a rolling pin. Melt the butter in a medium saucepan. Remove the saucepan from the heat and stir in the graham cracker crumbs and sugar. Press over the bottom and sides of the pan, then let set.

Measure the cream cheese and sugar into a large bowl or food processor and mix well to blend thoroughly. Add the cream and yogurt and mix again. Gradually add the lemon juice, whisking all the time. Turn the mixture into the pan on top of the graham cracker crust and chill in the fridge overnight to set.

Run a knife around the edge of the graham cracker crust to loosen the cheesecake, then push up the bottom or remove the sides of the pan and slide the cheesecake onto a serving plate.

Arrange the fruit on top of the cheesecake. Heat the red currant jelly in a small saucepan until melted, then carefully brush over the fruit. Let set. Serve chilled.

This is a good cheesecake for a party, as the sponge can be made in advance and frozen. Keep the cheesecake chilled once made, as it contains no gelatin and will soon soften in a warm room.

ANGEL SPONGE CHEESECAKE

SERVES 8

For the sponge
2 extra-large eggs
6 tbsps (75g) granulated
　　sugar
⅓ cup (55g) all-purpose
　　flour
½ tsp baking powder
¼ tsp salt

For the cheesecake
½ cup (115g) salted butter,
　　softened
¾ cup (150g) granulated
　　sugar
3 extra-large eggs, separated
finely grated zest and
　　juice of 2 oranges
¾ cup + 2 tbsps (200g)
　　full-fat cream cheese
1¼ cups (300ml) heavy
　　cream, lightly whipped

For decoration
confectioners' sugar, for
　　dusting
orange segments
mint leaves

Preheat the oven to 350°F. Lightly grease a 9-inch springform pan and line the bottom with parchment paper.

Measure the eggs and sugar into a large bowl and beat until the mixture is thick and light in color and the whisk leaves a trail when lifted out of the mixture.

Sift the flour, baking powder, and salt onto the beaten mixture and fold in lightly using a large metal spoon or spatula.

Turn the mixture into the prepared pan and tilt the pan to allow the mixture to spread evenly to the sides (don't worry that there appears to be little mixture for the size of the pan). Bake for 20–25 minutes, or until the sponge springs back when lightly pressed with your finger and has shrunk slightly from the sides of the pan. Let cool in the pan for a few minutes, then turn out, peel off the parchment paper, and finish cooling. Turn out and let cool on a wire rack.

Wash and dry the pan and then line the bottom and sides with parchment paper. When the sponge is completely cold, cut in half horizontally using a serrated or bread knife. Place one layer in the prepared pan, cut side up.

To make the cheesecake filling, measure the butter into a large bowl and beat until thoroughly softened. Add the sugar and beat again until light and fluffy.

Add the egg yolks, orange zest, strained orange juice, and cream cheese, and beat well until smooth and thoroughly mixed. Fold the whipped cream into the cheese mixture.

Place the egg whites in a large bowl and whisk until stiff but not dry. Fold them into the mixture.

Spoon the cheesecake mixture into the pan on top of the sponge and level the surface. Gently place the remaining sponge on top, cut side down. Cover with plastic wrap and chill in the fridge for about 4 hours, or until the cheesecake mixture is firm.

To serve, carefully remove the sides of the pan and gently peel away the parchment paper. Using an offset spatula or fish spatula, ease the cheesecake onto a serving plate. Dust the top with sifted confectioners' sugar and mark into sections with the back of a knife. Decorate with orange segments and mint leaves.

Apricot and orange is a lovely flavor combination. This is best served chilled.

APRICOT AND ORANGE CHEESECAKE

SERVES 10

For the crust
¾ cup (115g) graham
  crackers
¼ cup (55g) salted butter

For the cheesecake
1 × ¼-ounce (7g) packet
  powdered gelatin
¼ cup (60ml) warm water
1⅓ cups (175g) dried
  apricots
¾ cup + 2 tbsps (200ml)
  freshly squeezed orange
  juice
3 tbsps clear honey
finely grated zest of
  ½ orange
1 cup (225g) full-fat
  cream cheese
⅔ cup (150ml) full-fat sour
  cream
2 extra-large eggs, separated
½ cup + 1 tbsp (115g) sugar

For the topping
7 tbsps (100ml) heavy
  cream, whipped
5 small amaretti
  cookies, crushed
finely grated zest
  of 1 orange

You will need a 9-inch springform pan.

Place the graham crackers in a plastic bag and crush with a rolling pin. Melt the butter in a medium saucepan. Remove the saucepan from the heat and stir in the graham cracker crumbs. Press into the pan and let set.

Place the powdered gelatin in a small bowl and add the warm water. Stir for a few minutes until dissolved. Be sure never to boil any gelatin mixture as it will lose its thickening quality.

Meanwhile, place the apricots in a saucepan with the orange juice, bring to a boil and simmer gently for about 10 minutes, or until tender. Turn the apricots and any juice that hasn't been absorbed into a food processor and blend until smooth. Add the honey, orange zest, cream cheese, sour cream, and egg yolks and process again.

Mix the dissolved gelatin into the apricot mixture.

Place the egg whites in a large bowl and whisk until frothy. Add the sugar a little at a time, whisking well after each addition. Whisk until all the sugar has been added and the mixture is very stiff.

Turn the apricot mixture into the meringue and fold well together. Pour the mixture onto the graham cracker crust and chill in the fridge to set.

Loosen the edges of the pan and push up the bottom. Slip the cheesecake onto a serving plate. Mark the cheesecake into 10 wedges, then decorate the top with the whipped cream, amaretti crumbs, and orange zest.

A traditional cooked cheesecake. This recipe makes a good large cake, excellent for a party. The center dips a little on cooling—perfect to hold the fruit!

CONTINENTAL CHEESECAKE

SERVES 12

For the crust
1¼ cups (175g) graham
    crackers
⅓ cup (75g) salted butter
¼ cup (55g) demerara sugar

For the cheesecake
¼ cup (65g) salted butter,
    softened
1 cup + 2 tbsps (225g)
    granulated sugar
2⅓ cups (550g) full-fat
    cottage cheese or ricotta
⅓ cup (40g) all-purpose flour
finely grated zest and
    juice of 2 lemons
4 extra-large eggs, separated
¾ cup + 1 tbsp (200ml)
    heavy cream,
    lightly whipped

For the topping
about 3½ cups (450g) mixed
    summer fruits (red
    currants, black currants,
    blackberries, raspberries,
    and strawberries)
sugar, to taste
1 tsp arrowroot powder
⅔ cup (150ml) heavy cream,
    whipped

TIP

Use frozen mixed summer fruits, if fresh are unavailable. You don't have to use all the fruits suggested for the topping—choose your own combinations.

Preheat the oven to 325°F. Lightly grease a 9-inch springform pan and line the bottom and sides with parchment paper.

—

Put the graham crackers into a plastic bag and crush with a rolling pin. Melt the butter in a medium saucepan. Remove the saucepan from the heat and stir in the graham cracker crumbs and sugar. Press into the prepared pan and let set.

—

To make the cheesecake filling, measure the butter, sugar, cottage cheese or ricotta, flour, lemon zest and juice, and egg yolks into a large bowl. Beat until smooth. Fold in the lightly whipped cream.

—

Place the egg whites in a large bowl and whisk until stiff. Fold the egg whites into the mixture. Pour onto the graham cracker crust and bake for about 1½ hours or until set. Turn off the oven and leave the cheesecake in the oven for an additional 1 hour to cool.

—

Run a knife around the edge of the pan to loosen the cheesecake, and push the bottom up. Remove the parchment paper.

—

To make the topping, cook the red currants, black currants, and blackberries, if using, in 2 tablespoons of water in a saucepan and sweeten to taste. When the fruit has softened and released its juices, remove from the heat.

—

Blend the arrowroot powder with 2 tablespoons of cold water and add the cooked fruit and liquid from the saucepan. Return the mixture to the saucepan, allow to thicken, then let cool. Stir the raspberries and strawberries, if using, in with the other fruits, then pile on top of the cheesecake, leveling out evenly. Decorate the edge of the cheesecake with piped or spooned whipped cream.

This is a lovely, subtly flavored cooked cheesecake.

BUTTERMILK AND
SERVES 8 # HONEY CHEESECAKE

For the crust
¾ cup (115g) graham
   crackers
¼ cup (55g) salted butter

For the cheesecake
1 cup (225g) full-fat cream
   cheese
3 extra-large eggs, separated
2 rounded tbsps clear honey,
   plus extra to glaze
½ cup (55g) almond flour
⅓ cup (40g) all-purpose
   flour
1 cup + 3 tbsps (300ml)
   full-fat buttermilk
6 tbsps (75g) sugar
a handful of sliced almonds

Preheat the oven to 325°F. Lightly grease a 9-inch springform pan.

To make the crust, place the graham crackers in a plastic bag and crush with a rolling pin. Melt the butter in a medium saucepan. Remove the saucepan from the heat and stir in the graham cracker crumbs. Press into the prepared pan and let set.

Measure the cream cheese into a large bowl and beat until soft. Beat in the egg yolks along with the honey, almond flour, all-purpose flour, buttermilk, and 3 tbsps (30g) of the sugar.

Place the egg whites in a separate bowl and whisk until stiff. Whisk in the remaining sugar.

Fold the egg whites and sugar into the cheese mixture.

Spoon the mixture on top of the graham cracker crust and sprinkle the sliced almonds over the surface. Bake for about 1¼ hours, or until firm but still spongy to the touch. Turn off the oven, open the door, and allow the cheesecake to cool inside.

Loosen the sides of the cheesecake with an offset spatula, then remove the sides of the pan. Slide the cheesecake from the base of the pan onto a serving plate.

Gently heat the honey in a small saucepan and brush over the top of the cheesecake to glaze.

TIP
You'll find buttermilk with the yogurts and creams in supermarkets.

This makes a good, rich cheesecake. It is very moist, so there is no need for cream.

AUSTRIAN CURD CHEESECAKE

SERVES 10

⅔ cup (150g) salted butter, softened
1 cup + 6 tbsps (275g) granulated sugar
2⅓ cups (550g) full-fat cottage cheese or ricotta
4 extra-large eggs, separated
1¼ cups (115g) almond flour
¾ cup (115g) golden raisins
⅓ cup (55g) semolina
finely grated zest and juice of 2 lemons
confectioners' sugar, for dusting

Preheat the oven to 375°F. Lightly grease a 9-inch springform pan and line the bottom with parchment paper.

—

Place the softened butter in a large bowl and add the sugar and cottage cheese or ricotta. Beat well together until light and creamy.

—

Beat the egg yolks into the mixture one at a time, then stir in the almond flour, golden raisins, semolina, and the lemon zest and juice. Allow the mixture to rest for about 10 minutes. (This allows the mixture to thicken so that the golden raisins don't sink to the bottom of the cake when baking.)

—

In a separate bowl, whisk the egg whites until stiff but not dry and fold lightly into the mixture.

—

Turn the mixture into the prepared pan. Bake for about 1 hour or until firm to the touch. Cover the top of the cheesecake loosely with foil about halfway through the cooking time to prevent the top from becoming too brown. Turn off the oven, but leave the cheesecake inside to cool for about 1 hour. Allow to cool completely.

—

Loosen the sides of the cheesecake with an offset spatula, then remove the sides of the pan. Invert the cheesecake, remove the bottom of the pan and the paper, then turn back the right way up. Dust with sifted confectioners' sugar to serve.

This is a specialty of Florida, where limes grow on the low coral islands—the Keys.
My adaptation of the original recipe is very quick to make and delicious!

KEY LIME PIE

SERVES 8

For the crust
5 ounces (150g) ginger
    cookies
¼ cup (65g) salted butter
2 tbsps (30g) demerara
    sugar

For the filling
finely grated zest of
    1 large lime and juice
    of 4 large limes
1 × 14-ounce (397g) can
    full-fat condensed milk
1¾ cups + 2 tbsps (450ml)
    heavy cream

You will need an 8-inch springform pan.

Place the cookies in a plastic bag and crush with a rolling pin.
Melt the butter in a medium saucepan. Remove the saucepan
from the heat and stir in the cookie crumbs and sugar. Press over
the bottom and sides of the pan and let set.

Measure the lime juice, condensed milk, and 1¼ cups (300ml) of
the heavy cream into a mixing bowl and beat until well-blended.
Pour onto the prepared crumb crust and gently level the surface.
Chill in the fridge for several hours, until set.

Remove the pie from the pan.

Place the remaining cream in a large bowl and whisk until it
forms soft peaks. Spread the cream over the pie, then finish
with a scattering of grated lime zest. Serve well-chilled.

CAKE
DECORATIONS

ALMOND PASTE

You can buy very good premade almond paste, but if you do like to make your own, here is the basic recipe to make 3 cups (675g).

2⅓ cups (225g) almond flour
1 cup + 2 tbsps (225g) granulated sugar
1¾ cups (225g) confectioners' sugar, sifted
4 extra-large egg yolks or 2 whole extra-large eggs
about 6 drops of almond extract

Mix the almond flour and sugars together in a large bowl. Add the yolks or whole eggs and almond extract and knead together to form a stiff paste. Do not over-knead, as this will make the paste oily. Wrap in nonstick baking paper or a beeswax wrap and store in the fridge for an hour or up to 3 days.

To cover a cake with almond paste

There are two methods to cover a cake with almond paste; deciding which to employ really depends on the type of icing you are going to use. Fondant or ready-to-roll icing is best put over almond paste with rounded edges, using the first method. For royal icing, it is usually better to use the second method as it gives sharper corners to the cake. For both methods, start by standing the cake on a cake board that is 2 inches larger than the size of the cake.

METHOD 1

Lightly dust a work surface with sifted confectioners' sugar, then roll out the almond paste to about 2 inches larger than the top of the cake. Brush the cake all over with warmed apricot jam that has been pushed through a sieve.

—

Carefully lift the almond paste over the cake with the help of a rolling pin. Gently level and smooth the top of the paste with the rolling pin, then ease the almond paste down the sides of the cake, smoothing it at the same time.

—

Neatly trim excess almond paste off at the base. Use the excess for making holly leaves and berries; keep it wrapped in plastic wrap if not shaping immediately.

METHOD 2

Lightly dust a work surface with sifted confectioners' sugar, then roll out one-third of the almond paste to a circle slightly larger than the top of the cake. Using your cake pan bottom as a guide, cut the almond paste to the exact size.

—

Brush the cake all over with warmed apricot jam that has been pushed through a sieve. Lift the almond paste onto the cake and smooth over gently with a rolling pin. Neaten the edges.

—

Cut a piece of string the height of the cake including the layer of almond paste, and another to fit around the cake. Roll out the remaining almond paste and, using the string as a guide, cut the almond paste to size.

—

Brush a little more jam along the top edge of the strip as a seal, then roll up the strip loosely, place one end against the side of the cake, and unroll to cover the sides of the cake completely. Use a small offset spatula to smooth over the sides and the seams in the paste.

—

The table on page 400 shows you the quantities of almond paste needed to cover the tops and sides of various sizes of cakes.

ROYAL ICING

You can buy "instant" royal icing. However, if you do like to make your own, the recipe below makes enough to decorate an 8- to 9-inch round cake.

2 extra-large egg whites
4 cups (500g) confectioners' sugar, sifted
about 4 tsps fresh lemon juice

Place the egg whites in a large mixing bowl and whisk lightly with a fork until bubbles begin to form on the surface.

—

Add about half the confectioners' sugar and the lemon juice, and beat well with a wooden spoon for about 10 minutes until brilliant white.

—

Gradually stir in the remaining confectioners' sugar until the correct consistency for piping.

—

Once made, keep the icing covered with a damp cloth to prevent it from drying out and use as soon as possible.

HOMEMADE FONDANT ICING

There are some excellent varieties of fondant or premade icing available. However, if you prefer to make your own, here is the recipe to make 1¼ pounds (550g).

4 cups (500g) confectioners' sugar
1 generous tbsp light corn syrup
1 extra-large egg white

Sift the confectioners' sugar into a large mixing bowl, make a well in the center, and add the light corn syrup and egg white.

—

Knead together until the mixture forms a soft ball. Turn out onto a work surface lightly dusted with confectioners' sugar, and knead for about 10 minutes until smooth and brilliant white.

—

Add some sifted confectioners' sugar if the mixture is a bit on the sticky side. Wrap in plastic wrap and store in the fridge until required.

To cover a cake with fondant icing

Brush the almond paste with a little sherry, rum, or brandy (this has a sterilizing effect and also helps the icing to stick).

—

Roll out the icing on a work surface lightly dusted with confectioners' sugar, to about 2 inches larger than the top of the cake.

—

Lift the icing onto the cake, using a rolling pin for support. Smooth out evenly over the top of the cake with your hands, easing the icing down the sides of the cake.

—

Trim any excess icing from the base of the cake, then finish smoothing with a plastic cake smoother, or carefully with your hands. Let dry out at room temperature for about 1 week before decorating.

The table below shows the quantities needed to cover both the sides and top of various sizes of cakes:

Size of pan	Almond Paste	Fondant Icing
6-inch round pan 5-inch square pan	1½ cups (350g)	12 ounces (350g)
7-inch round pan 6-inch square pan	2 cups (450g)	1 pound (450g)
8-inch round pan 7-inch square pan	3 cups (675g)	1½ pounds (675g)
9-inch round pan 8-inch square pan	3⅓ cups (750g)	1¾ pounds (750g)
10-inch round pan 9-inch square pan	4 cups (900g)	2¼ pounds (1kg)
11-inch round pan 10-inch square pan	4⅓ cups (1kg)	2¾ pounds (1.2kg)
12-inch round pan 11-inch square pan	4¾ cups (1.1kg)	3 pounds (1.5kg)
13-inch round pan 12-inch square pan	6½ cups (1.5kg)	3½ pounds (1.6kg)

AMERICAN FROSTING

The "instant" American Frosting works perfectly well, but if you have a sugar thermometer, try this "proper" version.

2¼ cups (450g) sugar
2 extra-large egg whites

Place the sugar in a large, heavy-bottomed saucepan along with ½ cup (135ml) water and heat gently until the sugar has dissolved. Bring to a boil and boil to 239°F, as registered on a sugar thermometer.

———

Meanwhile, place the egg whites in a large deep bowl and whisk until stiff.

———

Allow the bubbles to settle, then slowly pour the hot syrup onto the egg whites, whisking continuously. When all the sugar has been added, continue whisking until the mixture stands in peaks and just starts to become matte around the edges.

———

Use to sandwich and top the Frosted Walnut Layer Cake (page 56). The frosting sets rapidly, so work quickly using an offset spatula. Let set in a cool place, but not in the fridge.

CRYSTALLIZED FLOWERS

You may want to decorate a special cake like the Sponge Christening Cake (page 136) with crystallized flowers. They are very simple to prepare but make a lovely finishing touch.

edible flowers (violets, pansies, camellias, primroses, little roses, and polyanthus)
a little beaten egg white
granulated sugar, for dusting

Brush the edible flowers with a little beaten egg white.

———

Dust with granulated sugar on both sides, then stand them on a wire cake rack in a warm place (over a radiator or on top of a warm stove, for example) and let sit until they are crisp and dry, which will take a few hours.

CHOCOLATE DECORATIONS

There are many decorations or finishing touches that you can make with chocolate. They're fun to do and look most impressive.

PERFECT CHOCOLATE CURLS

Place a clean baking sheet in the freezer for 15 minutes. Meanwhile, melt white, dark, or milk chocolate in a heatproof bowl over a saucepan of simmering water. Pour the melted chocolate onto the back of the cold baking sheet and spread out thinly. Let set, putting the baking sheet back into the freezer for a few minutes if needed. You want it to be completely set but not so hard that it would snap when bent. Hold a sharp knife at a 45-degree angle to the chocolate and either pull toward you or away from you as the chocolate curls around itself. You can adjust the angle and the pressure to have tighter or looser curls. After a few attempts you'll get the hang of it.

CHOCOLATE SHAPES

These can easily be made by melting the chocolate as with chocolate curls, then cutting it into squares or triangles with a sharp knife or cookie cutter. It helps to heat the knife or cookie cutter first. Use a round plain or fluted cookie cutter to stamp out circles.

CHOCOLATE LEAVES

Use a small paintbrush to spread melted chocolate evenly onto the underside of clean, dry leaves. Let set and then gently peel the leaf away from the chocolate, not the other way around.

HOW TO TEMPER CHOCOLATE

Tempering chocolate is the process of heating and cooling chocolate, then reheating it again, so that the fat crystals in the cocoa butter stabilize and become shiny and strong. Once tempered, the chocolate will keep its shininess and not become dull. It is perfect for coating cakes and individual chocolates.

Tempering has a reputation for being tricky to do, but, in fact, it is achievable at home if you have a thermometer.

There are two main methods of tempering:
1) The traditional, classic method of pouring melted chocolate onto a marble slab and spreading it backward and forward until cooled to the desired temperature.
2) The seeding method involves melting two-thirds of the chocolate being used, then adding the remaining one-third of unmelted chocolate and stirring until cooled to the desired temperature.

TEMPERING TEMPERATURES

Whether you want to temper dark, milk, or white chocolate, the method is exactly the same. However, the melting temperatures are different.

	Melting Temperature	Cooling Temperature	Reheating Temperature
Dark Chocolate	113–122°F	82–84°F	88–90°F
Milk Chocolate	104–113°F	80–82°F	86–88°F
White Chocolate	104°F	75–77°F	80–82°F

SEEDING METHOD

MAKES ABOUT 1 POUND (475G)

1 pound + 1 ounce (475g) dark, milk, or white
  chocolate drops or in a bar

You will need
1 medium heatproof glass bowl
1 medium saucepan
1 sugar thermometer or digital thermometer
1 rubber spatula

Pour approximately 1¼ inches water
into a saucepan and bring to a simmer
over medium-low heat. Once simmering, reduce
the heat to its lowest setting.

—

Chop the chocolate (if using a bar) very
finely with a large serrated knife or grate
the chocolate in a food processor.

—

Tip two-thirds of the chocolate into a
heatproof bowl and place over the saucepan.
Make sure the bottom of the bowl doesn't
touch the water, otherwise the chocolate
can overheat and burn (known as seizing).

—

Using a rubber spatula, stir the chocolate
continuously until it reaches melting
temperature (see temperature table).
Be careful not to let it go any higher.

—

Carefully remove the bowl from the heat
and add the remaining one-third of the
chocolate in small amounts, stirring slowly
and continuously, until you reach the correct
cooling temperature (see temperature table).

—

When the chocolate has reached cooling
temperature, place the bowl back over
the saucepan of very gently simmering water
and reheat, stirring continuously, until
the chocolate reaches the reheating
temperature (see temperature table).

—

Carefully remove the bowl from the heat
and test for temper by dipping the end of
a spoon in the chocolate. If the chocolate
has been correctly tempered, it will harden
evenly and set glossy within 5 minutes.

TIPS TO AVOID FAILURE

If your chocolate tempering doesn't work, you
can re-melt and start again from the beginning.

—

Use tempered chocolate immediately, as it
stays in temper only for as long as it stays
within the reheating temperature range.

—

Let tempered chocolate set in a cool place
at room temperature. Don't set it in the
fridge, as this can cause chocolate to bloom
(a white sheen) and lose its shine.

—

Another way to test for temper is to spread
a thin layer on a piece of parchment paper, wait
for 5 minutes, then try to peel the chocolate
from the paper. If you can peel it and it's not
blotchy, it's tempered.

—

Always use an accurate thermometer
and keep a close eye on the temperature.

—

Chocolate drops are easier to melt, as they
are smaller and of uniform size, plus there's
no chopping involved.

INDEX

Page numbers in *italic* refer to the illustrations

THANK-YOUS

About 33 years ago Lucy Young joined me to be my assistant. One of our first tasks was the TV series *Ultimate Cakes* for the BBC. At the time, we did a book to accompany the series, and about 15 years later, we added more cakes and updated the recipes to make the *Baking Bible*. Now we have modernized it again and added some new up-to-date bakes.

So, thank you, Luce, for being by my side and masterminding this book. And to Lucinda McCord, who tests the cakes here in our test kitchen—brilliant in every way.

To the lovely Isla Murray for creating all the cakes and bakes for the photographs: what a skill! And to Ant Duncan for the vibrant photos.

To Lizzy Gray for agreeing to give the book another boost, and to the very best editor, Jo Roberts Miller, who knows each recipe as well as we do!

To Nell Warner at BBC Books and to Emma and Alex at Smith & Gilmour.

Thank you, too, to our book agent, Caroline Wood, at Felicity Bryan Agency. We are lucky to have you looking after us.

And to my loyal readers—thank you. We hope you enjoy it.

Mary Berry